AFRICAN LITERATURE TODAY

14 Insiders and Outsiders

A review
Editor: Eldred Durosimi Jones
Associate Editor: Eustace Palmer
Editorial Assistant: Marjorie Jones

© Contributors 1984

All Rights Reserved. Except as permitted under current legislation no part of this work may be photocopied, stored in a retrieval system, published, performed in public, adapted, broadcast, transmitted, recorded or reproduced in any form or by any means, without the prior permission of the copyright owner

First published by Heinemann Educational Books 1984

First published in the United States of America 1984
by Africana Publishing Corporation

James Currey, Woodbridge, Suffolk

ISBN 978 0 85255 514 9

Transferred to digital printing

James Currey is an imprint of Boydell & Brewer Ltd
PO Box 9, Woodbridge, Suffolk IP12 3DF, UK
and of Boydell & Brewer Inc.
668 Mt. Hope Avenue, Rochester NY 14620, USA
website: www.boydellandbrewer.com

This publication is printed on acid-free paper

Contents

EDITORIAL vii

ARTICLES

Graham Greene Travels in Africa and Dadié Travels in Europe
    Marion A. Thomas, University of Strasbourg   1

A Touch of the Absurd: Soyinka and Beckett
    Catherine Obianuju Acholonu, Alvan Ikoku College of Education, Owerri   12

Laye, Lamming and Wright: Mother and Son
    Fritz H. Pointer, Luther College, Iowa   19

Feminist Criticism and the African Novel
    Katherine Frank, Fourah Bay College, University of Sierra Leone   34

Albert Camus, Aimé Césaire and the Tragedy of Revolution
    John Conteh-Morgan, Fourah Bay College, University of Sierra Leone   49

Africa under Western Eyes: Updike's The Coup and Other Fantasies
    Jack B. Moore, University of South Florida   60

On the Poetry of War: Yeats and J. P. Clark
    Obi Maduakor, University of Nigeria, Nsukka   68

Olaudah Equiano and the Tradition of Defoe
    S. E. Ogude, University of Benin   77

vi Contents

The Black Pseudo-Autobiographical Novel: *Miss Jane Pittman* and *Houseboy*
   Bede M. Ssensalo, California State University   93

Trans-Saharan Views: Mutually Negative Portrayals
   Kole Omotoso, University of Ife   111

The Backward Glance: Lamming's *Season of Adventure* and Williams' *Other Leopards*
   Funso Aiyejina, University of Ife   118

Charles Dickens and the Zulus
   Bernth Lindfors, University of Texas at Austin   127

REVIEWS

Wole Soyinka, *Aké: The Years of Childhood*
   'Molara Ogundipe-Leslie, University of Ibadan   141

Alan Paton, *Ah, But Your Land is Beautiful*
   Christopher Heywood, University of Sheffield   148

R. Sarif Easmon, *The Feud and Other Stories*
   Jack B. Moore, University of South Florida   151

Andrew Ekwuru, *Songs of Steel*
   Willfried Feuser, University College, Cardiff   157

James Gibbs, ed., *Critical Perspectives on Wole Soyinka*
   Richard Taylor, Bayreuth University   162

P. A. Egejuru, *Black Writers: White Audience. A Critical Approach to African Literature*
   John Conteh-Morgan, Fourah Bay College, University of Sierra Leone   164

Michael Etherton, *The Development of African Drama*
   Martin Banham, University of Leeds   169

Bruce King ed., *West Indian Literature*
   Willfried Feuser, University College, Cardiff   172

INDEX   178

Editorial

Although Africa has attracted the attention of non-African writers since the days of Herodotus, many Africans believe these writers largely misrepresented Africa and some avowedly, others implicitly, have set out to correct the record. Achebe was impelled by a desire to remind his people that they had a civilization – contrary to the record – before the white man came. There is an implication that Achebe wrote for his people as his audience. Why then write in English?

There was no doubt whom Olaudah Equiano intended to address in the eighteenth century with the interesting narrative of his life. He wrote in English primarily for the English when hardly any of his fellow Ibos shared his knowledge of that language; his model was Defoe both for his style – this is not surprising – and, according to Egude, for his fictionalizing of his autobiography, which may come as something of a surprise.

Is it possible to borrow language alone? Some critics who answer in the negative urge writers (however naïvely) to write in their own language. Ngugi now writes major works first in his native Gikuyu: a bold step forward, but he still employs the standard devices of the English novel form which he has borrowed to characterize and criticize his own society. Borrowing either of language or of style is only the beginning of the matter. Other writers have borrowed language, form and style to produce works which significantly define the African environment and stimulate ideas fundamental to the development of their societies. The fact that the plays of Wole Soyinka show a marked influence of the Theatre of the Absurd, particularly of the plays of Beckett, does not devalue their worth or their validity in Africa.

Defoe on Equiano, Beckett on Soyinka (Kafka on Laye, though not dealt with in this issue), the novel form on so many, illustrate widespread and differing European influences on African writers; what comes as a surprise in Equiano is not that his style derives from Defoe, but that his descriptions of Africa and the life of his people which read so convincingly as personal experiences also have other sources. Did Equiano borrow too much?

This is what raises important issues on borrowing. The borrowing of language is legitimate if the borrower remains his own man; if his ideas and his stance are truly his. African writers are judged by their success in representing essential truth whether in their own language or in a borrowed one.

Modern English and American writers have continued the tradition of Herodotus; Evelyn Waugh, Graham Greene, and John Updike, have among others set books in Africa comparatively recently. How different is their portrayal of Africa from that of Africans? To what extent do they see fellow human beings in this strange world? To what extent do they represent historical stereotypes? Since Africans are now beginning to pay Europe back in its own coin by commenting on their own travels in Europe, the comparison between Greene in Liberia and Sierra Leone, and Dadié in Italy is instructive. Greene sees monetary corruption in the idea of paying the devil/priest for his performance while Dadié sees the same corruption represented in the Bank of the Holy Spirit in Rome; the Zulus seem certain to have their own back on Charles Dickens!

The African diaspora, increasingly conscious of its roots, contributes a wider dimension to the continent of Africa, and quite significant fresh views of it from afar – different from the European view because it is an 'inside' view from 'outside', in a way that Waugh's brutally cynical and detached view could not be. There are remarkable similarities of stance but equally significant environmental differences between the exiles Wright and Lamming on the one hand and the indigenous Laye on the other. A whole issue of *African Literature Today* (no. 9) has been devoted to this backward glance from this new world, but still the subject fascinates. *Other Leopards* is particularly interesting because its author includes Arab Africa in his view and shows something of the North/South, Arab/Negro confrontation in the Sudan. (Most new world reminiscences are of sub-Saharan Africa.) What little cross-Saharan literature that exists – of sub-Saharan writers on Arab Africa and vice-versa – seems mutually unsympathetic. The Arab reception of Ayi Kwei Armah's *Two Thousand Seasons* is predictable, and shows the great divide within the continent itself.

Europe *has* influenced Africa, as Africans' use of the genres and languages of Europe has shown. The scene is now set for Africans to return the compliment, perhaps to move the two continents towards a better understanding of each other if not to Senghor's dream of cultural *métissage*.

Graham Greene Travels in Africa and Dadié Travels in Europe

Marion A. Thomas

The English writer Graham Greene and Bernard Dadié of the Ivory Coast both concern themselves with real problems of contemporary society. The two books selected here are Greene's *Journey Without Maps* (1936) and Dadié's *La Ville où nul ne meurt* (1969).[1] They are particularly valuable as they not only reflect a particular society but also a variety of problems: international cultural relationships, social discrimination and materialism. Personal reflections are woven among the comments on the journey, and tend to demonstrate that self-affirmation is deepened in proportion to contacts with others, provided that these contacts are engaged in with an open-minded attitude. Both books also reflect the increasing interest during the twentieth century in psycho-analysis and cultural anthropology. They are good examples of the various functions of the travel book as a literary form – suitable as a contribution to a more objective observation both of oneself and of one's own culture, as an encouragement to international contacts, and leading to the evaluation of the diverse contributions of different cultures towards the enrichment of our twentieth-century cosmopolitan way of life. Condemnation, scorn and fear of others are to be replaced by a sincere discernment. The difficulty of this open-mindedness, however, is not to be underestimated, as prejudice and exploitation have long histories.

Excellent background reading can be found in the scholarly study of early accounts of British travellers to Africa and of African characters in sixteenth- and seventeenth-century English literature, which appears in Professor Eldred Jones's book, *The Elizabethan Image of Africa* (University of Virginia Press 1971), and studies of more recent developments have been outlined by Willfried Feuser, 'A Tale of Tamed Tigers' (*African Literature Today*, 9, 1978, pp. 94–6), to which I would merely add one excellent French study by Léon-François Hoffmann, *Le Nègre romantique: personnage littéraire et obsession collective* (Payot 1973).

The journeys made by Graham Greene and Bernard Dadié in these books are both an examination of the present and a search for the past. Writing in the first person, the authors attempt to 'whisper in the reader's ear'. This engaging of the reader's close attention is an attempt to have him participate in the experience of the journey, identifying with the 'double' or 'persona' of the story. Dadié speaks in a personal, subjective way in parts of the book, and as a more distant narrator in other parts. This anonymous narrator includes the ancestors, and provides a more objective view of events. The alternation between subjectivity and objectivity explains the choice and personification of cultural, historic objects (such as the statue of Caesar Augustus), and allows a greater freedom of imaginative creativity.

A similar role in Greene's book is played by the references to the unnamed cousin who follows and accompanies him. The technique of double articulation also helps to express the fact that there is both a sense of being in one place and a sense of movement, which is very important in both books. In this connection also, the regularity of the rhythm is very meaningful, and a slowing of the pace occurs at moments of ease and relaxation of tension, or of deliberate heavy stress. An accelerated pace occurs to convey either urgency or lightness of mood. The pace of the journey is therefore skilfully used to intensify the meaning and mood of the reflections.

Graham Greene's choice of Liberia as a place to visit and write about in 1935 was initially the result of his reading a government report about conditions there. He noted that the interior forest region had not yet been developed industrially at all, and a trip there was an opportunity to explore the darkness and mystery of the unknown, as well as a return to a primitive stage of civilization: like returning to the innocence of early childhood. He does not hesitate to refer to cannibalistic societies as follows:

> That afternoon the doctor came in to talk about the bush societies....
> I am not an anthropologist and I cannot pretend to remember very much of what Dr Harley told me: a pity, for no white man is closer to that particular 'heart of darkness', the secret societies being more firmly rooted in Liberia than in any other country on the West Coast.... Every-

one in Ganta knew they were there, with their ritual need of the heart, the palms of the hands, the skin of the forehead, but no one knew who they were. The Frontier Force were active, searching for strangers. Presently the fear passed. The Manos round Ganta knew what the men were seeking, for they have their own cannibalistic societies, and though I said nothing of this to my boys and there were no Manos among the carriers, Laminah and Amedoo knew all about it. Laminah said to me one day, 'These people bad, they chop men', and they were happy to leave the Manos behind. This is the territory the United States map marks so vaguely and excitingly as 'Cannibal'. (JWM, pp. 173-4)

Of the commercialization developed by the French, he says, 'Perhaps even the cannibals on the Ivory Coast were now chiefly occupied in manufacturing baits for tourists' (JWM, p. 147).

Greene was aware that the American rubber company Firestone had plantations around Monrovia, and he planned to enter Liberia via an inland route through Sierra Leone, in a forest region he was to call 'the green tunnel' (JWM, p. 123). From this perspective, the journey was to make possible an exploration of his own unconscious and of mankind's past, a subject which was just becoming popular at the time.[2] The eminent French historian of African affairs, Robert Cornevin, has commented that while Liberia was the only Black African country to remain independent between the two wars, it was heavily controlled by the economic interests of the American Firestone company.[3] That situation and the economic relationships between Liberia and the United States have been outlined in English by Martin R. Delany.[4]

The search for the past in Dadié's book takes the form of an account of a trip to Rome at Easter, 1959. Rome is regarded as the seat of European culture as well as of the Roman Catholic Church, and the deep significance for Dadié of this concept of 'seat' or 'source' of religious and cultural traditions can best be understood by those who are aware of the importance of the seat, or throne, of Krinjabo in the Agni society in which Dadié was brought up. It is central to traditional ceremonies, and has conferred the general idea of 'guardian of traditions' upon the family seat throughout that ethnic group.

As Dadié observes people, places, and vestiges of ancient Roman culture around Rome, he becomes more and more aware of his African perspective and value system, and yet also of certain positive aspects he can use from the learning acquired from European teachers.

Both writers make some attempt to improve the images that Europeans and Africans have of each other and to lessen prejudices,

4 *Graham Greene and Dadié*

although it will be seen that Dadié's more cosmopolitan outlook leads him to greater progress in this direction. The ambivalent attitudes prevalent in both cultures have been described by Richard Bonneau in these words (my translation):

> Indeed, for the European, Africa is on the one hand the sea-coast and its palm-trees, the pleasures of hunting, and on the other hand the 'Green Hell'; but for the African, the West, both feared and admired, appears as the worst and the best of things.[5]

Despite falling into the stereotyped images already noted (darkness, cannibals, etc.), Graham Greene does try to make his English reader think more deeply about such words as 'civilization', explaining how it had become synonymous with exploitation in Sierra Leone, and describing its effect:

> Neither ILP nor Communist Party urges a strike in England because the platelayers in Sierra Leone are paid sixpence a day without their food. Civilization here remained exploitation; we had hardly, it seemed to me, improved the natives' lot at all, they were as worn out with fever as before the white man came, we had introduced new diseases and weakened their resistance to the old, they still drank polluted water and suffered from the same worms.... Civilization so far as Sierra Leone was concerned was the railway to Pendembu, the increased export of palm-nuts; civilization, too, was Lever Brothers and the price they controlled; civilization was the long bar in the Grand, the sixpenny wages. It was not civilization as we think of it, a civilization of Suffolk churches and Cotswold manors, of Crome and Vaughan. (*JWM*, p. 61)

Greene had, of course, been strongly influenced by Joseph Conrad's books, as well as by hearing his aunt's stories of her life in South Africa. J. Koyinde Vaughan spoke out, in a well-documented article which appeared in the review *Présence Africaine* (no. 14–15, 1957, pp. 210–2) against Greene's perpetuation of the image of Africa as a place of darkness. It must be noted, however, that Greene's use of the image extends to broader horizons: it becomes in this book a symbol of the moral decadence of England, and as such, contributes greatly to the importance of the work.

Greene also takes a real interest in some of the local customs, and especially in the personal role of the 'priest-devil' Landow (*JWM*, pp. 89ff). He compares the atmosphere of the bush school with a public school in England, and emphasizes the element of fear involved in both situations:

> Most natives ... will attend a bush school, of which the masked devil is the unknown head. Even the Christian natives attend.... The school and

the devil who rules over it are at first a terror to the child. It lies as grimly as a public school in England between childhood and manhood. He has seen the masked devil and has been told of his supernatural power; no human part of the devil is allowed to show. (JWM, pp. 89-90)

In this, he clearly reflects his own childhood attitudes towards his father and the school where the family had its home: Greene's father was the headmaster. He relates more of these experiences in *A Sort of Life*, 'The Lost Childhood' in *Collected Essays*, and in his other travel book, *The Lawless Roads* (all available in Penguin Books).

Dadié shows a comparable interest in folklore and legends, and his use of African proverbs is an important aspect of his book, accentuating the West African perspective in spite of using the language brought to his homeland by the European colonialists. The social significance of the use of the proverb has been explained by the Nigerian writer Emenyonu, who quotes the Igbo's description of it as 'the palm oil with which words are eaten'.[6] Dadié's style is alert and lively, with a humour which brings an attractive freshness to the criticism of social evils and injustices. In sharp contrast to Greene's slow, groping trek through the forest, Dadié flies by jet aircraft to Rome and beholds with astonishment the city which contains so many centuries of civilization and represents so much of western culture. This flight is an image of the rapid changes brought about by European colonization in Africa, and the astonishment translates the bewilderment with which the African may face the confusion of old and new ways of life.

Observations by the two writers on their respective journeys are noted in relation to personal recollections, both elements are skilfully combined and certain symbols selected. The images and symbols used merit some detailed consideration. There will be no attempt here to present an exhaustive interpretation of all the symbols used in the two books, but the following remarks should serve to demonstrate their multiple meanings and their relation to the social perspective of the two writers.

The symbols are the most striking and the richest single element in the structure of the works. Mircea Eliade has described the symbol as revealing the most profound aspects of reality which cannot be communicated in any other way.[7] Usually, a symbol cannot be explained because it appeals beyond its context to the observer's experience. It can serve an important social goal by facilitating communication and co-operation, as has been noted in a recent study by Altizer, Beardslee and Young.[8] As these writers have explained, the symbol's effectiveness depends largely on the skill of its user, as the object itself is relatively arbitrary.⁹ The symbol's main role is evocation, and it achieves this by connecting aspects or areas of experience which are different, and even sometimes in opposition.

In Greene's book, rats and insects feature prominently. Among the information that Greene had acquired before leaving England for the journey to Liberia was the following:

> The rat population may fairly be described as swarming, the wood and corrugated iron houses lend themselves to rat harbourage....
> The great majority of all mosquitoes caught in Monrovia are of a species known to carry yellow fever. (JWM, p. 17)

A native hut was regarded as synonymous with rats and insects by the character referred to in the book as 'Daddy', who had spent twenty-five years in Freetown, and who advised Greene against the trek through the forest region. Greene's own observations of the ants and bats begin when he stays at a hotel in Freetown (JWM, pp. 50–1), and from that point on, various insects and rats are mentioned with increasing, obsessive intensity. However, there is some humour in his descriptions of his host's efforts to rid the house of moths, cockchafers and beetles during the evening Greene spends at the border of Sierra Leone and French Guinea (JWM, p. 63). Later, in Bolahun, he expresses admiration for the Catholic missionaries' courage as they constantly face the risk of fever and the abundance of snakes, worms and rats (JWM, p. 84).

As swarms of moths fly round the paraffin lamps lit for the funeral ceremony of the Tailahun chief, Greene acknowledges not only a fear of moths which he says is inherited from his mother, but also his habitual reaction of avoiding any idea which is unpleasant to him, such as the concept of eternal life and damnation: 'But in Africa one couldn't avoid them any more than one could avoid the supernatural' (JWM, p. 96).

However, just as it was impossible to avoid the insects of the forest, he is obliged to learn to face up to them, and he compares this with a psychoanalytical process. As the trek progresses, the descriptions of the various insects, spiders and rats accompany his expressions of nervousness, boredom and frustration. When the path gets difficult, every living thing seems to be a snake or insect, and his reaction to the difficulty of the trek is reflected by the various emphases on them.

After walking for more hours of the day than usual to reach Duogobmai, and reaching that village ahead of his porters, he realizes that he will have to sleep without his equipment, and again, the observations on the rats reflect his disgust and frustration. He accepts the conditions he finds simply because they are unavoidable, but he is still afraid of catching malaria in a place so remote from any medical help. This leads to his recognition of how dependent he is on the willingness of his porters not to abandon him in the middle of the forest, and he yields to their requests for a rest day. However, this rest day at Duogobmai is full of problems and frustrations, expressed in two pages about the rats (*JWM*, pp. 130–2). Clearly, the descriptions of the rats are connected with the intensity of his mood of disgust.

At Zigita, he was disappointed at the non-appearance of the sorcerer, and he again writes about his impressions of disturbance by rats, although he finds that nothing in the hut was actually disturbed during the night at all.

The mood of rottenness is somewhat different at the Zorzor mission: there are beetles instead of rats, and this difference could indicate Greene's notion that evil in religious communities may take on a different expression from that in secular society. Later, he notes that the presence of insects is a sign of the absence of the corrupt and corrupting civilization such as he had observed on the coast of Sierra Leone and Senegal, as well as in Europe.

Using a rest house allotted to him at Bamakama (in French Guinea), he finds the hut full of insects and the smell of a dead rat under the floor. This, however, finally leads him to bury his fear of rats, and he arrives safely at Ganta to meet Dr Harley. Disagreeable conditions later on mostly give rise to comments on the destructiveness of invading goats or the presence of large spiders. Towards the end of the long trek through the forest region, where Greene notes the reappearance of signs of the decadent coastal civilization, the spiders represent the decay and the futility of progress, as well as his personal depression and fatigue.

Greene's trek as a whole is an image of man's struggle for survival in a decadent world. The rats, mosquitoes and other insects that disturbed him are not only physical realities, but also symbols of everything that torments and destroys man in today's world. Like the jigger that penetrated into his foot during the trek, and which he mentions repeatedly, evil is also within man. Jacques Madaule commented on this aspect of all Greene's writing, when he said in 1949: 'We are constantly aware of the catastrophes that assail us, and which show, in various ways, that evil is in man.'[10] Madaule comments that Greene's literary talent harmonizes with his Catholic view of the world.[11]

There are rare moments in Greene's book when one catches a glimpse of beautiful aspects of the forest, the sight of butterflies, a waterfall, or other sign of freshness and vivid colour; these reflect a very momentary pleasure or sense of relief, but are significant because they lighten the pervading oppressiveness of the other elements. Green's moral and spiritual perspective has been indicated by Madaule: 'The world in which we live, which has been corrupted by our sin, is a world in which there is a superabundance of evil, and it will continue that way until the end of time.'[12]

Bernard Dadié, also a Roman Catholic, perceives a similar malaise of civilization, but his manner of describing it differs considerably from Greene's. The spider is a popular character in regional folk-tales in the Ivory Coast, and not mentioned by Dadié in his travel book. When he refers to the flies and insects of the tropical forest, he uses them cleverly to connect in a humorous way two thoughts on anthropology and materialism which conclude thus: 'Donc la mouche est une nouvelle espèce de créature humaine qui vient, discute avec vous, et ensuite le ventre bien gros de nouvelles, s'envole se dégorger chez ceux qui le paient pour cette récolte' (La Ville, p. 39), which I roughly translate as: 'Therefore the fly is a new species of human being who comes to converse with you, and when he has had his fill of news, flies off to spill it out to those who pay him for these tit-bits.'

When Dadié mentions rats, the tone again contrasts with that used by Greene. On seeing a young Jewish woman during his journey, Dadié mentions the death of rats in a violent bush fire as an illustration of the atrocious torture of Jews in Europe (La Ville, pp. 20–1).

Repeatedly throughout the book, Dadié attributes most manifestations of aggressiveness to the accumulation of wealth, and observes that the spiritual influence of the Christ who was born in poverty is hardly apparent in a world controlled by the power of money. He reminds his reader that money came to his homeland along with European trade and colonization (La Ville, p. 20). And he includes a striking warning to young people against a thoughtless acceptance of the attraction to get richer, which easily leads to aggressive behaviour (La Ville, pp. 38–9).

Among Dadié's symbols are two objects representative of degenerate human enterprise: the Bank of the Holy Spirit which he sees in Rome, and the Cinzano advertisement board. The fact that Dadié has chosen objects made by man is meaningful. Man is the agent who spreads evil by his egoistic activities. The metal and stone of which these objects are built are neither good nor bad in themselves; that depends on the use made of them by man. The Bank of the Holy Spirit is the object selected by Dadié as the seat and symbol of the generalized usurpation of spiritual areas by materialism. He says:

> Men have progressed. God the Father, remaining in heaven, God the Son, nailed on the Cross, the very astute Romans, wishing to reconcile the irreconcilable, considered it opportune, beneficial, and good politics, to house God the Holy Spirit in a bank, the house of Mammon.... Has money become a holy spirit? (*La Ville*, p. 70)

Dadié notes the power of the wealthy with irony, and points to what could be achieved by a fairer distribution of wealth:

> Does this mean that, from now on, money, the spirit of the modern world, could play a more human rôle? Unite men, families, peoples, nations, instead of dividing them into the poor and the rich? Act as a leaven and not a brake? (*La Ville*, p. 70)

Both in Rome and at home, 'money is the liquor that goes most easily to the head' (p. 98). His sharp criticism is softened at some points: 'When there are so many ruins around and within one, one reaches the point of trying to reconcile the irreconcilable: Rome is at that point' (p. 86).

He aims his criticism more directly at the élite of the new young nations, referring to the fact that they are able to keep wealth from their countrymen by placing it in 'a mountainous, inaccessible place called Switzerland' (p. 155). Nor does the Papal estate escape sharp irony:

> Over there, in the distance, one can distinguish a powerful dome bearing a globe with a cross on it. It is the residence of the Pope, God's representative on earth.... Jesus Christ must have been born in a poverty they are ashamed of. Fortunately the Bank of the Holy Spirit was born. (p. 84)

During the visit to the Vatican described towards the end of the book, Dadié repeats the word 'golden' over and over again, and finally concludes: 'Take away the gold, and wouldn't that take from them all reason for living?' (p. 206). Dadié's sharpest criticisms are often expressed in this interrogative form, to provoke his reader's reflection rather than merely to express his own condemnation. It also allows for the humorous effect. His cool remark after the Pope's appearance may be quoted as a final comment on his satire: 'Besides, he is infallible.' (p. 207)

His criticism is directed not only towards leaders of the church and heads of government, but towards all who hold economic power and participate in the overturning of moral values. His adept juxtaposition of ideas and his well-turned phrases emphasize contrasts and achieve a penetrating, humorous effect.

His second symbol is the Cinzano advertisement board, the significance of which extends to all means of propaganda which influence other people's minds. Dadié mentions this advertisement board as soon as he leaves the airport in Rome, and he also associates with it his regret that the Romans seem to confuse their situation of 'holy city' with cultural superiority, and seem to dominate others with the approval of the Church.

The Roman ruins have a double function in this book: they are the symbol of ancient culture as well as of decadence. In devoting most of forty pages to the Roman history which he is reminded of by the ruins, statues and other monuments, Dadié not only demonstrates his wealth of knowledge of the details of this history, but also exercises his gift for rendering these historical accounts interesting to his readers by using a light tone, inserting amusing anecdotes, playing on words, and quoting proverbs. He interprets the presence of the ruins as meaning that Rome has not wanted to break with her past, a past which can still teach modern generations (p. 80). The decadence indicated is an absence of gratitude to illustrious ancestors such as Caesar Augustus, whose statue seems to serve only as a tourist attraction and as a source of lucrative gain – a materialistic, egoistic attitude observed in modern Rome as well as in modern African cities. Dadié is aware that modern industrialization has often been achieved at the cost of a lowering of moral values, and his is one of the prophetic voices greatly needed for today's world.

Commercialization of religious traditions is criticized by both writers. For Greene, it is an aspect which spoils the effect of the 'devil's dance' (JWM, p. 92). And he is reminded of an occasion during his childhood when missionaries visiting his school had impressed him by their preoccupation with money (JWM, p. 169). In Dadié's book, there is at first a note of surprise at the preoccupation with the sale of religious objects in Rome which he refers to in this way: 'Fetichism in this country is spread around ostentatiously in the streets.' (p. 112) Then a note of impatience: 'Is there anywhere in this city where they don't sell religious trinkets?' (p. 181) and he refers to the sale of portraits of the Pope as a flourishing industry, constituting most of the articles for sale in some places (p. 87). For both writers, a real religious piety does not involve this kind of commercialization. For Greene, there is also a more vaguely described sense of the supernatural, expressed in descriptions of the witch, the priest-devil, and the missionary doctor, and these harmonize with his themes of darkness and mystery. Dadié's book includes a fourth symbol: the butterfly, although it is only mentioned four times. Butterflies had been his childhood favourites during carefree hours at play, and this aspect may be noted in his pseudo-autobiographical novel, *Climbié*. Now, after long arduous efforts towards his country's independence, freedom is expressed by this symbol of the butterfly: freedom to be himself, just as on those days when he could forget the restrictions of school life and wander about day-dreaming. The butterfly which appears in Rome, a spirit of youthful spontaneity, promises him a happy, flourishing future. Only a very small part of the great city is filled with such laughter and song: the 'Song of the Butterfly' resounds in a small restaurant. Light and fanciful (p. 82), the butterfly represents hope, and poetic inspiration. It gives Dadié's book a note of hope for the future.

NOTES

1. Graham Greene, *Journey Without Maps*, London, Heinemann, 1936. In further extracts, *JWM*. Bernard Dadié, *La Ville òu nul ne meurt*, Paris, Présence Africaine, 1969. In further extracts, *La Ville*.
2. David Thomson, *World History from 1914 to 1961*, London, Oxford University Press, 1963 (1954), pp. 121–5.
3. Robert Cornevin, *L'Afrique noire de 1919 à nos jours*, Paris, Publications Orientalistes de France, 1973, p. 59.
4. Howard Brotz (ed.), *Negro Social and Political Thought, 1850–1920*, New York: Basic Books, 1966, pp. 73–9.
5. Richard Bonneau, 'L'Image de l'Occident dans le roman Négro-Africain – l'exemple ivoirien', doctoral thesis in comparative literature, Tours, 1975, p. 7.
6. Ernest Emenyonu, 'African Literature Revisited: A Search for African Critical Standards', in *Revue de Littérature Comparée* 48, 1974, p. 392.
7. Mircea Eliade, *Images et symboles*, Paris, Gallimard, 1952, pp. 13–14.
8. Thomas J. J. Altizer, William A. Beardslee and J. Harvey Young, *Truth, Myth and Symbol*, New Jersey, Prentice-Hall, 1962, p. 119.
9. ibid., p. 112. See also Alfred North Whitehead, *Symbolism: Its Meaning and Effect*, New York, Macmillan, 1958, p. 42.
10. Jacques Madaule, *Graham Greene*, Paris, Editions du Temps Présent, 1949, pp. 10–11.
11. ibid., p. 333.
12. ibid., p. 367.

A Touch of the Absurd: Soyinka and Beckett

Catherine Obianuju Acholonu

It is evident from Wole Soyinka's characterization, language, imagery, his themes, and above all his general style that he is fascinated by the absurd theatre. The Trials of Brother Jero, Jero's Metamorphosis, The Road, Madmen and Specialists, The Swamp Dwellers,[1] to mention only a few, often call to mind (some to a greater degree than others) the language, styles and themes of the plays of Albert Camus, Jean-Paul Sartre and, above all, those of Samuel Beckett, with whom this article will be concerned. This study will be confined to three plays by each author which will be treated jointly, since a single play of Soyinka's may show influences from more than one of Beckett's.

As in Waiting for Godot,[2] Soyinka's characters in Madmen and Specialists are tramps (cf. the touts in The Road). Aafaa and his mates are beggars and to earn their living they move from place to place like the tramps Vladimir and Estragon, Pozzo and Lucky in Beckett's play. In these two plays the chief characters are drop-outs from society. Soyinka makes use of human deformity in the same way as does Beckett: his characters are either old, invalid, ailing or nursing wounds. Blind men play leading roles, as in the second part of Waiting for Godot, where Pozzo is blind; in Endgame[3] the hero Hamm is a blind invalid in a wheelchair; in The Road, Murano – who is to enlighten Professor about the Word – is blind; in The Swamp Dwellers it is the beggar from the north who is blind, while in Madmen and Specialists Blind Man plays a leading role. The message of Beckett's Not I is also ingeniously incorporated in Madmen and Specialists. Not I[4] is a play without action. There are no characters but only a mouth which is seen and heard as it gives the life history of its female character. This idea is echoed in the opening of Madmen and Specialists when the beggars stake parts of their bodies to throw dice:

Goyi	Why leave me out? I still want to try.
Blind Man	You have nothing left to stake.
Cripple	You're just a rubber ball, Goyi. You need a hand to throw with, anyway.
Goyi	I can use my mouth.
Aafaa	To throw dice? You'll eat sand my friend.

In *Madmen and Specialists* the language is condensed to the barest minimum so that the characters (especially the tramps) make very short sentences that are full of meaning. This is reminiscent of Beckett's style, and that of other existentialist writers.

Cripple	Your turn, Aafaa.
Aafaa	What for?
Cripple	A penny is something.
Aafaa	Not for me.
Goyi	Give her a pennyworth, then.
Aafaa	Can't be bothered.
Blind Man	Go on. Don't be mean.

(*Madmen and Specialists*, p. 10)

Hamm	You're leaving me all the same.
Clov	I'm trying.
Hamm	You don't love me.
Clov	Once!

(*Endgame*, p. 14)

Soyinka's characters make use of foul and degenerate language, and this is similar to the language Beckett's disillusioned characters indulge in. Both authors make extensive use of sordid, frightening and disgusting images. Like Vladimir and Estragon in Beckett's play, Soyinka's tramps stink: 'He has stinking breath and I have stinking feet' (*Waiting for Godot*, p. 46).

Like Beckett's plays, *Madmen and Specialists* is infested by such vermin as fleas, bugs, rats, dogs and by the greatest of all vermin – man.

Professor in *The Road* is Soyinka's version of Beckett's Pozzo in *Waiting for Godot*. Like Pozzo, Professor is mad, and like him he has lost touch with the realistic world, implicit in their lack of notion of time. Professor reads time from a watch that has ceased to work, while Pozzo reads the years from his own. Both are seekers after something (though more pronounced with Professor than with Pozzo), and that thing is the meaning of life; in *The Road* it is the Word. Pozzo uses Lucky as his guide, his eye; in much the same way Professor uses blind Murano.

14 Soyinka and Beckett

> Pozzo But for him (Lucky) all my thoughts, all my feelings would have been on common things. *(Pause with extraordinary vehemence.)* Professional worries: *(calmer)* Beauty, grace, truth of the first water, I knew they were all beyond me.
>
> (*Waiting for Godot*, p. 33)

The blind beggar in Soyinka's *The Swamp Dwellers* echoes Pozzo in his reference to time. When asked how long he has been blind Pozzo replies:

> Pozzo I woke up one day as blind as Fortune...
> Vladimir And when was that?
> Pozzo Don't question me! The blind have no notion of time.... Have you not done tormenting me with your accursed time! It's abominable! When! when! One day is that not enough for you, one day like any other day....
>
> (*Waiting for Godot*, p. 89)

Likewise, in *The Swamp Dwellers* Makuri asks the blind beggar:

> Makuri And you have been on the road for... how long did you say?
> Beggar I have lost all count of time. To me, one day is just like another... ever since my sight became useless.
>
> (*Swamp Dwellers*, p. 90)

Soyinka's rhetorical devices are akin to those of Samuel Beckett though sometimes more acidic. Both authors indulge in lexical and syntactic gymnastics so that the result is usually ambiguity, pun, paradox and irony which are pointers to the ingenuity of the authors. In *Endgame*, when Nell, Hamm's ageing mother, tells Clov 'desert!' (p. 23) by which she means that he should clear off, Clov interprets the word as 'She told me to go away into the desert' (p. 23), the suggestion being that the world is an arid land, a desert, a wasteland where men's lives languish. Soyinka uses language in the same way. The Old Man in *Madmen and Specialists* refers to man in society as:

> the cyst in the system ... the dog in dogma, tick of heretic, the tick in politics ... a dot in the i of ego, an ass in the mass ... the pee of priesthood, the pee pee of perfect priesthood, oh how dare you raise your hindquarters you dog of dogma and cast the scent of your existence on the lamp-post of Destiny you HOLE IN THE ZERO OF NOTHING. (p. 76)

The expressions 'cyst', 'tick', 'ass', 'pee', 'pee pee' may appear meaningless at first glance especially as they are derived from those words succeeding them. They are part of what I call Soyinka's lexical gymnastics. But they are all pregnant with meaning. These sickening images portray man as a useless but irritating outgrowth of the body (cyst), a parasitic vermin (tick), a mere bottom or buttocks (ass), an excrement (pee), and an animal (dog). These images find their equivalents in Beckett, especially in *Waiting for Godot*, where man is referred to as 'that bog' (p. 15), 'the slobber ... the slaver ... a cretin ... a goitre' (p. 26).

In fact Soyinka's themes are echoes of those of Samuel Beckett. His characters are gripped by the same hopelessness in which Beckett's characters find themselves. In *Madmen and Specialists* 'Hope is dead' (p. 67), and for the characters in *Endgame* 'nature has forgotten us' (p. 16). Both authors realize that 'truth hurts' (*Madmen and Specialists*, p. 7) as is evident from the observations of their characters who point out the horror of thinking. For Vladimir and Estragon in *Waiting for Godot*, 'What is terrible is to have thought' (p. 64). Aafaa in *Madmen and Specialists* is horrified by the fact that the old man teaches the disabled men to think, thus 'placing a working mind in a mangled body' (p. 37).

Soyinka's existentialist plays are populated by the old, the ailing, the disabled or people nursing wounds. These are Beckett's vehicles too. It is a device to demonstrate the sordid plight of man. Both authors allude to the entanglement of man, a condition from which there is no escape. In *The Road*, this idea is symbolized by the ever-present spider spinning his web. And in *Waiting for Godot* Pozzo, alluding to Lucky's extraordinary dance, says, 'Do you know what he calls it? ... The Net. He thinks he's entangled in a net' (p. 40). Soyinka's spider's web originated here.

Beckett's characters in *Waiting for Godot* blame God for the hopelessness of their condition which is worsened by his 'divine apathia divine athambia divine aphasia' (p. 43). Their incessant waiting for a Godot they cannot identify, who never shows up, and who, they know, will never show up, is absurd in the sense that it is the only content of life and this content is empty. Religion offers the only consolation to man, but it offers only a delusive hope. Beckett's atheistic message, delivered through his characters' numerous heresies, is that this content of life is in itself empty and man's life shall be wasted here on earth: 'One day we were born, one day we shall die, the same day, the same second, ... they gave birth astride of a grave, the light gleams an instant, then it's night once more' (*Waiting for Godot*, p. 89). The heresy of Soyinka's characters culminates in their parody of the Gloria: 'As – Was – Is – Now As Ever Shall Be ...' (p. 40). With the word 'As', Soyinka establishes a mysterious code that forms the focal point of the themes of his play. Its relevance in

Madmen and Specialists is akin to that of The Word in *The Road* and of Godot in *Waiting for Godot*.

Soyinka's *The Swamp Dwellers* has many things in common with *Endgame*. The four characters that populate the play are the only people left living, and they are 'living-dead'. They find themselves in a cell under the ground while on the earth's surface all is dead and quiet. One gets the impression that death is hovering on the earth's surface looking for victims just as the marshes are lying in wait for travellers in *The Swamp Dwellers*. The Serpent which is the god of this land lives in the marshes and is the symbol of death itself. Makuri's speech 'This is the end. This is as far as human beings can go ...' (p. 89), is reminiscent of Hamm's observations in *Endgame*: 'It's the end, Clov, we've come to the end' (p. 50), 'there's nowhere else' (p. 14), 'outside of here it's death' (p. 45).

Like Beckett, Soyinka uses water in *The Swamp Dwellers* as a symbol of death, contrary to the conventional use of this symbol. The height of this sinister symbolism is Beckett's recurring picture of a honeymoon on the river where the bride and groom usually find themselves (at the climax of their intercourse) struggling against death by drowning.

> Vladimir Do you remember the gospels?
> Estragon I remember the maps of the Holy Land. Coloured they were. Very pretty. The Dead Sea was pale blue. The very look of it made me thirsty. There's where we'll go for our honeymoon. We'll swim. We'll be happy.   (*Waiting for Godot*, p. 12)
> Nell We once went out rowing on lake Como. (*Pause*) On April afternoon.
> Nagg We had got married the day before.
> Nell Engaged.
> Nagg You were in such fits that we capsized. By rights we should have been drowned.   (*Endgame*, p. 20)

This symbol is incorporated into *The Swamp Dwellers*.

> Makuri Come on, my own Alu. Tell old Makuri what you did on the night of our wedding.
> Alu No.
> Makuri You're a stubborn old hen.... Won't you even tell how you dragged me from the house and we went across the swamps, though it was so dark that I could not see the white of your eyes?
> Alu My mother said I had to say it on my bridal bed.
> Makuri Just where we stood. Go on say it again.
> Alu 'Where the rivers meet, there the marriage must begin. And the river bed itself is the perfect bridal bed!'

Makuri (thoughtfully): A-ii ... The bed of the river itself ... the bed of
the river (Bursts out suddenly into what appears to be illogical
laughter). We did not know the swamp came up as far as that
part of the stream ... the ground ... gave ... way beneath us!
(The Swamp Dwellers, pp. 85-6)

Though there are many similarities in the styles and themes of the two authors, yet there is a significant point of divergence in their philosophies. Both authors proclaim doom for mankind, but whereas Soyinka sees man as the creator of his troubles, Beckett's man is helpless and incapable of changing the fate to which nature has confined him. Soyinka sees little hope for mankind: since as a result of his evil tendencies man has brought doom upon himself, he can save himself by denouncing evil, but there is little hope of his doing so. The problem of Beckett's man is existential. He is evil but he does not have a chance to improve on himself and there is no need to try, for life is a cul-de-sac. The only thing that is certain is that the world is a burial place, 'the end is in the beginning ...' (Endgame, p. 44) and 'we are born astride of the grave' (Waiting for Godot, p. 89). Man is to be pitied for he has no choice and cannot prevent his birth. You cannot blame yourself for being born; nor can you blame your parents, for according to Nagg, Hamm's father, 'if it hadn't been me it would have been some one else' (Endgame, p. 38), nor can you place the blame on God, because Beckett does not believe in the existence of God; for him life is one unfathomable farce.

Samuel Beckett is a very radical and contagious writer. There is no doubt that he has had a profound influence on modern writers all over the world. Wole Soyinka has not escaped the touch of the magic staff of that great writer. On the contrary, much of Soyinka's fame, brought about by his introduction of 'something new and different' into African literature, stems from Beckettsian elements in the styles, language and themes of his plays.

NOTES

1. Wole Soyinka, The Jero Plays contains The Trials of Brother Jero and Jero's Metamorphosis, London, Methuen, 1973. The Trials of Brother Jero is also included in Three Plays, London, Rex Collings, 1973. The Road, London and New York, Oxford University Press, 1965. Madmen and Specialists, London, Methuen, 1971. The Swamp Dwellers is included in

Five Plays, London and New York, Oxford University Press, 1964. It is also included in *Three Plays*, London, Rex Collings, 1973.
2. Samuel Beckett, *Waiting for Godot*, London, Faber, 1956.
3. Samuel Beckett, *Endgame*, London, Faber, 1958.
4. Samuel Beckett, *Not I*, London, Faber, 1973.

Laye, Lamming and Wright: Mother and Son

Fritz H. Pointer

Camara Laye, the first of two children, was born in ancient Kouroussa at the head of the Niger, in Upper Guinea, on 1 January 1928. Kouroussa, which is geographically part of the western Sudan, has known historical civilization for a thousand years or more, and its inhabitants (approximately 8,000 in 1939) are still deeply rooted in the tradition of Islam and the ancient traditions of Africa.

Although Guinea was under French influence, forming part of former French West Africa, in spite of the French having *assimilation* as a direct aim, African rural life away from towns was then little touched. The impact of French civilization was probably more superficial in a small town like Kouroussa than in a modern city such as Conakry; thus life in the countryside continued, under French administration, in its traditional way.

Kouroussa is far into the interior of Guinea, on the rich fertile plain. The capital, Conakry, 400 miles away on the coast, is so unknown and strange to many of the inhabitants of the interior that it is like another country. Camara Laye's mother typifies this perception, as can be seen from the extreme apprehension she felt when he first went away to school. From his autobiographical *L'Enfant noir*, we read:

> Depuis une semaine, ma mère accumulait les provisions. Conakry est à quelque 600 kilomètres de Kouroussa et, pour ma mère, c'était une terre inconnue, sinon inexplorée, où Dieu seul savait si l'on mange à sa faim. Et c'est pourquoi les couscous, les viandes, les poissons, les ignames, les riz, les patates s'entassaient. Une semaine plus tôt déjà, ma mère avait entamé la tournée des marabouts les plus réputés, les consultant sur mon avenir et multipliant les sacrifices. Elle avait fait immoler un boeuf à la mémoire de son père et invoqué l'assistance de ses ancêtres, afin que le bonheur m'accompagnât dans un voyage qui, à ses yeux, était un peu comme un

départ chez les sauvages; le fait que Conakry est la capitale de la Guinée, ne faisait qu'accenteur le caractère d'étrangeté du lieu où je me rendrais.[1]

For a whole week my mother had been collecting provisions for me. Conakry is about 400 miles from Kouroussa, and to my mother it was an unknown if not an unexplored land where God alone knew if I would get enough to eat. So she gathered couscous, meat, fish, yams, rice and potatoes. The week before, she had gone to the most celebrated marabouts to consult them about my future and make sacrifices. She had offered up an ox in memory of her father and had invoked the spirits of her ancestors that good fortune might attend me on a venture which in her eyes was rather like going to live among savages. The fact that Conakry is the capital of Guinea only served to accentuate its strangeness.[2]

Camara Laye's mother is the personification, the metaphor of all African women; the incarnation of maternal principles in domestic truth and social morals. There is nothing here of the *Oedipus Tyrannus*; the chance of being exposed as an infant, then rescued, then adopted by a king, then by one coincidence killing his father, and then by another coincidence marrying his father's widow are impossible in this context. The preparations for Camara's journey to Conakry are not a private matter, nor are they occasioned by capricious or abnormal affection, but involve his immediate and extended family – ancestors, uncles and the community – and consulting the most celebrated marabouts and offering up an ox as sacrifice. All of this was to look after the young Camara's spiritual and physical needs. The night before he was to leave for the technical school in Conakry, he could not sleep; he was depressed, upset and woke several times during the night. He heard groans and went to his mother's hut where he heard her tossing and moaning quietly on her bed. He asked himself pensively:

> Est-ce que la vie était ainsi faite, qu'on ne pût rien entreprendre sans payer tribut aux larmes? (*EN*, p. 181)
>
> Was this what life was going to be like? Were tears a part of everything we did? (*DC*, p. 139)

This rupture in Camara's life: this wrenching separation at the tender age of fifteen from mother and motherland is the central thematic image around which *L'Enfant noir* is based. As alluded to earlier, Laye was being sent to Conakry, from Kouroussa, for a course of technical study at the École Georges Poiret, a Technical College. Near the time of departure his mother reluctantly instructs him to 'Cours vite faire tes adieux maintenant!' ('Run and say your goodbyes now!') The sensitive portrayal that follows gives eloquent testimony to the communal context enveloping the youthful Laye, and by metaphorical extension the youth of rural Africa.

> J'allais dire au revoir aux vieilles gens de notre concession et des concessions voisines, et j'avais le coeur gros. Ces hommes, ces femmes, je les connaissais depuis ma plus tendre enfance, depuis toujours je les avais vus à la place même où je les voyais vu disparaître: ma grandmère paternelle avait disparu! Et reverrais-je tous ceux auxquels je disais à présent adieu? Frappé de cette incertitude, ce fut comme si soudain je prenais congé de mon passé même. Mais n'était-ce pas un peu cela? Ne quittais-je pas ici toute une partie de mon passé? (*EN*, p. 183)

> I had to go and say farewell to the elders of our concession and to those of the concessions nearby. I went with a heavy heart. I had known these men and women since I was a baby. I had always known them. I had watched them living in this place and I had watched them disappear from it too. My father's mother had disappeared! Would I ever again see these people to whom I was now saying farewell? Overcome by doubts, I felt suddenly as if I were taking leave of the past itself. And wasn't that just what I was doing? Wasn't I leaving a part of my life behind me? (*DC*, p. 140)

Here Laye expresses the timeless circle of life; from birth, through life, to death — the essence and unity of the human experience. For Laye, this essence is the people of his community who nurtured and reared him since infancy. Leaving them was like leaving a part of his life behind. It is not in the normal order of things for a fifteen-year-old to be severed from home and family, simply to go to school. This certainly particularizes the African experience of the 1940s. By that I mean that it is unlikely that an African born in the United States or the West Indies would have to leave home to attend secondary school. Most probably, even in the 1940s there would have been a school in the area, if not in the neighbourhood. Like that of other rural African youths, Laye's academic and secular life is very particular; it is, however, Laye's relationship with his mother that provides a metaphor and symbol for the relationship with one's family and land. One does not leave family and home every day.

The image Laye provides is both typical and universal. It has neither ethnic, nor national, nor empirical boundaries. What distinguishes Camara Laye (or Richard Wright or George Lamming) is his visualization, his memory and perception, his interpretation and aesthetic recreation of an otherwise banal experience.

This is not an 'existential' experience, especially in Laye's case; it has nothing to do with man's responsibility for forming his own nature, or stressing the prime importance of personal decisions, personal freedom or personal goals. Quite the contrary: Laye, like most of us, is not responsible for his own decisions or goals at the age of fifteen; and unlike the experience of some of us, the collective principles of his community precluded such individualism; thus the foresight and insight of Laye's community decided for him, until he would reach the age of accountability. Laye, like the rest of us, is a product of his context, a victim of his childhood.

In traditional African life, the individual does not and cannot exist alone, except corporally. He owes his existence to other people, including those of past generations and his contemporaries. He is simply part of the whole. Laye belongs to this context; a context that stipulates that only in terms of other people does the individual become conscious of his own being, his own duties, his privileges and responsibilities towards himself and towards other people.[3] Laye's social context, as presented in *L'Enfant noir*, is not one in which the individual makes his own choice of moral, political and/or social conventions; rather, 'the individual can only say "I am, because we are; and since we are, therefore, I am."'[4] Therefore, leaving the warmth, comfort, and security of his motherland and mother was a trying experience for the entire community; like snapping the link of a chain, a link that resists the rupture.

> Quand je reviens près de ma mère et que je l'aperçus enlarmes devant mes bagages, je me mis à pleurer à mon tour. Je me jetai dans ses bras et je l'étreignis.
> — Mère! criai-je.
> Je l'entendais sangloter, je suntais sa poitrine douloureusement se soulever.
> — Mère, ne pleure pas! dis-je. Ne pleure pas!
> Mais je n'arrivais pas moi-même à refréner mes larmes et je la suppliai de ne pas m'accompagner à la gare, car il me semblait qu'alors je ne pourrais jamais m'arracher à ses bras. Elle me fit signe qu'elle y consentait. Nous nous étreignîmes une dernière fois, et je m'éloignai presque en courant. Mes soeurs, mes frères, les apprentices se chargèrent des bagages. (*EN*, pp. 183–4)

> When I returned to my mother and saw her standing in tears beside my luggage, I too began to weep. I threw myself into her arms. I begged her not to go with me to the station, for I thought that if she did I should never be able to tear myself away from her arms. She nodded consent. We embraced for the last time and I almost ran out of the hut. My sisters and brothers and the apprentices carried my luggage. (*DC*, p. 140)

Laye's feelings are genuine and pure; complementing a clear and honest picture. The English translation has collapsed, ever so slightly here, but the essence has been maintained. Mother and son embraced. They shed tears in each other's arms. Everyone is standing. Sisters, brothers and apprentices are all supportive. His father is also firmly present; the strong figure of another theme. It is the 'nod' from his mother that releases him, a fledgling, to take his leave. The experience is contextualized by Laye's subtle, neutral use of the much maligned 'hut'; a word in his adept hands that gets stripped of its pejorative use and prejudice, and substitutes a warm, womb-like aura that envelops and seduces the reader with a simple yet profound sense of maternal loss.

Another novelist, Richard Wright, treats a similar experience; where the loss, the separation, is more psychological than physical. At the age of twelve, Wright was inured to hunger and instability; experiences that even time could not erase; a sense of the world derived from his relationship with his mother and family; a sense that was more esoteric than typical. Wright's precocious cynicism convinced him that the meaning of living came only when one was struggling to wring a meaning out of meaningless suffering. Wright acutely challenges our understanding of the mimetic principle in art, that 'Art imitates Nature'.

We must see what sense can be made of words like truth, probability, realism when they function within the context of a mimetic system such as autobiography. The uniqueness and truth of Wright's childhood is told with brutal realism. Wright was the first African–American novelist to depict the plight of the urban masses, and the first to approach this material in terms of the tradition of naturalism and urban realism. Richard Wright, in laying bare his suffering, helps us to suffer less. In the following extract from his autobiography, *Black Boy, A Record of Childhood and Youth*,[5] Wright reveals and illuminates another vision of the mother/son relationship and of maternal separation and loss. To borrow an engineering expression, 'the critical path' of Laye and Wright parallel each other in many ways. Wright also writes imagistically, for example;

> We left Clarksdale (Mississippi); my mother rode on a stretcher in the baggage car with Uncle Edward attending her. Back home, she lay for days, groaning, her eyes vacant. Doctors visited her and left without making any comment. Granny grew frantic. Uncle Edward, who had gone home, returned and still more doctors were called in. They told us that a blood clot had formed on my mother's brain and that another paralytic stroke had set in.
>
> Once, in the night, my mother called me to her bed and told me that she

could not endure the pain, that she wanted to die. I held her hand and begged her to be quiet. That night I ceased to react to my mother; my feelings were frozen. I merely waited upon her, knowing that she was suffering. She remained abed ten years, gradually growing better, but never completely recovering, relapsing periodically into her paralytic state. The family had stripped itself of money to fight my mother's illness.... Her illness gradually became an accepted thing in the house, something that could not be stopped or helped.

My mother's suffering grew into a symbol in my mind, gathering to itself all the poverty, the ignorance, the helplessness, the painful, baffling, hunger-ridden days and hours; the restless moving, the futile seeking, the uncertainty, the fear, the dread; the meaningless pain and endless suffering. Her life set the emotional tone of my life, colored the men and women I was to meet in the future, conditioned my relation to events that had not yet happened, determined my attitude to situations and circumstances I had yet to face. A somberness of spirit that I was never to lose settled over me during the slow years of my mother's unrelieved suffering, a somberness that was to make me stand apart and look upon excessive joy with suspicion, that was to make me self-conscious, that was to make me keep forever on the move, as though to escape a nameless fate seeking to overtake me. (BB, p. 87)

In contrast to Laye's essentially collectivist context, emphasizing a more common feeling of an almost equitably shared loss, he even uses the plural pronoun 'we', i.e. 'Were tears a part of everything *we* did?' One can, however, see that the core image for Laye and Wright is mother and son, embroidered with other members of the immediate and extended family. Each writer went to his mother in the night summoned by tears to his mother's bedside. The tears of Laye's mother are tears of deep emotional pain because her son is leaving; there are no visible tears in Wright's mother's eyes: her eyes are vacant, vacant from a paralytic stroke. Her intense pain was physical. So painful that she had called her son to her bedside to tell him she could no longer endure it, that she wanted to die. Baggage, luggage, suitcases abound in both writers' imagery in the examples cited here. Baggage because the young Camara is being sent from his bucolic Kouroussa homeland to urban Conakry. Baggage because the youthful Wright's mother must travel in 'the baggage car' on a stretcher, from their rural home in Clarksdale, Mississippi, eventually to the urban metropolis of Chicago. Richard Wright's nocturnal experience with his mother seems more private, as is the author's response to it. Michel Fabre, Wright's superlative biographer, states,

> Even if Wright exaggerates his precocity when writing his autobiography, it is important to remember that the future stages of his develop-

ment all proceeded from his intensely tragic sense of human existence, which was existential long before he knew the word.[6]

Wright's own words give credence to Fabre's observations. Viewing the experience, in retrospect, as an author some years later, Wright's literary explanation leans towards the existential, if by existential is meant that the essence of being is to be; that man is responsible for forming his own individual nature, through individual choice and goals. Wright says he made such choices and set such goals;

> At the age of twelve ... I had a conception of life ... a sense of the world that was mine and mine alone ... an attitude toward life that was to endure, that was to make me seek those areas of living that would keep it alive, that was to make me skeptical of everything while seeking everything, tolerant of all and yet critical. (BB, p. 88)

The existential possibility here is 'to ... seek those areas of living that would keep it alive.' If this 'it' refers back to 'living' or to Wright's 'sense of the world', it is Wright's view alone. A view predicated on the unique relationship between Wright and his mother, which as author he does not attempt to disperse or share with other family members in terms of their intellectual and emotional composition as characters.

Unlike Richard Wright, Camara Laye did not suffer from this kind of extreme uncertainty and insecurity. Neither did he develop an inflexible idea of life, which combined a thirst for reality with the conviction that only heated struggle would give existence a meaning wrenched from suffering.[7] Laye grew up in well-established and settled surroundings, in a traditional African way of life not greatly troubled by European influences. In his own society, he might almost be said to belong to the privileged classes – if it is possible to talk of 'privilege' in a communal society.[8] Joyce A. Hutchinson, editor of a text of L'Enfant noir, writes,

> Laye himself has no doubts about the value of his traditional way of life; his memories of his childhood and his family are almost sacred; his only regret is that he left too early to understand all the mysteries and that he will now never understand them. But the other doubt and the uncertainty exist – the doubt as to whether he was right to leave, the feeling of being uprooted. From the beginning he has, as it were, a foot in two worlds: first in the town and the country, where he feels different from the country boys; and later in Africa and Europe.[9]

In spite of the particularity of their cultural context, one can recognize the pan-African, if not universal, dimensions of Laye's and Wright's experience of maternal loss. African literature, of Africa and the diaspora, provides a plethora of works conveying this theme and imagery. Ezekiel Mphahlele's *Down Second Avenue*[10] opens with a picture of his family, including his brother, sister, paternal grandmother, father and mother in Pretoria. Separation and loss come as a result of his mother's death. She was a diabetic and had had a stroke when Mphahlele went to her bedside for the last time;

> She didn't speak much, except to say, 'I feel very, very tired, like I'd been walking miles and miles'.
>
> After a week, it turned out that I had seen and heard my mother speak for the last time that day I left her in bed. I received a telephone call to say that she had passed away, in grandmother's arms. A diabetic coma had done it. She was forty-five.[11]

Mphahlele's intellectual and emotional response is, like Wright's, existential; as may be gleaned from this observation from the same work, 'But all in all perhaps I led a life shared by all other country boys. Boys who are aware of only one purpose of living, to be.'[12]

The mother/son relationship is a seed from which grows much of a novelist's thematic and imagistic material. The quality of that relationship, for better or worse, is like the soil in which one's primary and most lasting influences are rooted. Being is simply not enough, if one is not also concerned with the quality of being. The novelist should not just be concerned that we have life, but that we have it more abundantly. In his autobiography, *Blame Me On History*, Bloke Modisane recreates the thoughts and feelings of maternal loss occasioned by involuntary exile. Remembering the image of his mother he writes:

> I saw her begin to die of the thought that I was deserting her without a protector, and I prayed for the words to persuade her to understand that I was sick with shame for the selfishness which was driving me to betray the love of a mother who needed me more than the sanity I claimed to be losing.
>
> 'Who are you leaving me with?' she said, her eyes having abandoned the hope of tears. 'What is to become of us? What will happen to you in a strange country with people you don't know? Who will look after you?'
>
> 'Mama, I'm not going there to die,' I said. 'Soon our country will be right, all will be well and I will come back ...'
>
> I had seen her eyes wet with grief and several times I kept delaying the journey ... yet I knew that the longer I stayed the greater were increased the chances of being stabbed to death or being arrested on charges under the Immorality Act.[13]

Still Modisane had to wrestle with the terrifying thought that he might never see his mother or homeland again. He knew, as a black South

African, that for as long as South Africa remained white, for so long he would be an exile from the country of his birth. These are but a couple of examples, from Southern Africa, of this prevalent pan-African literary theme, others could be cited.

These are some of the novelists of the 1930s to 1950s, including Laye, Wright and Lamming, who were victims of a transition, from family to the larger world, from rural to urban, too abrupt to be easily assimilated.

To connect the third point of our pan-African triangle, we turn to the West Indies and the autobiographical novel of the gifted George Lamming, *In the Castle of My Skin*. Once more we see the protagonist/author, faced with the travail, the difficult labour of creating a separate identity away from mother and motherland. Lamming recreates the scene of his departure from Barbados, sharing much the same imagery and emotional trauma of maternal loss that characterizes Camara Laye and Richard Wright.

> My mother had been packing for almost a week. One would think she was leaving too. Tonight I shall be cock in the yard at a farewell party, and two days later I see them for the last time.
>
> I don't remember anything except the singing. They shouted 'for he's a jolly good fellow' which, of course, I have never been. When I review these relationships they seem so odd. I have always been here on this side and the other person there on that side, and we have both tried to make the sides appear similar in the needs, desires and ambitions. But it wasn't true. It was never true. When I reach Trinidad where no one knows me I may be able to strike identity with the other person. But it was never possible here. I am always feeling terrified of being known; not because they really know you, but simply because their claim to this knowledge is a concealed attempt to destroy you. That is what knowing means. As soon as they know you they will kill you, and thank God that's why they can't kill you. They never know you. Sometimes I think the same thing will be true in Trinidad. The likenesses will meet and make merry, but they won't know you. They won't know the you that's hidden somewhere in the castle of your skin.[14]

Lamming's impending and inevitable estrangement is closer to Wright's interpretation than it is to Laye's; particularly in terms of the cognitive and emotional postures the former discloses. The responses of Lamming and Wright, in the instances cited, reveal the rootlessness, ambiguity of identity, and individualism (as opposed to individuality) of the deculturized. Deculturation refers to the process whereby, at the meeting of two cultures, one consciously and deliberately dominates the other and denies it the right to exist, by directly and indirectly questioning its validity as a culture, denigrating it, making its carriers objects of ridicule and scorn, and thus finally leading to its questioning by the very people whom it has nurtured and given an identity and a positive being.[15]

Aside from the apparent lack of collectivist values, of a more clearly defined cultural context, both Lamming and Wright express their concern for this aspect of maternal loss by an appeal to personal, existential, self-knowledge and self-definition. There is Wright's 'conception of life ... that was mine and mine alone', and Lamming's 'They won't know the you that's hidden somewhere in the castle of your skin'.

Laye's background was different. He came from a secure and respected background, which had been very little affected by the advent of Europeans; he never aspired to be European but had always considered himself an African. He is, therefore, not unduly obsessed with the problem of identity, and finds no need to proclaim his individuality or existential self. Laye's self-concept comes from and is part of the collective society; his individuality is derived from and assured because of his society, not in spite of it, or in opposition to it. Though the experience of estrangement is common to each of these authors, what distinguishes one from the other is the perception and interpretation of that experience through artistic narrative imagery.

The essential thematic image under consideration here is that of mother and son; and by implication, family and child or community and individual. It is, undoubtedly, one of the most popular in all fiction; it involves the people we know, or think we know best. It is the seeming finality, like snipping the umbilical cord; the sense of permanent loss, like turning one's back for all time on home and family that characterizes the intellectual and emotional disposition of Wright and Lamming, more so than Camara Laye; and Wright, it seems, more so than Lamming. To offer even more obvious evidence of this, Wright's autobiographical *Black Boy* is not dedicated to his mother but to his sister, Ellen Wright and his daughter, Julia Wright 'who live always in my heart'. On the other hand, Lamming's *In the Castle of My Skin* is dedicated 'To my mother and Frank Collymore whose love and help deserved a better book'. These observations are concerned less with the quality of the relationship of each of these authors to his mother and home than with the quality of their literary response, in words and pictures, to that relationship, and what the relationship itself offers as artistic motivation or aesthetic expression. Staying with the evidence provided by the opening dedication of each author's work, the original Paris edition of Laye's

L'Enfant noir opens with the only poem I've ever seen bearing Camara Laye's name...

A Ma Mère

Femme noire, femme africaine
Ô toi ma mère je pense à toi...

Ô Dâman Ô ma mère, toi qui me portas
sur le dos, toi qui m'allaitas
toi qui gouvernas mes premiers pas
toi qui la première m'ouvris les yeux
aux prodiges de la terre,
je pense à toi...

Femme des champs, femme des rivières
femme du grand fleuve, Ô toi, ma mère,
je pense à toi...

Ô toi Dâman, Ô ma mère, toi qui
essuyais mes larmes, toi qui
me rèjouissais le coeur, toi qui
patiemment supportais mes caprices,
comme j'aimerais encore être près de toi,
être enfant près de toi!

Femme simple, femme de la resignation,
Ô toi, ma mère, je pense à toi...

Ô Dâman, Dâman de la grande
famille des forgerons, ma pensée
toujours se tourne vers toi
la tienne à choque pas m'accompagne,
Ô Dâman, ma mère, comme, aimerais
Encore être dans ta chaleur,
Être enfant près de toi...

Femme noire, femme africaine,
Ô toi, ma mère, merci; merci pour
tout ce que tu fis pour moi, ton fils,
si loin, si près de toi!   (EN, p. 7)

To My Mother

Black woman, woman of Africa
O my mother, I am thinking of you...

O Daman, O my mother, you who bore me
upon your back, you who nursed me,
you who watched over my first faltering steps,
you who first opened my eyes
to the wonders of the earth,
I am thinking of you ...

O you Daman, O my mother, you who
dried my tears, you who
patiently bore with all my many caprices,
how I should love to be beside you once again,
to be a little child beside you!

Woman of simplicity, woman of resignation,
O you, my mother, I am thinking of you ...

O Daman, Daman of the great
family of blacksmiths and goldsmiths, my thoughts
are always turning towards you,
and your own thoughts accompany me at every step,
O Daman, my mother, how I should love
to be surrounded by your loving warmth again,
to be a little child beside you ...

Black woman, woman of Africa,
O you, my mother, thank you; thank you for
all that you have done for me, your son,
who, though so far away, is still so close to you! (*DC*, p. 5)

Laye's mother came from Tindican, a small village near Kouroussa, where her father had also been an able smith. His uncles were farmers and Laye's visits to them and to his maternal grandmother give insight into the agricultural life of upper Guinea. Laye's mother, however, had inherited the mysterious powers of her caste, 'qui fornit la majorité des circonciseurs et nombre de diseurs de choses cachées' (from which the majority of circumcisers and many soothsayers are drawn'). Laye gives some examples of his mother's powers and of her authority and the respect she commands in her society. He also explains how her family, the Daman, had for its totem the crocodile (*EN*, p. 4). The crocodiles in the Niger River – a river called 'Djoliba' by the villagers – are a danger for everybody except the members of the central family because these animals are regarded as their totems. When the fifteen-year-old Laye is about to leave for

Conakry, his mother procures for him some water which is believed to have 'eau magique qui a nombre de pouvoirs et en particulier celui de developper le cerveau'; *EN*, p. 182 ('a magic potion possessing many qualities particularly that which develops the brain'). Laye's attitude towards these mysteries and the mysteries themselves are the topic of quite another discussion. We know that Laye was submerged but emerged from a traditional African context with identifiable social, and perhaps for our purposes more importantly, artistic influences. Let us, for the moment, take repose in his tentative conclusion,

> ce mutisme des choses, des reasons profondes, des choses, conduit au silence; mais il suffit que ces choses aient été évoquées e leur impénétrabilité reconnue. (*EN*, pp. 59–60)

> the mystery of things, their how and why, conduces to silence. It is enough for such men to observe things and recognize their impenetrability. (*DC*, p. 53)

Laye's mother was an impressive person. Born immediately after twins she possessed supernatural powers and was often consulted by the village people. Camara Laye describes her deeds simply as he remembers them. He makes no attempt to explain or interpret those deeds, but states resignedly,

> Je ne veux rien dire de plus et je n'ai relaté que ce que mes yeux ont vu. Ces prodiges – en vérité, c'étaient des prodiges – j'y songe aujourd'hui comme aux événements fabuleux d'un lointain passé. Ce passé pourtant est tout proche: il date d'hier. Mais le monde bouge, le monde change, et le mien plus rapidement peut-être que tout autre, et si bien qu'il semble que nous cessons d'être ce que nous étions, qu'au vrai nous ne sommes plus ce que nous étions, et que deja nous n'étions plus exactement nous-mêmes dans le moment ou ces prodiges s'accomlissaient sous nos yeux. Oui, le monde bouge, le monde change; il bouge et change a telle enseigne que mon propre totem – j'ai mon totem aussi – m'est inconnu. (*EN*, p. 91)

> I do not wish to say more, and I have told you only what I saw with my own eyes. These miracles – they were miracles indeed – I think about now as if they were the fabulous events of a far-off past. That past is, however, still quite near: it was only yesterday. But the world rolls on, the world changes, my own world perhaps more rapidly than anyone else's; so that it appears as if we are ceasing to be what we were, and that we were not exactly ourselves even at the time when these miracles took place before our eyes. Yes, the world rolls on, the world changes; it rolls on and changes, and the proof of it is that my totem – I too have my totem – is still unknown to me. (*DC*, p. 184)

Laye recreates life in his Mandinka community as an existence full of beauty and meaning. It is a sheltered and protected life. Yet at an early age he became aware that his destiny would lead him out of this society. The thought of leaving his family and community is hardly palatable, but the technical and industrial knowledge needed by that same community demanded that he leave. His final exit is particularly hard on his mother, who does not want to hear of his going away. After Conakry, he returns to Kouroussa briefly before being sent to Paris for further study. His mother pleads with him;

> – N'aurai-je donc jamais la paix? dit-elle. Hier, c'était une école à Conakry; aujourd'hui, c'est une école en France; demain... mais que sera-ce demain?... Ta place est ici!... Mais à quoi pensent-ils dans ton école? Est-ce qu'ils se figurent que je vais vivre ma vie entière loin de mon fils? Mourir loin de mon fils? Ils n'ont donc pas de mère, ces gens-là? Mais naturellement ils n'en ont pas; ils ne seraient pas partis si loin de chez eux s'ils en avaient une! (*EN*, pp. 250-1)

> 'Am I never to have peace?' she said. 'Yesterday it was the school in Conakry; today it's the school in France; tomorrow ... what will it be tomorrow?... Your place is here!... What are they thinking about at the school? Do they imagine I'm going to live my whole life apart from my son? Die with him far away? Have they no mothers, those people? They can't have. They wouldn't have gone so far away from home if they had. (*DC*, p. 184)

What a contrast between this gentle, nostalgic book and Richard Wright's bitter account of his tragic childhood. Laye's childhood was happy; he was surrounded with love and care and grew up in comparative security. Wright's childhood was all poverty, hunger and hatred, the seeming *sine qua non* of black American life. Laye describes his childhood with a touch of romanticism, and he leaves the world of his parents with sadness and regret. By contrast, Richard Wright describes his youth with brutal realism, and as an experience he would rather cast off and forget.

The differences in cultural contexts and childhoods of Camara Laye, Richard Wright and George Lamming gave birth to unique re-creations, interpretations and evaluations of a social relationship, or experience, that is at the same time pan-African and universal. The relationship each describes is unique and yet typical; unique in the sense that only the experience and genius of Camara Laye alone could produce *L'Enfant noir*, or Wright *Black Boy*, or Lamming *In the Castle of My Skin*; typical because their re-creation of meaningful fiction typifies the special problems and concerns of the African novelist, in Africa and the diaspora. Their work also reminds us of the impossibly simple yet complex task of many novelists: the synthesis of experience and technique into a fictional, albeit autobiographical, construct that affirms the possibilities of the human imagination and memory.

NOTES

1. Camara Laye, *L'Enfant noir*, Paris, Librairie Plon, 1953, pp. 179–80. In following extracts, EN – *L'Enfant noir*.
2. Camara Laye, *The Dark Child*, translated from the French by James Kirkup, New York, Farrar, Straus and Giroux, 1969, pp. 137–8. New York, Noonday Press, 1954. In following extracts, DC – *The Dark Child*. Also published as *The African Child*, Glasgow, Fontana/Collins, 1955.
3. John S. Mbiti, *African Religions and Philosophy*, New York, Praeger, 1969, p. 108; London, Heinemann, 1969.
4. ibid., p. 109.
5. Richard Wright, *Black Boy, A Record of Childhood and Youth*, New York, Harper and Brothers, 1937; London, Longman, 1970. In following extracts, BB – *Black Boy*.
6. Michel Fabre, *The Unfinished Quest of Richard Wright*, translated from the French by Isabel Barzun, New York, William Morrow & Co., Inc., 1973, p. 32.
7. ibid., p. 32.
8. Camara Laye, *L'Enfant noir*, ed. Joyce A. Hutchinson, London and New York, Cambridge University Press, 1966, p. 4.
9. ibid., p. 5.
10. Ezekiel Mphahlele, *Down Second Avenue*, London, Faber, 1959; Berlin, Seven Seas Publishers, 1962; New York, Doubleday, 1971.
11. ibid., p. 155.
12. ibid., p. 17.
13. Bloke Modisane, *Blame Me On History*, New York, E. P. Dutton & Co., 1963, p. 292.
14. George Lamming, *In the Castle of My Skin*, New York, Collier Books, 1970, p. 291; London, Longman Drumbeat, 1979.
15. Daniel P. Kunene, *The Heroic Poetry of the Basotho*, London and New York, Oxford University Press, 1972, p. xi.

Feminist Criticism
and the African Novel

Katherine Frank

One of the most controversial issues in contemporary discussion of African literature is whether or not various western critical approaches and methodologies are suitable for or even adaptable to African writing. Can we come to *Things Fall Apart* or *Bound to Violence*, for example, with the same expectations and critical tools that we bring to bear on *Jude the Obscure* or *Portrait of the Artist*, or should we seek instead to bring about what Eldred Jones has called the decolonization of African literature? Much of the current debate centres on whether such established critical orientations as the New Critical, Neo-Aristotelian, biographical, historical, archetypal, Freudian, structuralist, poststructuralist, and deconstructionist schools are truly cross-cultural modes of literary analysis. And further, whether African literature requires its own Black Aesthetic in order to posit appropriate and searching ways of understanding a body of writing that has few cultural and historical affinities with the 'Great Tradition' of western literary history.[1]

Rather than risk facile generalizations about the universal law of literary criticism versus the claims of an African aesthetic, I would like to skirt the larger issue in order to explore the relevance of one particular kind of western criticism – feminist criticism – to one particular genre of African literature – the novel. Though feminist criticism now seems securely entrenched in western literary circles – with numerous scholarly journals devoted to feminist thought, and women's studies programmes and departments flourishing at many American and British universities – it has yet to gain legitimacy or even visibility in African literary studies. Lloyd Brown's *Women Writers in Black Africa* (1981) is the first full-scale treatment of African women writers and his brief bibliography shows how little has preceded his pioneering study: the token article on Flora

Nwapa now and then in *African Literature Today* or *Research in African Literatures*, a 1977 number of *Ba Shiru* devoted to women and Africa, Kenneth Little's study of the image of urban women in African literature, and a sprinkling of articles on or interviews with women writers such as Grace Ogot, Buchi Emecheta, Rebeka Njau, and Bessie Head scattered in various journals. As Brown notes in his introduction, 'women writers of Africa are the other voices, the unheard voices, rarely discussed and seldom accorded space in the repetitive anthologies and the predictably male-oriented studies in the field.'[2] Until the present moment, in fact, African literary studies has been an almost exclusively masculine domain, largely because the scholars and critics who have mapped it out are nearly all men, who have tended to ignore the admittedly small but still significant number of African women writers and women-related issues in African literature.

Thus in contrast to other western approaches, feminist criticism has had virtually no impact on African literature. But before speculating on whether and how this situation might be remedied, we need a clearer notion of what feminist criticism involves beyond an interest in women writers and women-oriented issues in literature. It is a mistake, in fact, to talk about feminist criticism as if it were a single, codified critical methodology. In reality, there are a number of feminist criticisms covering a broad spectrum from the sociological, prescriptive, and polemical to the formalist, rarefied, and aesthetic. Perhaps the best way of covering this wide terrain is to describe the various species of feminist criticism, along with some notable examples, and then attempt to gauge the usefulness each kind might hold for African letters. It is also important to note at the outset where, as they say in the States, this kind of criticism is 'coming from'. By far the greater number of its practitioners are American scholars who have largely concentrated their energies on nineteenth- and twentieth-century British literature, especially women novelists from Jane Austen to Virginia Woolf.

Kate Millett's *Sexual Politics* (1969), the first 'classic' of feminist criticism, however, focused on twentieth-century male writers, and in the years since its publication it has become something of a prototype of 'stereotypical' or 'images of women' feminist criticism.[3] Millett's study exposed the sexist, reductive images of women perpetrated by such novelists as Henry Miller, Norman Mailer, D. H. Lawrence, and Jean Genet, and it quickly spawned a number of similar studies of figures such as Dickens, Thackeray, Trollope and other male writers who have been less than charitable to their female characters. The underlying impulse of such stereotypical criticism is usually political, even moral. For generally the critic is saying in essence, 'look at how so-and-so portrays women characters; how unfair, or how demeaning, or how chauvinistic!' In addition, there is an implied standard of realism in such 'images of women' criticism because an author's 'images' or 'stereotypes' are evaluated according to how faithfully, or more often faithlessly, they reflect how women 'really' are. Stereotypical feminist criticism, then, is both descriptive and evaluative, but judgement is passed in accordance with sociological and moral rather than aesthetic criteria. And herein reside the limits to its usefulness. It may be interesting to observe that Dickens' women characters come in three versions: angels, coquettes or femme fatales, and hags, but there is little left to say about them.

And yet when Millett's book first appeared such observations seemed in the nature of revelations and were widely emulated. Images of women in literature were carefully classified, and anthologies put together with table-of-contents headings such as 'the Mother', 'the Angel', 'the witch', 'the bitch-goddess'. And feminist scholars speculated, with good cause, on the effects upon readers of such damaging stereotypes, just as Afro-American critics have denounced stereotyped portrayals of Blacks in American literature. 'Images' criticism indeed is not a peculiarly feminist phenomenon. In the States it has characterized Black, Chicano, and Jewish as well as women's studies. It would seem, in fact, a necessary initial critical strategy or phase of any group that feels culturally oppressed or beleaguered.

Thus it is not surprising that the few feminist studies that have been done in African literature are stereotypical ones: Abioseh M. Porter's essay on images of women in Ngugi and Njau, for example,[4] Kathleen McCaffrey's article on images of women in the works of selected West African writers and film makers,[5] and, most extensively, Kenneth Little's recent book, *The Sociology of Urban Women's Image in African Literature*.[6] Little's study is remarkably similar to the sort of 'images' work done by American feminists ten or so years ago. He covers some thirty writers – most of them male novelists – and comes up with a number of 'role categories' for their female characters including girlfriends; good-time girls; wives; free women; mothers; workers and political women; and courtesans and prostitutes.

Little's diligent and thorough study should probably exhaust the stereotypical vein of feminist criticism in the African novel, and also perhaps reveal its fundamental dead-endedness. For stereotypical criticism concentrates on the least interesting elements of any given text. Stereotypes are by definition inimical to subtle, complex, and convincing characterization. They signal artistic failure, and thus an 'images of women' criticism necessarily concentrates on inferior literary works or on the flawed aspects of successful ones.

At the opposite extreme of the sociological and political orientation of stereotypical criticism is the aestheticism of three other related but still distinct modes of feminist criticism – the stylistic, generic and archetypal approaches. What immediately distinguishes these is their primary focus on the text – the particular literary work divorced from its author and environment – so that these three approaches are feminism's equivalent to formalism or New Criticism. It might appear that all feminist criticism must be implicitly contextual, that it is unavoidably concerned with the gender of writers and their attitudes toward women, but stylistic criticism at least attempts to retain a rigid fidelity to text over context. The limited success and few examples of this attempt probably reflect its inherent difficulty. The inconclusiveness, for example, of Mary Ellmann's *Thinking About Women* (1968) and Patricia Meyer Spacks' *The Female Imagination* (1972) expose the troubles encountered when critics start asking whether women use language differently from men, whether there is such a thing as a female style, and if there is, then what do we do with stylistic 'transvestites' like Samuel Richardson who writes like a woman, and George Eliot who writes like a man? And where do all those Victorian women scribbling under the cloak of a male pseudonym like the Bell brothers in Yorkshire fit into this vexed issue of gender and language and style? Lady Elizabeth Rigby, an early reviewer of *Jane Eyre*, guessed the female identity of Currer Bell because, she asserted, no man could have described the upholstery with the care and precision of Charlotte Brontë. But this is less a reflection of a female style than of sex roles. Women are taught to take notice of the upholstery and men are not. No doubt we could think of equivalent female concerns in the African novel – Emecheta's detailed descriptions of cloth patterns and colours in her novels, for example, or all the cooking and gossiping that goes on in Nwapa's novels. But we are saying less about a feminine style when we notice such concerns than confirming the truism that writers write best when they write about what they know best. Victorian women were experts on interior decoration while African women know about cloth and food and the lives of their neighbours.

Feminist generic and archetypal criticism has proved more fruitful than this sort of question-begging stylistic approach. In fact, two of the finest feminist studies to appear in recent years, Ellen Moers' *Literary Women* (1977) and Sandra M. Gilbert and Susan Gubar's *The Madwoman in the Attic* (1979) are superb examples of these two approaches.[8]

Moers' study, as it turns out, is rooted in various historical and sociological issues despite its main concentration on the kinds of literary genres, influences, and patterns of imagery that have characterized writing by women. Like Ian Watt in *The Rise of the Novel*, Moers explores the historical reasons behind the adoption of certain genres – most notably, women writers' appropriation in the nineteenth century of the novel of domestic realism and the gothic, and she explains the historical and sociological reasons as to why these became peculiarly feminine literary forms.

One might similarly investigate, I think, the two distinctive kinds of novels being written today by contemporary African women, for in some respects they seem to be recapitulating the literary history of their Victorian women predecessors. Even after accounting for the important shaping influence of indigenous African literary forms, it is striking to see the sharp contrast between what amounts to the African domestic realism of Buchi Emecheta's and Flora Nwapa's novels, books concerned with women's private, family lives – their experience of courtship, marriage, and childbearing – and the psychological 'gothics' of Rebeka Njau and Bessie Head who write mind-bending books about the psychic entrapment, madness and flight of African women profoundly alienated from the domestic worlds of Emecheta's and Nwapa's novels.

Archetypal criticism carries on this preoccupation with distinctive female forms, but intra- rather than inter-textually. Moers' concluding chapters on the kinds of metaphors used by women writers – for example, birds and bird cages, open plains and ravines in contrast to phallic mountains – anticipates Gilbert and Gubar's far more systematic and comprehensive approach in *The Madwoman in the Attic*. Their title comes from *Jane Eyre*, and it identifies the pervasive concern with enclosure, imprisonment, and entrapment that Gilbert and Gubar found among nineteenth-century women writers, their recurrent fantasy of flight and escape, and finally their obsession with madwomen, ghosts, and doubles. They show that Bertha Mason, the madwoman imprisoned in Mr Rochester's attic, is no less a double of Jane Eyre than is Helen Burns. She is an archetype of the rage and passion of circumscribed nineteenth-century womanhood, just as Helen Burns is the saintly 'angel in the house', to use Virginia Woolf's phrase, of Victorian romance. There are a host of other metaphors and images that Gilbert and Gubar explore in their massive study, in addition to their acute discussion of the use of male pseudonyms, the influence of authors such as Milton upon women writers, the devious use of autobiography in women's fiction and so on. But the analysis of female archetypes – the identification and hypothesized rationale for them – remains the most valuable contribution of the book, and also the aspect of it that may most easily be translated to the African novel. If the madwoman in the attic is the spectre that haunts woman-authored nineteenth-century English fiction, it is the madwoman in the village who haunts the novels of Rebeka Njau and Bessie Head, the barren wife in Nwapa's books, and finally and perhaps most significantly, it is the slave girl – including the slave girl buried alive at the command of her male master – who becomes the archetype of African female experience in the novels of Buchi Emecheta.

Such archetypal criticism serves a dual function. Quite obviously, images of womanhood such as the female lunatic, childless wife, and slave girl speak worlds about their authors' vision of what it means to be a woman in a particular environment, whether it be nineteenth-century Yorkshire or twentieth-century Lagos. But quite apart from this sociological interest, archetypes also give us insight into a writer's artistic gifts – the way in which she transforms experience into art by creating telling and effective symbols, images, and metaphors for her vision. Archetypal criticism, then, is both descriptive and evaluative, and in one special case – that of the androgyne, the archetype of the fusion of maleness and femaleness – it has also been prescriptive.

In 1973 the American critic Carolyn G. Heilbrun published what on the surface seemed a modest enough literary study entitled *Toward a Recognition of Androgyny* that quickly became a rallying call for an androgynous orientation not merely in feminist literary criticism but in the women's movement as a whole. Though ostensibly a critical study, with 'androgynous readings' of Greek myths, *Wuthering Heights*, Ibsen, and Henry James among others, in reality *Toward a Recognition of Androgyny* is a rather utopian work calling for an end to rigid sex roles and the creation of an androgynous society. 'I believe that our future salvation,' Heilbrun says in her introduction, 'lies in a movement away from sexual polarization and the prison of gender.' 'Androgyny,' she continues, 'suggests a spirit of reconciliation between the two sexes; it suggests further, a full range of experience open to individuals who may, as women, be aggressive, as men, tender; it suggests a spectrum upon which human beings choose their places without regard to propriety or custom.'[9]

Heilbrun did not invent the concept of androgyny. It was Coleridge who first insisted that 'a great mind must be androgynous', while it was Virginia Woolf who made androgyny a literary ideal in her pioneering study of women writers, *A Room of One's Own*. What Heilbrun did was update Coleridge and Woolf to the sexual revolution and women's movement of the 1970s, and for a time androgyny – as literary archetype, sexual ideal, and political panacea – enjoyed an enormous vogue. In literary studies this meant that certain so-called androgynous writers whose sexual identity was not immediately apparent in their work or who seemed to combine a feminine and masculine point of view, became extremely popular, increasingly taught in the classroom, and incessantly written about in scholarly monographs and journals.

But from the very beginning there were problems inherent in the concept of androgyny. It was unclear, for example, whether androgyny implied sexual equality or sexlessness, and whether it sought to abolish or fuse sexual stereotypes. Further, did it seem to endorse bisexuality or asexuality? There was, in fact, an intractable fuzziness about androgyny not merely in literary criticism, but in the social sciences as well that cast doubt on its validity and usefulness. It tended to label, even obscure, rather than illuminate the writers and works with which it was associated, so that in the last two or three years it has gradually faded out of feminist literary crticism though it appears to have retained some currency in psychology and sociology.

I bring it up here, then, because for a period it was one of the dominant modes of feminist literary criticism, and was applied in an evaluative as well as analytical fashion: 'androgynous writers' such as Emily Brontë and Woolf were praised over female or feminist ones like Austen and Charlotte Brontë and Edith Wharton. Androgyny's unsuitability to African literature seems to me obvious. The world of the African novel – whether a traditional, colonial, or post-independent world – tends to be a sexually defined, even sexually polarized, one, with rigidly decided sexual roles that deny androgynous transcendence. One could make a case, however, for an androgynous interpretation of Buchi Emecheta's quite recent book, *Destination Biafra*. This is an ambitious, if very uneven, war novel whose militantly feminist heroine possesses both feminine and masculine characteristics. Attractive, Oxford-educated Debbie Ogedemgbe is a nurturing woman who seeks to defend and protect the women and children victimized during the Biafran war, but the masculine, aggressive side of her character is shown when she joins the army, smokes cigarettes, tosses grenades, and refuses to marry her English lover at the end of the novel.

Unfortunately, however, the polemical woodenness of Emecheta's heroine –Debbie's propensity to spout slogans rather than credible dialogue – her stature as a rather mechanical hybrid of feminine and masculine traits, and the lack of psychological complexity in her portrayal all bring home the shortcomings of androgyny as a literary ideal. It seems unlikely that Emecheta's bold if flawed attempt to imagine an androgynous African woman will be imitated, though one hopes that more women writers will subscribe to Emecheta's feminist vision. Whatever future African writers, both men and women, may dream of, then, it is not likely to be Heilbrun's promised land of androgyny. As archetype and social panacea androgyny is a myth, a compelling, attractive, but ultimately unrealizable illusion, and African fiction rarely indulges in such flights of fantasy, concerned as it is above all with the wounds of the past and the ills of the present.

Sociological and historical feminist criticism wholly eschews this visionary idealism of androgyny. Instead of theorizing about a futuristic asexual or bisexual world that will liberate women to write, it concentrates on the peculiar cultural, environmental, and historical forces that have sometimes produced and encouraged, but more often frustrated and silenced, women writers. Elaine Showalter's *A Literature of their Own: British Women Novelists from Brontë to Lessing* (1977) is a model of this sort of historical/sociological approach.[10] Showalter, indeed, has written the definitive history of British women novelists in the nineteenth and twentieth centuries – a quite different story, as it turns out, from that traced in Ian Watt's, Arnold Kettle's, David Cecil's, or Walter Allen's 'standard' surveys of English prose fiction.

In *A Literature of their Own* Showalter unearths a hidden female literary history, or 'sub-culture' as she calls it, by reviving 'minor' figures like Mary Braddon, Margaret Oliphant, Dorothy Richardson and others who provide continuity between 'touchstone' writers such as the Brontës and George Eliot and Virginia Woolf. And just as importantly, Showalter explores the conditions under which these women wrote – the pressures, obstacles, and limitations they endured – with a number of highly interesting findings. Like most modern African women, Victorian women were less educated than men, a fact which had obvious deleterious effects upon their writing. Again like many women African writers, they tended to be unmarried or if married, childless or with only one or two children. Mrs Gaskell, penning her novels in the family dining room with numerous children underfoot, was the exception who proves the rule. Most often, nineteenth-century women writers wrote in isolation, even secretly like Jane Austen who pushed her manuscripts under the blotter whenever anyone entered the parlour, and many only felt free to write openly when they were forced to earn a living after the death of a husband, father, or brother left them without financial support. It was virtually unheard of for a nineteenth-century woman to choose the profession of author or 'man of letters' deliberately, though again we have a glaring but solitary exception in George Eliot. Instead of the public careers of Dickens or Thackeray or Trollope, we find nineteenth-century women scribbling novels surreptitiously late into the night, often with an acute sense of guilt, often for cash, and often under the disguise of a male pseudonym. Such conditions quite obviously impeded the free play of creativity, and yet nearly half of the great Victorian novelists in England were women.

Showalter, furthermore, traces the historical development of women's writing in England from an initial phase of imitation or emulation of male models – a Feminine period from the Brontës to the 1880s – followed by a Feminist protest period coinciding with the suffrage movement in England in the last twenty years of the century; and finally culminating in what Showalter calls a Female phase initiated by the great psychological women's novels of Dorothy Richardson and Virginia Woolf in the first three decades of this century. As is the case in male-oriented literary history, Showalter found that women writers read, responded and reacted to each other's work, finding strength, inspiration and sometimes monitory caveats in the writing of their predecessors and contemporaries.

Crucial to Showalter's reconstruction of a women's literary history was the recovery – sometimes amounting to *discovery* – of forgotten, neglected women writers whose works were long out of print, their reputations and even their very existence effaced from the annals of literature. Resuscitating figures like Braddon or Oliphant, Showalter found, was often valuable work in itself, quite apart from the gaps these writers filled in the history of women's writing. Thus very closely related to historical/sociological feminist scholarship is another critical category involving the discovery or recovery of 'lost women', as one feminist journal calls these neglected figures. This sort of endeavour, in fact, is perhaps the most exciting and rewarding species of feminist criticism. In the past decade, all sorts of women writers have been rescued from literary oblivion by feminist scholars who have introduced or reintroduced them into the established canons of American and English literature. Their works have then been reissued, and their lives often made the subjects of new feminist biographies. To name just a few of the discoveries of recent years: Margaret Fuller, Kate Chopin, Agnes Smedley, and Charlotte Perkins Gilman in American literature; and Mary Wollstonecraft, Mary Shelley, and Dorothy Richardson in English literature.

Less dramatically, perhaps, the historical/sociological and recovery modes of feminist criticism are also changing, sometimes radically changing, the way we read figures who have never been lost. By placing the Brontës and George Eliot and Virginia Woolf in the context of *women's* literary history, Showalter gives us new eyes for old texts, shows us how the books of these women were shaped by and reflected the world that engendered them, and in the process, destroys such misleading and incomplete stereotypes as Emily Brontë as a kind of Yorkshire oracle, Charlotte Brontë as a bitter, plain little governess, George Eliot as the mouthpiece for the positivism of George Henry Lewes, and Woolf as the Grande Dame of Bloomsbury. All these women were writing about the experience of women in their own worlds – sometimes with bitterness and frustration, sometimes with qualified hope. And it is through this feminist lens – from within as it were – that our final category of re-evaluative criticism proceeds, producing at times entirely different books from those we read about in *The Great Tradition* or *An Introduction to the English Novel.*

These last three related areas of feminist criticism – the historical/sociological, discovery/recovery and re-evaluative – are those which hold the most promise for African literature, especially for the African novel. For it is only through a systematic application of these approaches that we can hope to answer certain fundamental questions about African fiction and African women novelists. Questions such as: Why are there so few women writers in Africa? Should we swell their ranks by including white figures such as Olive Schreiner, Doris Lessing, and Nadine Gordimer; in other words, is gender or race the most significant defining characteristic of a writer? What educational, marital, and familial circumstances foster and thwart writing by African women? Who do African women writers read and seek to emulate as literary models? Why have so many of them ceased to publish after writing only a novel or two (Rebeka

Njau is a notable example of this phenomenon)? Can we trace a women's African literary history in the two brief decades that have elapsed since Nwapa, the first widely-known woman novelist in Africa, brought out *Efuru*? Is there, that is, some sort of development stretching from Nwapa's early work to recent novels by Buchi Emecheta, Ama Ata Aidoo, and Bessie Head? How can we go about recovering the pre-Nwapa 'lost lives' in African literary history – women writers such as Adelaide and Gladys Casely-Hayford, Mabel Dove-Danquah and others whose work is out of print or still in manuscript in university archives? And how can we rescue and re-evaluate people like Nwapa and Aidoo and Ogot from the parentheses and footnotes of male-oriented, male-authored African literary history?

A systematic attempt to answer such questions, it seems to me, would result in an invaluable contribution to both African and women's studies, and would also go a long way towards establishing a peculiarly African kind of feminist criticism. Clearly, several of the modes of feminist scholarship – most notably the archetypal, historical/sociological, recovery and re-evaluative approaches – can be modified and even enhanced to fit the needs and conditions of African fiction. But quite apart from the adaptability of western feminist criticism to the African novel, there are a number of key issues, themes, motifs and problems in African writing that need to be explored from a feminist perspective in order to see how such issues are portrayed by women writers and how they affect the lives of women in their novels.

The best way of discussing these concerns, I think, is historically, not in terms of when particular books were written, but rather according to the period in which they take place. In a manner somewhat analogous to Showalter's three-phase chronology of the history of women's fiction, African literature has often been studied in terms of the three historical periods that dominate it: the pre-colonial or traditional, the colonial and the post-independence eras. Now certain problems of African experience are associated with each period, and these problems take on a new dimension and meaning when they are viewed from a feminist point of view.

With several striking exceptions such as Ouologuem's *Bound to Violence*, traditional African life, before the incursion of the white man, is usually the object of nostalgic celebration in the African novel. And yet women writers such as Buchi Emecheta and Flora Nwapa do not reflect this vision of a lost golden age that we find in African male writers. For African women, Emecheta and Nwapa show, traditional life was often full of hardship and oppression. In their books we see the traditional African woman as a mere chattel, property to be passed on from father to husband, exhausted while still young by ceaseless childbearing, or broken-hearted and humiliated by barrenness. And in her recent *So Long a Letter* Mariama Bâ shows how all these oppressive characteristics of traditional life have been retained and perpetuated in the post-independent, westernized Muslim family.

Emecheta's, Nwapa's, and Bâ's grim vision of the traditional African woman, especially as seen in Emecheta's archetype of the slave girl, has been criticized, however, by some literary critics and historians who trace all the ills suffered by African women to colonialism. According to scholars such as Maryse Conde and Kathleen M. McCaffrey, it is the sexist white values of the colonial invaders which have oppressed African women and wrested from them the independence and dignity they enjoyed in their traditional village world.[11] For with the advent of colonialism the new conflict between rural and urban values is introduced into the African novel, and along with it a heated debate over which environment – the village or the city – is most hospitable towards and supportive of the needs and desires of women. A further extension of this conflict can be found in Emecheta's first two books and Aidoo's *Our Sister Killjoy* in which not even westernized, urban Africa can answer the hopes of Emecheta's and Aidoo's heroines who are forced to flee their homelands and seek new lives in Europe. They flee, that is, to the very land of the colonialists whom Conde, McCaffrey and other critics insist are the paramount oppressors of African womanhood. Thus there is a seemingly irresolvable critical argument over the plight of African women in the colonial era, and the argument fails to lessen in the novels set in post-independent Africa.

The fundamental problem that seems to face the contemporary African fictional heroine is that she is torn between two antagonistic identities: her communally-bred sense of herself as an African, and her feminist aspirations for autonomy and self-realization as a woman. Feminism, by definition, is a profoundly individualistic philosophy: it values personal growth and individual fulfilment over any larger communal needs or good. African society, of course, even in its most westernized modern forms, places the values of the group over those of the individual with the result that the notion of an African feminist almost seems a contradiction in terms.

It is this inherent paradox that is the major thrust of an article by Beatrice Stegeman on 'The New Woman in Contemporary African

Novels'. African communalism, as Stegeman explains, 'implies a standard or value of submergence rather than self-realization. In traditional African societies, the role of each citizen is to perpetuate the status quo, to assure continuity of the clan, to work within tradition.' The 'new woman', or feminist, as Stegeman goes on to show, rebels against such traditionalism because she evinces 'a theory of personhood where the individual exists as an independent entity rather than a group member, where she is defined by her experiences rather than her kinship relations, where she has responsibility to realize her potential for happiness rather than to accept her role, where she has indefinable value rather than quantitative financial worth, and where she must reason about her own values rather than fit into stereotyped tradition'.[12]

Stegeman does an excellent job of defining this key issue of African tradition versus feminist individualism, but perhaps because she limits her discussion to novels by male writers she pays little attention to the toll exacted by this conflict in works by women novelists. Most striking are the price of madness in Njau and Head, and that of exile, deracination, and isolation in Emecheta. Only Mariama Bâ in *So Long a Letter* is able to envisage a reconciliation of African consciousness with feminist aspiration. Her heroine, Ramatoulaye Fall, struggles for fulfilment within her Islamic, Senegalese culture, unlike her friend Aissatou Bâ who divorces her husband when he takes a second wife and in the manner of Emecheta's heroines educates herself and then pursues a professional career abroad. Ramatoulaye submits to her husband's polygamy, but as she herself affirms, she 'survives'. And we see that the lives of her daughters will be different; they will have marriages of equality rather than oppression. But Ramatoulaye's hope is not merely a vicarious one to be realized in the lives of her daughters. At fifty, the mother of twelve children, widowed, no longer beautiful, Ramatoulaye nevertheless is able to imagine a future for herself. She closes her 'long letter' to Aissatou with, 'I warn you already, I have not given up wanting to refashion my life. Despite everything − disappointments and humiliations − hope still lives on within me. It is from the dirty and nauseating humus that the green plant sprouts into life, and I can feel new buds springing up in me'.[13]

This crucial problem of feminism in conflict with traditionalism that Bâ alone among contemporary women novelists in Africa resolves − the problem of the African woman torn between her desire for independence and fulfilment and the claims and constraints of her society − is the most striking and controversial issue in contemporary African fiction by and about women. But it is also one more manifestation of the fundamental opposition between western and African values that permeates African literature and critical writing on it. Thus we seem to return full circle to my original question of whether European-style literary criticism can or should be used on African texts. I doubt if there is a definitive yes or no answer to this debate, but I hope I have suggested a number of ways in which a feminist approach could shed new light on the African novel. Far from being the narrow, doctrinaire methodology denounced by its detractors, feminist criticism is distinguished by its flexibility and variability, and thus could have a complex and extensive utility in African studies. There is almost certainly a women's history of African literature to be written. I have tried to show, also, how such an approach could identify and explore female archetypes, and discover, recover and re-evaluate women writers in Africa.

And finally, feminist criticism seeks to create an environment in which writing by and about women will thrive and increase. Several years ago the American novelist and short-story writer Tillie Olsen wrote a critical work entitled *Silences* which explored not what women have written but rather what they have failed to write because of social, historical and critical obstacles that have conspired to keep them silent. 'Literary history and the present', Olsen wrote, 'are dark with silences'.[14] If this is true for western women, it is probably doubly true for African women. There are surely vast silences here to be broken, silences of African women who have ceased to write or who have never written at all because they have felt there was no audience to hear their words. Feminist critics, like all critics, seek to reconstruct, analyse, account for and judge literary works. But before all this, they accept the responsibility to listen attentively, to abort silence, to encourage women writers in Africa to take up their pens. Ideally, then, our task would be an unending one because in a literary realm where writing by and about women is flourishing, there will always be a great deal more to be said.

NOTES

1. For various positions on this critical debate see: the first chapter of Charles R. Larson's *The Emergence of African Fiction*, Bloomington, Indiana University Press, 1972; Ernest Emenyonu, 'African Literature: What Does It Take to Be Its Critic', in *African Literature Today* 5, London, Heine-

mann, New York, Africana, 1971; three articles in *African Literature Today* 7, London, Heinemann, New York, Africana, 1975: D. S. Izevbaye, 'The State of Criticism in African Literature', Solomon Ogbede Iyasere, 'African Critics on African Literature: A Study in Misplaced Hostility', and Bernth Lindfors, 'The Blind Man and the Elephant'. Also of interest in *ALT* 7 are Adeola James' review of Eustace Palmer's *An Introduction to the African Novel*, and Eustace Palmer's 'A Plea for Objectivity: A Reply to Adeola James'.
2. Lloyd W. Brown, *Women Writers in Black Africa*, Westwood, Connecticut, Greenwood Press, 1981, p. 3.
3. Kate Millett, *Sexual Politics*, 1969; rpt. New York, Avon Books, 1970, London, Hart-Davis, 1971; London, Virago, 1977.
4. 'Ideology and the Image of Women: Kenyan Women in Njau and Ngugi', in *Ariel*, 12, no. 3, July 1981.
5. 'Images of Women in West African Literature and Film: A Struggle Against Dual Colonization,' in *International Journal of Women's Studies*, 3, no. 1, Jan.–Feb. 1980.
6. Little's study is published by Macmillan. My discussion derives from excerpts published in three issues of *West Africa*, 3 September 1979; 10 September 1979; 17 September 1979.
7. Mary Ellmann, *Thinking About Women*, New York, Harcourt, Brace and World, 1968; London, Virago, 1979, Patricia Meyer Spacks, *The Female Imagination*, New York, Alfred A. Knopf, 1972; London, Allen and Unwin, 1976.
8. Ellen Moers, *Literary Women: The Great Writers*, New York, Anchor Books, 1977; Sandra M. Gilbert and Susan Gubar, *The Madwoman in the Attic: The Woman Writer and the Nineteenth-century Literary Imagination*, New Haven and London, Yale University Press, 1979.
9. Carolyn G. Heibrun, *Toward a Recognition of Androgyny*, New York, Harper Colophon Books, 1973, pp. ix–xi.
10. Elaine Showalter, *A Literature of Their Own: British Women Novelists from Brontë to Lessing*, Princeton, Princeton University Press, 1977; London, Virago, 1978.
11. Maryse Condé, 'The Female Writer in Modern Africa: Flora Nwapa, Ama Ata Aidoo, and Grace Ogot', in *Présence Africaine*, no. 82, 1972, pp. 132–43. For McCaffrey, see note 5 above.
12. Beatrice Stegeman, 'The Divorce Dilemma: The New Woman in Contemporary African Novels', in *Critique: Studies in Modern Fiction*, 15, no. 3, 1974, pp. 90–2.
13. Mariama Bâ, *So Long a Letter*, trans. Modupé Bodé-Thomas, London, Heinemann (AWS 248), 1981, p. 89.
14. Tillie Olsen, *Silences*, New York, Delacorte, 1978, p. 6; London, Virago, 1980.

Albert Camus, Aimé Césaire and the Tragedy of Revolution

John Conteh-Morgan

The association of the names of Albert Camus and Aimé Césaire for the purposes of a comparative literary study may come as a surprise.[1] No two writers could be more different. In the first place, Camus was born to a family of French colonists who had settled in Algeria as far back as 1871, while Césaire's parents were indigenous Martinicans who, though French in theory and by law were, by the history and realities of their island, more like a colonized people. Secondly, in spite of all his disclaimers, Camus' plays and novels display several common characteristics with those of existentialist writers such as Sartre and Malraux. His imaginative writings like theirs, therefore, give a considerable amount of attention to philosophical questions such as alienation, loneliness, suffering and death. Césaire on the other hand belonged to the Négritude school of writers whose literary activities show an intense preoccupation with cultural and sociopolitical issues. The fragility of freedom in newly-emergent nations, the evils of colonialism, the vitality of African cultures and so on are themes that figure prominently in his works.

Despite these significant differences in their social background and in the orientation of their writings, however, Césaire and Camus exhibit a link which makes an association of their names not unreasonable, and a comparison of their plays *Les Justes* (1949) and *La Tragédie du roi Christophe* (1963)[2] illuminating. This link is their common tragic sensibility. By this I mean their shared concern for the facts of suffering and evil in human experience, their similar preoccupation with the role of destiny in human affairs and their common perception of life as the locus of irresolvable conflicts between human aspirations and reality. It is perhaps natural, in the light of the above, that both writers should show great interest in the tragic form and should wish to try it as a mode of literary expression.

Of course, the objection might be raised at this point that while both authors are indeed possessed of a tragic sense, this is expressed very differently. It could be argued that Césaire, for example, explains human suffering in terms of social, political and psychological factors. Camus on the other hand sees it as a metaphysical problem, a fundamental feature of the human condition which is therefore irreducible, in the tradition of Rousseauist romanticism, to external social and political forces.

This objection is certainly weighty. However, it loses much of its force when it is remembered that after 1945,[3] probably because of his experience of World War Two and the immense suffering that it entailed, Camus became increasingly aware of the moral problem of inter-human evil. He came to the conclusion that far from just being a hopeless clod who was entirely acted upon by some evil and impersonal deity, man often intensified his suffering by his unmeasured reaction to the tragic nature of existence. Camus saw politics in general, and the politics of revolution in particular as one such reaction;[4] as an attempt by men to take control of their destiny and to settle it in purely historical terms. But because of its pretensions to absoluteness, Camus contends that this attempt only succeeds in increasing the suffering which it set out to abolish. Thus like Malraux in *La Condition humaine* (1933), Camus came to a clear and profound understanding of politics as a powerful force, a modern form of destiny which brings men to grief in the manner of the ancient gods of tragedy. It is precisely this conception of politics as destiny, explored in *Les Justes*, that gives this play its striking similarity to *La Tragédie*, and which provides the ground for an interesting comparison of both works. Indeed Césaire himself invites such a comparison, if only because he thinks it will help to dispel ideas of a pessimistic and nihilistic Christophe that seem to be gaining ground among certain critics:

> Pour moi, Christophe n'est pas nihiliste.... il suffirait de (le) comparer... aux héros de Camus que l'on trouve dans *Les Justes*. Eh bien, ce jeune homme, cette jeune femme qui sont des terroristes et qui vont lancer une bombe sur le Grand-Duc... ça n'a aucun rapport avec Christophe..., il me semble.
>
> For me, Christophe is not nihilistic.... One would only need to compare

(him) to Camus' heroes in *Les Justes* to realize this. Now this young man, this young girl who are terrorists and shall be throwing a bomb at the Grand-Duc ... have nothing in common with Christophe ... it appears to me.[5]

Leaving aside for the moment the debatable question raised here of whether Christophe has nothing in common with Camus' hero and his comrades in *Les Justes*, one is struck by the need Césaire feels to contrast his protagonist with that of Camus. This need would not have arisen, one suspects, if Césaire had not been aware of some affinity – perhaps thematic, perhaps structural – between the two plays. The elucidation of this affinity and of possible differences will constitute the substance of this paper.

Although set in different historical periods, early twentieth-century Tsarist Russia in the case of *Les Justes*, and early nineteenth-century colonial Haiti in *La Tragédie*, these plays are linked by their common theme of rebellion against tyranny; a rebellion which finds expression in *Les Justes* in the assassination, by a young group of terrorists, of the Grand-Duc Alexandrovitch. In *La Tragédie*, it takes the form of a heroic attempt by the visionary hero Christophe to liquidate vestiges of French colonialism in his country, to unite his people and instil in them a sense of dignity and freedom. However, both these attempts – one conceived in an effort to hasten 'la libération du peuple russe' (the liberation of the Russian people) (*Théâtre*, p. 310), the other in a bid to give Haitians, among other things, 'la faim de faire et le besoin de perfection' (the thirst for achievement and the need for perfection) (*La Tragédie*, p. 138) – turn out to be tragically paradoxical, for the means envisaged or actually used by the heroes are in sharp conflict with the noble ends that inform their movements. It is this conflict between noble ends and ignoble means that constitutes the crucial drama and tragedy in both plays. What I intend to do in this article is to examine the exploitation of this conflict by each author.

Les Justes and *La Tragédie* revolve, as has been observed, around a tragic dualism, a structural antagonism whose most immediate application is in the hiatus between the intentions and achievements of the respective heroes, between their ethics and their politics. Right from the beginning, to take the case of *La Tragédie* first, the protagonist emerges as a man who is impelled by a noble ideal – that of giving his people their lost sense of identity, a distinct cultural personality which he sees as a prerequisite for any act of authentic development.

He wants to put an end to their alienated state as a people who have been taught to despise themselves by slavery and colonialism. Using a rare and uncharacteristic image borrowed from nature, he compares his project with that of a farmer whose task it is to nurture carefully a plant which has been forcibly uprooted from its natural environment and transplanted elsewhere. What Haitians need, he tells Pétion, is not just formal liberty but:

> quelque chose grâce à quoi ce peuple de transplantés s'enracine, boutonne, s'épanouisse, lançant à la face du monde les parfums, les fruits de la floraison.
>
> something thanks to which this nation of transplanted people will sink roots, put out buds, blossom out and send on to the face of the world the perfumes and fruits of their luscious beauty.
>
> (La Tragédie, p. 23)

Unlike his rival Pétion who thinks of freedom as a gift or an entrenched article in a constitution, Christophe thinks of it as a conquest which can only become real and lasting through action and concrete achievement. It is, indeed, in the light of this conviction that he mobilizes his people into the task of building an enormous citadel that should stand as a living testimony to their spirit of endeavour and greatness:

> ce peuple doit so procurer, vouloir, réussir quelque chose d'impossible!... Porté par nos mains blessées, le défi insensé! ... je dis la Citadelle la liberté de tout un peuple.
>
> these people must obtain, aim at and achieve something impossible! ... Carried by our wounded hands, the mad challenge! ... I mean the Citadel, the liberty of an entire people.
>
> (La Tragédie, p. 63)

Through the experience of the manual labour involved in constructing this monument, the Haitians will be transformed (so Christophe thinks), into regenerated citizens. They will discover the exacting realm of responsibility; be drawn from their passivity and inaction to participate, as they have never done before, as actors and not just as spectators in the making of their destiny. They will, finally, obliterate their past as a slave people washed helplessly, hither and thither by the waves, and finally washed on some sterile, stony island ('Ilôt pierreux, milliers de nègres demi-nus que la vague a vomis un soir.' (stony inlet, thousands of half-naked negroes vomited one evening by the waves), in Christophe's vivid image of disgust (La Tragédie p. 38)) to become a proud nation whose existence will signal, in the hero's words, the definitive 'Annulation du négrier' (Death of the slave trader) (*La Tragédie*, p. 63).

Such then is the soaring vision that informs King Christophe's actions. But such also is the vision which, in its essentials, informs the movement of Kaliayev and his comrades in *Les Justes*. Admittedly, their ends are not as specific and as clearly worked out as Christophe's. As characters they do not come alive; they are not sufficiently individualized in the way Christophe is.[6] Camus' hero and his comrades can even be accused of indulging in woolly sentimentalism. But to imply, as Césaire has done,[7] that they have nothing in common with his protagonist because they are nihilistic is to confuse them with the historical 'Just Assassins' after whom they are patterned, and who, indeed, were partly influenced by the nihilistic theories of contemporaries such as Bakunin and Nechayev.[8]

But far from being impelled by that sense of despair which could lead to blind destruction, Kaliayev and his comrades are selfless and positive in their determination to rid the Russian people of the shackle of Tsarist tyranny: 'nous abattrons la tyrannie' (we shall overthrow tyranny), says Stepan (*Théâtre*, p. 309) a view that is echoed by character after character in the play.

Annenkov Toute la Russie saura que le grand-duc Serge a été exécuté à la bombe ... pour hâter la libération du peuple russe.

All Russia will know that the Grand-Duc Serge has been killed by a bomb ... to hasten the liberation of the Russian people.

(*Théâtre* p. 310)

Kaliayev Nous tuerons pour bâtir un monde où plus jamais personne ne tuera! Nous acceptons d'être criminels pour que la terre se couvre enfin d'innocents.

We shall kill to build a world where never again shall anyone be killed! We accept to be criminals so that the world will at last be covered with innocent people.

(*Théâtre*, p. 322)

Like Christophe, Camus' protagonist and his comrades are fighting to preserve something greater than themselves. Like him too, they have consented to take part in revolutionary activity so that others might derive joy in life: 'pour donner une chance à la vie' (to give an opportunity to life), in Kaliayev's words (*Théâtre*, p. 322); 'pour que', in Vastey's justification of Christophe's activities, 'il n'y ait plus de par le monde une jeune fille noire qui ait honte de sa peau et trouve dans sa couleur un obstacle à la réalisation des voeux de son coeur' (so that no black girl in the entire world will any longer be ashamed of her skin and find in its colour an obstacle to the accomplishment of her heart's desires). (*La Tragédie*, p. 82)

It is thus clear at this point that despite the different historical and political contexts in which they operate, Christophe on the one hand, and Kaliayev and his comrades on the other are united by their unmistakable assertion of solidarity around common human values, such as justice and liberty, and their attempts to change the political conditions that violate them. It is in this sense that both plays can be said to be ultimately about ethical values. But in so far as the protagonists are also committed to giving concrete expression to these values, through violent action if necessary, *Les Justes* and *La Tragédie* are also about politics, or more precisely about revolutionary politics. Ethics and politics: such are the twin poles around which both plays revolve. It is the conflict between them that gives both *Les Justes* and *La Tragédie* their basic dramatic structure and that gives rise in both plays to a sense of tragedy.

The possibility of such a conflict in Césaire's play is announced from the very first scene of Act I, where Christophe explains to Pétion that he is prepared to use force, to have recourse to the sword in the pursuit of his ideals. What the Haitian people need, he asserts, is a leader, 'qui au besoin *par la force* l'oblige à naitre à lui-même' (who through *force* if need be, obliges them to self-regeneration) (*La Tragédie*, p. 23, my italics). The dramatic tension of the first Act of *La Tragédie* is based on the feeling that a set of critical actions are about to take place; that in spite of all the pleas for moderation from Madame Christophe and Wilberforce, Christophe is about to pass into action, to implement his designs in their totality without due consideration for the only-too-human fallibility of his subjects, the inertia of nature and the inescapable realities of a three-hundred-year history of slavery and colonization:

> ce peuple doit se procurer, vouloir, réussir quelque chose d'impossible! Contre le sort, contre l'Histoire, contre la Nature.

> these people must obtain, aim at, accomplish something impossible! Against destiny, against History, against Nature.
>
> (*La Tragédie*, p. 62)

Consumed by a Romantic all-or-nothing vision of action in time, Christophe rapidly gets to the position where he forgets the concrete individuals whom he set out to defend. He removes his political means from the sphere of moral judgement, arguing that only the ends they are meant to serve could be used to justify them. The reader is therefore hardly surprised when in Act II, in a bid to further his ends, he decrees forced marriages, has those whose revolutionary ardour is less than total executed, and justifies tyranny which he pledged to abolish during his enthronement, as a legitimate means of furthering liberty.

It is not the least of tragic ironies in this play that a man who is so obsessed with constructing a state and with moulding the personality of his people should choose destruction as his favourite weapon. This paradox is not lost on the Deuxième Dame who exclaims:

> Le charmant paradoxe! En somme le roi Christophe servirait la liberté par les moyens de la servitude.
>
> What a charming paradox! In short King Christophe would serve liberty by using the methods of slavery. (La Tragédie, p. 80)

nor on the Deuxième Paysan who observes:

> je me dis comme ça que si nous avons rejeté les Blancs à la mer, c'était pour l'avoir à nous cette terre, pas pour peiner sur la terre des autres, même noirs.
>
> I tell myself this that if we have thrown the whites into the sea, it was to have to ourselves this land and not to labour on the land of others, not even blacks. (La Tragédie, p. 74)

As the African page boy accompanying his coffin remarks, Christophe is indeed 'bifaced' (La Tragédie, p. 152), a contradictory figure in whom coexist mutually exclusive opposites.

> patience et impatience, défaite et victoire ... force de jour marée du noir.
>
> Patience and impatience, defeat and victory ... force of day and tide of night. (La Tragédie p. 152)

Determined to abolish suffering when the play opens, he discovers at the end that he has only intensified it.

This rivalry between moral idealism and practical politics is also at the heart of Les Justes. Like Christophe, Kaliayev is conscious of the necessity of violent action if he is to succeed in accomplishing his objectives, and he decides to use it. But unlike the hero of La Tragédie who exults in it, violence, even in the service of a higher cause, is very much against Kaliayev's nature. Basically a poet, he shows great sensitivity to beauty and evinces a profound taste for life in all its fullness:

la vie continue de me paraître merveilleuse. J'aime la beauté, la bonheur. C'est pour cela que je hais le despotisme.

life continues to appear marvellous to me. I like beauty, happiness. That is why I detest despotism.

(Théâtre, p. 322)

It is because of this strong attachment to life that he experiences intense anguish at the thought of being the prime actor (in so far as he is charged with assassinating the Grand-Duc) in a movement that seeks to uphold life by destroying it.

Thus unlike his bitter critic Stepan who, in the manner of Christophe, is prepared to be ruthless in his effort to rectify the evils of society, Kaliayev argues for the observance of ethical propriety, for the respect for human life without which the revolution, even if successful, would betray its origins.

But while Kaliayev accepts the unquestionable moral superiority of his position, he also sees some positive value in Stepan's attitude. Not to carry out his task against the Grand-Duc would be to renounce his desire for a just society and to capitulate to the tyranny perpetuated by him. Yet he is convinced that to assassinate him is tantamount to entering into a pact with evil. Kaliayev is caught, in other words, in a conflict between his love and respect for life which forbid violent action against anyone, and his unswerving commitment (which he shares with Stepan) to a form of social justice which, in the context of his situation, pre-supposes, at the very least, violence against the Grand-Duc. His dilemma is similar to that of the 'Rebel' about whom Camus writes in L'Homme révolté:

Si je renonce à faire respecter l'identité humaine, j'abdique devant celui qui opprime ... Si j'exige que cette identité soit reconnue pour être, je m'engage dans une action qui pour réussir, suppose un cynisme de la violence et nie cette identité.

If I give up attempts to have human dignity respected, I abdicate to the oppressor ... If I demand that this dignity be taken into consideration, I commit myself to a line of action which, to be successful, presupposes a cynical attitude towards violence which denies this dignity.

(Essais, p. 690)

Kaliayev's predicament lies in his acute awareness of the fact that in his just rebellion against social evil, he is forced to commit murder in the name of a human nature which itself forbids such action. His tragedy, like Christophe's, thus derives from the antagonism between the moral demands and the practical requirements of the revolution. Or does it really? Freeman has demonstrated[9] that there is some uncertainty in *Les Justes* as to what actually constitutes the hero's tragic predicament. For side by side with his ideas on the inviolability of all life, Kaliayev is convinced that the evil involved in taking the life of a tyrant can be made good of perfectly, if the assassin in turn freely pays for his crime with his life:

> Je sais maintenant que je voudrais périr sur place, à côté du Grand-Duc.
> ... c'est la seule façon d'être à la hauteur de l'idée, c'est la justification.

> I now know that I would like to perish on the spot, beside the Grand-Duc.
> ... It is the only way to be worthy of the idea, it is its justification.
>
> (*Théâtre*, p. 323)

On no account, however, should one act against innocent people since not even death will constitute sufficient atonement for such action. It is on the basis of this admirable but untenable theory of redemptive suffering that Kaliayev refuses to throw the bomb at the Grand-Duc when the latter is accompanied by children.

Now a man who argues like Kaliayev – that there is a limit that cannot be overstepped in the name of an ideal without tarnishing the latter – can only be truly tragic[10] if, through no fault of his own, he violates his self-imposed law. In other words, Camus' hero would only have been tragic if he had been granted a reprieve, contrary to his wishes, or if he had unwittingly acted against the children. As it turns out, however, he is able to assassinate the Duke (thus satisfying his need for a fair society) without simultaneously destroying those moral principles of the movement which are so dear to him. It is precisely because of this good fortune that he emerges not as a tragic character, but as what Freeman appropriately describes as a 'lucky' hero: lucky in so far as he is not confronted a second time with a situation in which he must choose between his moral integrity, which proscribes violence against the innocent, and his social commitment.

It is in Camus' failure to exploit this conflict to its limits that reside the basic differences between *La Tragédie* and *Les Justes*. In terms of dramatic structure, for example, Césaire achieves an extremely pure line to his play, with his protagonist moving inexorably and relentlessly from a phase in Act I in which he is brimming with noble ideas and impelled by visions of grandeur for his people, to one in the last Act in which he experiences total disillusionment, suffering and failure. At no point in the drama is there even the hint of a possible escape for him from that fearful logic of events unleashed by his uncompromising thirst for the absolute. Christophe's trajectory can indeed be described, as Césaire himself does, as 'une course effrénée à la mort' (a mad rush unto death).[11] But Christophe does not only die, he lives long enough to witness the total destruction of his ideals, to see his people for whom he had dreamt only greatness rise up in arms against him. His statement to Hugonin: 'Chacune de tes paroles s'encombre d'un débris de mes rêves' (Each of your words is littered with debris of my dreams) (*La Tragédie*, p. 39) is a tragic recognition, an *anagnorisis*, of the distance separating his dreams from reality.

If *La Tragédie* describes, in its dramatic movement, a *descent* into inevitable death and destruction, *Les Justes* on the other hand describes an *ascent* from near-destruction to certain redemption. Unlike Christophe for whom affliction is the definitive experience and anxiety and despair the dominant mood, Kaliayev goes through anguish only temporarily; that is during the moments preceding his throwing of the bomb. For the rest of his life, events unfold according to *his* plans. He is arrested and tried, offered the possibility of a reprieve which he rejects, and is finally executed – all as he personally wanted it. Thus his death does not constitute a loss, as in the case of Christophe, but a fulfilment: an apotheosis. It is actively sought and obtained.

Kaliayev reconciles harmoniously, in a way Christophe does not, ethics and politics and it is precisely because of this that he cuts the figure of a martyr rather than that of a tragic hero, as Camus would have liked. How can he be tragic when he chooses his fate; when he is the master and not the victim of circumstances? Furthermore, tragedy should evoke responses of pity; pity at the undeserved misfortune of a man who is neither bad nor 'pre-eminently virtuous and just'. The hero of *Les Justes* is not only just, he is perfect. He has no *harmatia*, so that unlike Christophe for whom we feel only sympathy and pity, we gasp at his luck and admire his integrity.

It could be said in conclusion that although both authors set out to write tragic dramas based on the conflict between the moral demands and the practical requirements of revolution, only Césaire succeeds in this task. *La Tragédie du roi Christophe* shows revolutionary activity as it *is* in real life, with its turmoil, paradoxes, compromises and betrayals. *Les Justes* on the other hand depicts it as it *ought* to be. In Camus' play tragic suffering is held out as a real possibility at the beginning; it is intellectually perceived and analysed by the hero, but it never becomes a lived experience.

NOTES

1. Although very rare, such associations are not altogether absent. In their study of Césaire's poetry, M. and S. Battestini hint at a possible influence of Camus' *Homme révolté* (1952) on Césaire's idea of revolt. See *Aimé Césaire, écrivain martiniquais*, Paris, Fernand Nathan, 1967, p. 7. One can also consult a more recent article linking both writers, in the present author's 'Politics as tragedy: Aimé Césaire's *La Tragédie du roi Christophe*, in the light of Albert Camus', *L'Homme révolté*, Ba Shiru (forthcoming).
2. Aimé Césaire, *La Tragédie du roi Christophe*, Paris, Présence Africaine, 1970 (hereafter referred to as *La Tragédie*). References to *Les Justes* will be taken from Albert Camus, *Théâtre, Récits, Nouvelles*, Paris, Gallimard Bibl. de la Pléiade, 1962 (hereafter referred to as *Théâtre*).
3. For a study of Camus' conception of tragedy and its evolution, see my doctoral dissertation: *Concepts of Tragedy in the Writings of Albert Camus*, Unpublished D. Phil thesis, Sussex University, 1978.
4. For a rather dated but classic critique of this theory of revolution, see Jean-Paul Sartre, 'Réponse à Albert Camus' in *Les Temps Modernes*, Août 1952, pp. 334–53.
5. David Dunn, 'Interview with Aimé Césaire on a new approach to *La Tragédie du roi Christophe* and *Une Saison au Congo* Cahiers Césairiens,' 4, 1980, p. 2.
6. For a detailed study of Christophe, from a point of view of his style, see my article 'Development: growth or creation? A note on the image of the builder in Aimé Césaire's *La Tragédie du roi Christophe*', *Présence Francophone* (forthcoming).
7. David Dunn, op. cit. p. 2.
8. For an analysis of the 'Just Assassins' and their relationship with the philosophy of Bakunin, see Albert Camus, *Essais*, Paris, Gallimard, Bibl. de la Pléiade, 1965, pp. 560–79 (hereafter referred to as *Essais*).
9. E. Freeman, *The Theatre of Albert Camus: A Critical Survey*, London, Methuen, 1971.
10. For an exposition of *Les Justes* in terms of tragedy see *inter alia*, E. Freeman, op. cit. pp. 99–118, Patricia Little, 'Albert Camus, Simone Weil and Modern Tragedy' in *French Studies*, January 1977, pp. 42–51.
11. David Dunn, op. cit. p. 5.

Africa under Western Eyes: Updike's *The Coup* and Other Fantasies

Jack B. Moore

There are few American writers more exasperating than John Updike. Few writers have more technical skills than he. Practically no major American writer possesses his dazzling verbal skill. He is highly productive as a short-story writer and novelist. He is concerned with the demands of his art and yet he seems equally involved with the health (or sickness) of the American state. As accurately as Norman Mailer if not as solipsistically (Mailer seems himself the target of all his popguns) he has boomed like the man-of-war in *Heart of Darkness*[1] salvo after salvo into the decaying tangle of American national behaviour – not to try to destroy it but to clear away the rot and let the good stock (if there is any left) take deeper root and flourish. One cannot imagine a writer with more gifts than he, and yet though novel after novel of his is far better than most of what his contemporaries are capable of producing, nearly all appear ultimately unsatisfactory, the later ones rarely achieving the anxious grace of *Poorhouse Fair, Rabbit, Run,* or *The Centaur.*[2]

The Coup[3] is a typical, and typically good, Updike performance. Its plot concerns a mythical African country called Kush, where the 'life expectancy is thirty-nine years, the per capita gross national product $79.00, the literacy rate 6%'. The leader of this mildly and ineffectually socialistic state is Colonel Hakim Félix Ellelloû, a partly American-educated man with characteristics of Leopold Senghor, Sekou Touré, Julius Nyerere, Chaka the Great – and, one suspects, John Updike. An intellectual, an autocrat, a philosopher and moralist, a womanizer and a purist, a would-be man of the people,

Ellelloû's intelligence and imagination dominate the novel. His wit is captivating, the perfect (perhaps too perfect since too readily available) outlet for Updike's marvellous descriptive artistry: 'His little hooked nose alone,' Ellelloû says of the shrunken, deposed king he will soon behead, 'had resisted the reshaping of time and sat in the centre of his face like a single tart fruit being served on an outworn platter.' This king contains in his cell objects of 'fantastic workmanship that only extreme poverty coupled with faith in an afterlife produces'. The skill of such phrasing is not merely verbal. The first description encapsulates the decline and sad condition of a once-great and powerful man. The second remark penetrates into the cultural conditions found perhaps only in very poor, very religious and non-technological nations where monotonous ornateness is not computerized and mass produced.

The novel does not always succeed at the verbal level. Ellelloû has a predilection for pseudo-profundities such as 'a barefoot man is not poor until he sees others wearing shoes'; slightly off-target metaphors – for example when he says a woman's 'breasts were the shape of freshly started anthills'; and sometimes just plain corny language, which no matter how ornately laid out is still corny: of himself and his love Ellelloû claims that 'our fatigue was a tower to which each night we added another tier'! But these occasional infelicities can be permitted a writer who takes such constant verbal risks, who writes nearly always at a high pitch that is bound sometimes to waver in the wind of his rhetoric. In fact, the over-writing is also sometimes a positive element of the book since within the perspective of the novel's narrative point of view it communicates Ellelloû's charming but not always wise exuberance.

What is wrong about the novel in a truly destructive sense, and what is ultimately wrong about so many of Updike's novels is that his technique – though often stunning – is not accompanied by the ability to make his audience care much about the characters he has created or about what happens to them. His satire is often funny but it tends to depict familiar caricatures rather than individuals who convince readers of their humanity, no matter how foolishly the characters act. Satire tends to diminish the depth of characters, but the great prose fiction satirists such as Swift and Voltaire managed to create major and even minor characters whose vices and follies were rooted in people we could sympathize with or despise, such as the extremely likeable Candide or the rather sad Yahoo nurse who alone laments Gulliver's departure from Houyhnhnm land, or Shrike the cruel, tortured tormentor of Nathanael West's Miss Lonelyhearts.

These people seem to have real feelings even though at some other technical level they are only opportunities for their creators to illustrate some thematic point.

The American satiric novelist Nathanael West also created characters in his brilliantly morbid novels who had much of their human dimension ruthlessly cut away. They become what West said he wanted to produce in *Miss Lonelyhearts*[4] – cartoons, filled with stereotyped grotesques; yet most of West's major characters retain the ability to experience and administer what seems like real pain, so that they become more than just decorations in their creator's terrifying, satanic abstraction. Even the most savage satire need not produce characters we do not care much about.

Updike's main character, Félix Ellelloû, desires to maintain or rather to establish his nation's integrity while both America and Russia press limited but binding aid upon the desiccated land. Like the Fisher King of a modern waste land, Ellelloû seeks through a personal quest to revitalize himself and his increasingly sick nation, travelling in space around his mainly barren country and in time back through his life, most frequently to the land of his college years, America, described here as elsewhere in Updike's recent fiction as a spoiled, pimply-faced brat with no class, who will never grow up. Updike appears to be wanting, as is so common among western novelists, to locate some possibility for personal salvation in Africa, but the world he describes in his mythical Kush will not support that burden as it trades most of its presumably special connection to the miracle of existence for an ersatz society of corrupting, mock affluence doled out by a modern mega-corporation interested only in fast bucks.

Updike's satire on America is amusing but not deep, partly because it is peopled with witless characters who have the shallowness of stereotypes shown on American situation comedy television series, worn masks for stale pies in the face: a militant black who finally trades in his worn revolutionary rhetoric for a place in the establishment; a white and fake liberal woman who sleeps with blacks to assuage her white guilt, and for sexual kicks; the woman's bewildered and bigoted daddie, middle-class to his nigger-hating core. None of these stuffed dolls has the reality Ellelloû in his quest possesses, and the effect of this lack is an artistic disjuncture. A man we are supposed to feel real pity for, whose agony presumably should pain us, is surrounded by the kind of 'vidiots' who represent people in commercial dramatizations, who help create a trivial context which it is difficult to be seriously affected by.

A similar aesthetic disjuncture haunts the African portions of Updike's novel. When Elleloû, a funny, insightful, very human man most of the time, cuts off his former king's head, he sees it held before him, he says, 'at arm's length, as the centre of an opposing basketball team demonstrates his intimidating one-handed grip'. The words are catching but at the expense of character. Elleloû does not seem to be hiding his emotions here: rather, he seems to feel almost nothing. The king has been real and affecting to this point, yet his beheading has no more honesty to it than one of those imaginative, fake deaths in the James Bond films. Later in the book, after an excruciatingly painful (to an American) description of how sacred land in Kush has been turned into a Disneyworld through American-style technology and entrepreneurial skill, Elleloû orders the execution of a mob of gawking, insensitive, bussed-in tourists. This sequence follows the mysterious journey of intense suffering and (supposedly) enlightenment that Elleloû has undertaken, a section of the book with deeply religious and mythic implications. Elleloû very realistically describes his sufferings during this psychologically intense trip. What then are we to make of the flippant way he orders the deaths of the tourists? The insouciant wiseacre, joking so murderously, cannot possibly be the same man who has just scratched and crawled his way over the harshest imaginable terrain to reach his personal goal.

Comparisons between similar novels by disparate authors are odious and yet inevitable. Evelyn Waugh's *Black Mischief*[5] is a more slashing, anti-African novel, Chinua Achebe's *A Man of the People*[6] more politically revealing, Saul Bellow's *Henderson the Rain King*[7] is more psychologically powerful, Camara Laye's *The Radiance of the King*[8] more intricate in its revelation of the mystery of existence, Ayi Kwei Armah's *The Beautyful Ones Are Not Yet Born*[9] more penetrating in its exploration of human filth, Conrad's *Heart of Darkness* infinitely more terrifying in its depiction of the horrors of the western mind and the human heart. To its credit, John Updike's *The Coup* contains some of the better elements of all these novels about African leadership, and yet is not exactly imitative of any one of them. But Updike never seems quite to have decided what kind of book he wants his to be: satire, tragedy, absurdist melodrama – he writes as though he is almost afraid to commit himself totally to any single or dominant approach. Cruder novels about Africa and the West have left clearer impressions of success than this one though few have been written with a finer intelligence. But intelligence is not enough when you are writing about Africa; you need the novelist's equivalent of largeness of soul too, and this (student of theology though

Updike may be) – along with the ability to curb aspects of his talent in order to get at the truth of what he sees – is what Updike lacks. Africa is too big for him, though the American press has generally conceded that his depiction of Kush is one of the novel's great successes.

In *Henderson the Rain King*, Saul Bellow's Africa is large and incomprehensible, clearly a projection of the mind of its narrator, the bumbling Henderson, who never shows us Africa at all but only reveals a large, odd land that is the fancy of an awkward, but endearing and relentlessly forward-looking Rain King. Once away from constricting America, Henderson jumps almost immediately into a loose corner of Africa's ancient heart, a world of fable like everything else in Henderson's charmed and silly life. Henderson shows that white men of imagination come to Africa not as Dr Livingstone supposedly did, to save souls, but to find their own (though some like Conrad's Kurtz lose theirs). But even though Henderson's view of Africa is naturally distorted (since the land he penetrated is really impervious to him) we can glimpse through his dreams a few true shapes: just enough to let us know the place is real enough to the people inside it, if not to Henderson. The political infighting is crafty and vicious, the struggle for domination sincere.

There is something otiose (a word I think Updike would approve of – Ronald Firbank used to employ it regularly and nicely) about the African characters engaged in Updike's local squabbles, something faintly ridiculous. After all, when you live in a country like America, perhaps the most productive and destructive nation the world has yet known, the trickles of power that seep into lesser nations are perhaps inevitably comic (until they discover large oil reserves). Of course they are not funny, but in *The Coup* they invariably seem so. A real coup, even in a small place, is not at all funny although in a big place you can look at it through a reverse political microscope. There are really no 'lesser nations', though Updike's Kush seems 'lesser'. Any country is totally important and totally real to the people living in it. Updike's presentation of Kush and its inhabitants reduces the piece of African space the nation supposedly encompasses to the diminished size of a parody. I remember once in Ghana seeing a marvellous Twi reworking of *Antigone* that seemed absolutely correct in its awareness of the delicate political and personal conflict the original play is about. The play made the Twi kingdom as large as ancient mythic Thebes. Updike's Kush could never contain such a play, even though his book's protagonist Ellelloû would certainly be intellectually capable of appreciating the old tragedy. Updike's

Africa coincides with the Africa of many American imaginations, a place that could not possibly exist, except sometimes erotically in popular trash like *Mandingo*, or sentimentally as the homeland of Alex Haley's *Roots*.

Perhaps the western novel best compared with *The Coup* is not Bellow's burly *Henderson the Rain King*, made more real by the chunks of accurate anthropological lore dropped throughout its African landscape like signposts in a strange wilderness, but the more fragile and satiric *Black Mischief* by Evelyn Waugh, which makes only scant pretence of creating an Africa of serious significance. Waugh's African stage-set can only exist impossibly – as did in reality the weird colonials he describes in his art-deco Africa, and the denatured Africans who so ludicrously try to ape the whites that Waugh wants us to think *they* think are their monkey betters.

Waugh's honest and straightforward racism is only mitigated by what appears to be his dominating streak of inhumanism. In *Black Mischief* nearly everyone is shown in the worst possible (and most artificial) light. The contempt in which most of the Africans in the book are held by most of the English ruling class is perhaps exceeded only by the contempt the children of the ruling class feel towards their parents and their own class. The well-meaning stupidity of the African Emperor Seth seems almost innocent next to the networks of ignorance flung throughout the 'Azanian' territory by the other Europeans who occupy positions of diplomatic authority in Waugh's sinister land of mystery, as comic as it is killing. Waugh's African farce is also as clever as it is chilling: playing at love with sappy Prudence, Waugh's hero Basil tells her 'I'd like to eat you', and she replies, 'So you shall, my sweet'. And so he does: later, after the facade of a modern kingdom which Basil has set up is devastated as easily as a Hollywood set is struck, he unknowingly eats Prudence in a cannibalistic ritual with Africans friendly to him. And Prudence's death is real: Waugh twists from comedy into violence as quickly as a joke hanging can break a neck. Missionaries or nubile white ladies in the pot has for a long time been the favourite western joke about uncivilized African kingdoms, as well as a serious justification back home for many a profitable punitive expedition. Yet, quite as clear in the book as the African fall from grace – the cultural poor taste that cannibalism signifies (or rather the African failure to have achieved a redeeming fall from grace through their cultural childishness – kids will eat anything) – is the depravity of the western civilization which at the conclusion to *Black Mischief* is evacuating its privileged colonials from warring Kush. This advanced civilization had just finished mangling itself in World War One and was on the brink of renewed self-mutilation on a scale unknown in Africa, in World War Two. The western society Waugh described in *Black Mischief* was in the process of dismantling itself, eating itself in a grand exhibition of self-cannibalism worse than that of Saturn, who only devoured his children.

So Waugh's racism seems another local version of his inhumanism: he hates everybody. The racism along with the inhumanism produces a consistent satirical point of view that the more well-meaning, politically liberal writer Updike lacks. His Americans are mostly fools but there is no resonance to their folly. Most are well-intentioned enough such as Ellelloû's white wife who wants to atone for centuries of oppression by sleeping with her black man: nailed in bed instead of on a cross. In *Black Mischief* a few élite Africans want to become British. In *The Coup* an entire village of workers lives apparently happily in a bad reconstruction of America during the late 1950s, eating cheeseburgers and listening to Doris Day singing the cynic's national anthem: 'Que Sera, Sera'. What will be, will be. The liberal American both loves and hates his country. The worst thing that could happen to Africa, Updike probably fears, would be to turn into another America. But at the same time I suspect he thinks their cheeseburgers wouldn't be as good as American ones. For after all, haven't we heard that even in Russia, tight American blue jeans are the craze on the black market? Blue jeans – those symbols of fake egalitarianism which are vestiges of the splendidly exploitable Wild Western myth of freedom and justice and opportunity and a gun for all. The Russians want to beat the Americans but still they want to get into their sexy trousers. Yes, the liberal loves the land he hates.

Waugh ridiculed African civilization for its pretentiousness on the surface and barbarism below – but he made the same satiric attack upon European society, sometimes reversing his charges. Updike seems stuck between treating Africa seriously and at the same time being unable to. This contradictory attitude is reflected in Ellelloû's adventures during the last half of the novel; Ellelloû is now stumbling over the hot, moonish terrain of Kush trying to discover the source of its dryness, now getting trapped into a stupid confrontation with an American public relations expert who seems to have wandered in from a low grade farce. It is as though one of the questing Arthurian knights, Gawain perhaps, were suddenly to confront Jerry Lewis playing the Green Knight.

So Updike himself veers to and fro in his African book, nearing the power of *Henderson the Rain King*, coming close to the poisonous satire of Black Mischief, sometimes writing precisely and realistically about his African leader, then turning him into an almost Chaplinesque victim of modern times, but never really settling down into a consistent artistic attitude. That he comes close to so many varied artists suggests his range, that he falls short of each demonstrates his finally deficient grasp, at least in this novel, of the artistic control he needs to master his undoubted talents. That American readers may still prefer his version of Africa to those of the standard indigenous African novelists is as understandable as was the western search for the mountains of the moon, the source of the Nile in the fabled regions of the interior. Sometimes the truth is so hard it hurts to get at it.

NOTES

1. Joseph Conrad, Heart of Darkness, London, William Blackwood, 1902; Penguin, 1973.
2. John Updike, Poorhouse Fair, New York, Knopf, 1977.
   Rabbit Run, New York, Knopf, 1960; London, Penguin, 1969.
   The Centaur, New York, Knopf, 1963; London, Penguin, 1970.
3. John Updike, The Coup, New York, Knopf, 1978; London, Penguin, 1980.
4. Nathanael West, Miss Lonelyhearts, New York, New Directions, 1962.
5. Evelyn Waugh, Black Mischief, London, Penguin, 1980.
6. Chinua Achebe, A Man of the People, London, Heinemann (AWS 31), 1966; New York, Doubleday, 1967.
7. Saul Bellow, Henderson the Rain King, New York, Viking, 1959; London, Penguin, 1966.
8. Camara Laye, The Radiance of the King, London, Collins, 1956; New York, Macmillan, 1970.
9. Ayi Kwei Armah, The Beautyful Ones Are Not Yet Born, London, Heinemann (AWS 43), 1969; Boston, Houghton Mifflin, 1968.

On the Poetry of War: Yeats and J. P. Clark

Obi Maduakor

The publisher's notice on the back cover of the Longman's edition of J. P. Clark's *Casualties* (1970)[1] pays tribute to Clark by comparing him to Yeats. *Casualties*, says the publisher, 'is the work of a poet who, like W. B. Yeats, saw his country's tragedy whole and has transmuted it to poetry through the quality and power of his vision'. That compliment must have been gratifying to Clark, for he himself prefaced the poems in this collection with a quotation from Yeats: 'we have no gift to set a statesman right', which was Yeats' reply to Edith Wharton, who had asked him for a war poem.[2] The other inscription from Auden – 'No metaphor ... can express/A real historical unhappiness' – reaffirms the traditional view of art as mimesis. Yeats shares this opinion also: 'art,' he says, 'is but a vision of reality';[3] that is, art can at best reproduce an echo, not the actual shock of a real historical unhappiness. The allusion to Yeats then suggests that Clark was conscious of Yeats' role as a poet who made poetry out of a situation of civil war, and that in writing about the Nigerian Civil War in lyric terms he himself was consciously recalling Yeats.

But the quality of the verse in *Casualties* indicates that the implication of Yeats' remark to Edith Wharton was lost on Clark. Yeats did not mean that the artist is powerless before the powers that be, but that art should not concern itself with politics and ideology. The ideal subject-matter for poetry would have been, in Yeats' opinion, an heroic past, heroic passion, heroic moods and aristocratic tradition, but where the poet is compelled to comment on public events as Yeats so often had to, his public utterance must be couched in a stylized idiom.

Yeats' euphemism for all poetry that is not redeemed by style is rhetoric. The word is fraught with opprobious connotations in

Yeats. In poetry, the vices of rhetoric include prosaic language, trivial metaphor, unseasoned use of image or symbol, opinion or propaganda, moral earnestness, political eloquence, abstraction, psychological discursiveness. These weaknesses were most obvious in the work of the Young Ireland poets who were in ascendancy shortly before Yeats emerged on the Irish literary scene. These poets, Yeats wrote, 'turned poetry ... into a principal means of spreading ideas of nationality and patriotism'.[4] In the poetry of the English Victorians, rhetoric reared its head in the form of moral earnestness. 'My generation, because it disliked Victorian rhetorical moral fervour, came to dislike all rhetoric.'[5] Rhetoric is at the root of Yeats' dismissal of the war poetry written by some English soldier-poets of the First World War such as Wilfred Owen and Siegfried Sassoon, although the reason given is that 'passive suffering is not a theme for poetry':

> I have a distaste for certain poems written in the midst of the Great War ... I have rejected these poems for the same reason that made Arnold withdraw his *Empedocles on Etna* from circulation; passive suffering is not a theme for poetry.[6]

Rhetoric is here synonymous with sentimental self-pity.

There is not much of sentimental self-pity in Clark's *Casualties* but the collection suffers from what would have seemed to Yeats as serious rhetorical blemishes. The first originates from Clark's conscious effort not to be sentimental. He is aware of the need to establish a correct distance between him and his material, and the question of distance is all the more urgent because of the public character of the material that Clark is dealing with. It is indeed to distance himself from his subject that Clark wrote in verse in the first instance. He had half a mind, he said, to write in prose 'this personal account of some of the unspeakable events that all but tore apart Nigeria'; but he chose poetry because the 'paths of poetry are not open to many' (*Casualties*, p. 54). One of the means by which he hoped to escape from topicality is to use animal personae as his objective correlatives – squirrels, cockerels, rats and vultures. The presence of these animals lends the poems an aura that is African: but it is not enough that the poems should be African. They should also move the reader, and retain a mood that is appropriate for the tragic theme. Clark's animals recall the animal characters of folk tales. In their poetic context they frequently diffuse rather than reinforce the tragic mood. The overall atmosphere is folksy. In *Vulture's Choice*, the tragic impact is dissipated by the vulture's casual attitude to serious issues.

Perhaps the tone of nonchalance is intentional, but it is not appropriate for the subject. And, of course, the poem irritates by the prosaic flatness of the vulture's replies to his unnamed interlocutor:

> Then I shall eat it for breakfast.
> Then I shall eat her for lunch.
> Then I shall eat both for the night. (p. 5)

Of these folksy poems only two, *What the Squirrel Said* and *The Cockerel in the Tale*, are aesthetically satisfying. *What the Squirrel Said* is successful in form as a note of warning sounded by a morally conscious village sentinel, the squirrel, who had sensed some danger in the air. The poem seeks to recapture the strident cry of an agitated sentinel by means of repetition and structural uniformity of the opening couplets which are antithetically and morally balanced against each other:

> THEY KILLED the lion in his den
> But left the leopard to his goats.
> They killed the bull without horns
> But left the boar to his cassava. (p. 13)

The poem *The Cockerel in the Tale* relies for its effects on the rhetorical devices and the verbal structure and phraseology of Yoruba traditional poetry, especially hunter's song (*ijala*):

> he who woke up the lion
> And burnt down his den over his crest,
> He who the same night bagged
> A rogue elephant, not sparing his brood,
> He who in the heat of the hunt
> Shot in the eye a bull with horns
> They say never gored a fly, hooves
> That never trod on cocoa or groundnut farm,
> Stood,
> Alone on the trembling loft of the land. (p. 8)[7]

Clark's squirrels, cockerels, and rats, whether they function as poetic personae or as protagonists are inadequate as vehicles for a tragic experience. They do not convincingly sustain the weight of the tragic experience that inspired the poems. They fail, in this regard, as vehicles for poetic emotion. Clark has heroic animals such as lions, bulls, and elephants, but they are frequently caught up in passive roles in their contexts which add nothing to the dramatic effect. The effect is different in Okigbe's *Path of Thunder*, for instance, where elephants pound the earth and magic birds dive through the air. Only in the poem *The Beast* did Clark endeavour to give vigour to his verse by placing his symbolic animals in a context of action:

> Wind from the dragon takes possession
> Of masks; dung from the dragon
> Makes catacombs of cities and farms;
> With mere drippings the dragon sets
> Rivers on fire, flames of this lick
> Mangroves to salt. (p. 31)

That verse, however, does not sound good enough as poetry; the rhythm is somewhat mechanical and too easily predictable because of Clark's tendency to enumerate or itemize, but the verse moves forward even if on stilts.

The verse foreshadows a technical weakness that is more fundamental in *Casualties*: that is, Clark's descriptive technique. His language is frequently descriptive, affirmative and declamatory and does not evoke a mood, or order emotions. He has dispensed with the allusive, the suggestive technique that renders the poetry of *Song of a Goat* so powerful. In *Casualties*, language is neither given a fresh exploration nor exploited for its emotive responses. The poems possess, as a result, a narrative flavour which diminishes their effects as lyrical songs. *The Burden in Boxes* and *The Reign of the Crocodiles* read like allegorical tales. This is so because certain key words in these poems such as 'box' and 'gifts' have been shorn in their context of their potency as processional images; their meaning in the poem is so obvious that they have become allegorical metaphors rather than poetic images. It is not, however, Clark's allegorical tendencies alone that are disquieting; his mode of address is tactless. In *The Burden in Boxes* one encounters such disappointing lines as

> Open the boxes was the clamour
> Of monkeys above tides. Open them all!
> or
> Bring us the bearers of the gifts
> The gifts left us in boxes at
> The crossroads, bring them out, we say,
> So we may see them in the market place. (p. 6)

Leader of the Hunt and *Return Home* have an interest that is more important to the historical researcher than to a lover of poetry. *July Wake* has a good beginning. Clark starts the poem off with the technique of juxtaposing without what Marshall McLuhan calls 'the copula of logical enunciation':[8] 'Glint of SMG, flare of mortar, tremor/Of grenades occupying ministry/And market' (p. 23), but six lines later he resumes his narrative tone signalled with a modified version of the conventional folk formula for beginning a story. From this moment onwards the verse slackens and loses much of what has been gained by the juxtapositional technique of the beginning.

Conversations at Accra has some dramatic vitality; the poem reads like a scene in a play. Language is used to suggest gesture and action, and to mark variations in tone in a conversational dialogue; but to be dramatic is not to be lyrical, and sometimes the dramatic flights descend to the level of melodrama; and above all, the entire poem has its own share of the general descriptive taint that diminishes the poetic effects of most of the poems in *Casualties*. At one point in the conversation, Character A bursts in on the reader with the following statement:

> You mean tie a thorough hound
> To a tree and set a common cur
> As guard over him? Oh, boy, oh boy
> Before you rush to the next post
> There would be reversal of roles, and you
> At the end of the leash. (p. 17)

The poem *Season of Omens* underscores what must be seen as Clark's major problem in *Casualties*, that is, the problem of transmuting the events of a political occasion into art. The original intention to write *Casualties* in prose was deep-rooted. *Season of Omens* is a straightforward reproduction of a piece of journalistic information that has not been transformed by the personality of the artist. In the poem, a political occasion overwhelms personality rather than personality subduing the occasion. As a result we have objective reportage rather than a subjective reshaping of an event:

> WHEN CALABASHES HELD petrol and men
> turned faggots in the streets
> *Then came the five hunters*
> When mansions and limousines made
> bornfires in sunset cities
> *Then came the five hunters*
> When clans were discovered that were not in the book
> and cattle counted for heads of men
> *Then came the five hunters.* (p. 11)

Yeats' *Easter 1916* is an occasional poem but it has transcended the occasion it depicts by the dominance of Yeats' personality over the event. By the time Yeats wrote the poem his poetics had undergone a radical transformation: 'I planned to write short lyrics or poetic drama where every speech would be short and concentrated, knit by dramatic tension'.[9] Yeats had learned to strip his verse of the decorative embellishments of his early poetry. He had strengthened his style. His contact with Synge and his experience at the theatre had revealed to him the merits for lyric poetry of dramatic utterance. Words had begun to obey his call so that his poetry bears evidence of what he considered to be the hallmark of style: 'the natural words in the natural order'.[10] These developments are reflected in the poetry of the middle period. In *Easter 1916* his mode of address is direct and dramatic, his syntax is passionate, his rhythms are musical, his tone is controlled. The result is a poem that is remarkable for its lyric beauty and its emotional intensity: 'All changed, changed utterly,/A terrible beauty is born'. (CP, p. 178)

The last line has a tragic resonance that charms and frightens; the emotional quality that it conveys is one that is likely to endure. The poem is an elegy that celebrates heroic will in the abstract by embodying it in the particular. Yeats' personality has so transformed the occasion that inspired the poem that it has become a personal reinterpretation of history and not a poetic restatement of it. *September 1913*, also an occasional piece, takes its inspiration from a situation that is the diametrical opposite of the heroic moments celebrated by its companion, *Easter 1916*, but it has successfully transformed anger and contempt into a permanent lyric by the magic of Yeats' 'subtle rhythm' and the coherence of his 'organic form':[11]

> What need you, being come to sense,
> But fumble in a greasy till
> And add the halfpence to the pence
> And prayer to shivering prayer, until
> You have dried the marrow from the bone?
> For men were born to pray and save:
> Romantic Ireland's dead and gone,
> It's with O'Leary in the grave. (CP, p. 106)

When Yeats comes to write about the Irish Civil War itself, he achieves greater complexity in his poetry by seeing the Irish situation in a context that is local and yet universal. His syntax retains its natural momentum as in *Easter 1916* and *September 1913*, and his form continues to be organic, but the troubles in Ireland confirmed Yeats' belief in the twenties in what he called the 'growing murderousness of the world'.[12] The poem *Nineteen Hundred and Nineteen*, for instance, which arose out of the Black and Tan terrorism in Ireland in the year 1919, was originally entitled *Thoughts upon the Present State of the World*. That poem together with its companion piece, *Meditations in Time of Civil War*, reinforce a pattern of awareness foreshadowed in *The Second Coming*. Both poems (the later ones) are strongly informed by a sense of an ending. Irish history, they suggest, is passing through an apocalyptic moment represented by the burning of the great ancestral houses in the local counties. The burnings provided Yeats with an image that confirmed his belief in the continuity of historical flux:

> That country round
> None dared admit, if such a thought were his,
> Incendiary or bigot could be found
> To burn that stump on the Acropolis. (*CP*, p. 205)

In Eliot the 'Unreal City' is every city – Jerusalem, Athens, Alexandria, Vienna, London. In Yeats the burning country is modern Ireland, the Acropolis, and, by extension, Agamemnon's ancient parapets in 'Leda and the Swan'. Viewed in their Yeatsian contexts the burnings become, in the words of T. R. Henn, 'part of the repeating pattern of history'.[13]

Clark is unable to weave into the texture of his verse implications that go beyond his immediate concerns. His poetry generally lacks breadth. Images with resourceful potential are not explored beyond the attractions of their initial appeal. Emotions are not charged to a high pressure point where they can explode themselves into cathartic resolution. Even sorrow is not allowed to yield the fullest possibilities of its impact. The absence of breadth is remarkable in *Song, Skulls and Cups, Vulture's Choice, The Usurpation*, to name only a few examples. The question of breadth is less related to the length of the poem than to the sweep of thought and the curve of emotion within the poem itself. Even the relatively longer poems than those just mentioned rush hurriedly to a close, like *Death of a Weaver Bird, Exodus, Aburi and After*. Clark's poetry does not always move us because it has no heave and swell. This point is not to be taken personally against the poet; it is merely a permanent feature of his poetic temperament. Clark is not capable of giving a poetic subject-matter a sustained treatment. It is for this reason that Ulli Beier thinks of him as a 'spontaneous poet'.[14] In most of the poems in *Casualties* the poetic flame is hardly allowed to go beyond a given flicker. What Clark needed to do was compress the whole experience that informed *Casualties* into one or two lyrics of some length, but in devoting nearly a book of poetry to the Nigerian Civil War he diversified his feelings, thereby weakening the power of his verse.

There are, however, some poems in the volume that tend to salvage Clark's poetic credibility. The poems *Dirge*, *The Casualties*, and *Night Song* are exempted from the general blemish that weakens the aesthetic merit of most of the poems in *Casualties*. These poems possess a compactness of structure and a tone that matches Clark's tragic theme. In *Dirge*, for instance, the emotional intensity is sustained through the repetition of the initial words 'tears' and 'fear' and by a conscious parallel in the structure of the lines; both devices enhance the tragic mood while lending speed and vigour to the verse:

> Earth will turn a desert
> A place of stone and bones
> Tears are founts from the heart
> Tears do not water a land
> Fear too is a child of the heart
> Fear piles up stones, piles up bones
> Fear builds a place of ruin
> O let us light the funeral pile
> But let us not become its faggot. (p. 28)

Clark comes closer in lines such as these to Wole Soyinka and Christopher Okigbo who also wrote about the Nigerian Civil War or anticipated it. It is their tough diction, their non-declamatory use of language, their surer sense of tragic emergency that make Soyinka and Okigbo more successful than Clark as war poets. These two poets do not possess to the same degree Yeats' technical expertise, nor do their images match the all-inclusive allusiveness of Yeats' poetic images, yet their poetry is likely to outlive their time as Clark's *Casualties* might not.

NOTES

1. J. P. Clark, *Casualties*, London, Longman, 1970; New York, Africana, 1970.
2. A. Norman Jeffares, *A Commentary on the Collected Poems of W. B. Yeats*, London, Macmillan, 1968, p. 189.
3. W. B. Yeats, *Collected Poems*, New York and London, Macmillan, 1950, p. 159. Further references to this volume appear in the text after the abbreviation CP.
4. W. B. Yeats, *A Book of Irish Verse*, London, Methuen, 1920, pp. xix–xx.
5. W. B. Yeats, *Essays and Introductions*, London, Macmillan, 1961, p. 497.

6. W. B. Yeats, *The Oxford Book of Modern Verse*, Oxford, The Clarendon Press, 1936, p. xxxiv.
7. For structural similarities between Clark's poem and the Yoruba Ijala, see *Salute to the Olu-oje Lineage*, lines 12–13, 23–4, 30–1, and 37 in S. A. Babalola, *The Content and Form of Yoruba Ijala*, Oxford, The Clarendon Press, 1966, pp. 130–5.
8. Marshall McLuhan applied this phrase to the technique of Pound, Eliot and the French symbolists. See his essay, 'Tennyson and Picturesque Poetry', *Essays in Criticism*, 3, July 1951, p. 271.
9. W. B. Yeats, *Essays and Introductions*, p. 521.
10. Dorothy Wellesley, ed., *Letters on Poetry from W. B. Yeats to Dorothy Wellesley*, London, Oxford University Press, 1964, p. 126.
11. For the allusion to Yeats' 'subtle rhythm' and his 'organic form', see *Essays and Introductions*, p. 248.
12. W. B. Yeats, *Autobiography*, New York, Collier Books, 1974, p. 130; London, Macmillan, 1955.
13. T. R. Henn, 'W. B. Yeats and the Poetry of War', in *Proceedings of the British Academy*, 51, 1965, p. 304.
14. Ulli Beier, 'Three Mbari Poets', in *Black Orpheus*, 12, 1963, p. 47.

Olaudah Equiano and the Tradition of Defoe

S. E. Ogude

Defoe and Equiano have one thing in common: they sought to present Africa to eighteenth-century England and ultimately, Europe. On the face of it their motives appear to be mutually contradictory. But as I shall demonstrate, Equiano ends his dismal narrative on a note that dominates Defoe's African vision: that Africa is a potential market for England, then already on the verge of industrialization and that British policy should take cognizance of this fact. This strange convergence of vision appears to have been ignored by commentators on both Equiano and Defoe.

Equiano wrote a single book on Africa – his purported autobiography and indeed, his only book.[1] Defoe wrote several books on Africa. For the purpose of this essay, I shall concentrate on Equiano's single book and relate it to Defoe's *The Adventures of Robinson Crusoe* (1719),[2] *The Life, Adventures and Pyracies of the Famous Captain Singleton* (1720),[3] and *Colonel Jack* (1724).[4] I shall examine Equiano's text from several perspectives and I shall compare the narrative method, content and the point of view against the background of Defoe's fiction.

Equiano's *The Interesting Narrative* has for long been accepted as an autobiography. This is because Equiano's assertions and use of circumstantial evidence appear to have the compelling force of truth. Yet when we analyse the book, especially the first part, several questions arise which we cannot satisfactorily answer. One such question centres on the authenticity of *The Interesting Narrative*. Equiano took for granted the credulity of eighteenth-century Englishmen about distant places when he wrote his account of Africa. That the authenticity of his account was never called into question in the eighteenth century may be explained by the fact that eighteenth-century Englishmen tended to take an indulgent attitude towards tales of distant places, and perhaps because of the growing interest in the customs and manners of other peoples.[5]

It is easy to show that the opening chapter is not autobiographical in the ordinary sense of the word, and therefore it will be much easier for us to regard the subsequent chapters as essentially fictional; even where Equiano treats historical events, he finds it easier to create fiction out of reality and thereby he paints a much more poignant picture of the slave's misery. The question then, is: how much faith should be put on the introductory chapter of *The Interesting Narrative*?

Unfortunately the first chapter which forms the basis of *The Narrative* cannot seriously be regarded as history. It is true that it deals with the principal character of the narrative but the 'facts' presented in the chapter were already some thirty years old before they were put down in writing. By his own evidence, Equiano was some eleven or twelve years old when his story began. He was carried away from his culture into an entirely different world at this tender age, and if we may assume that he wrote his history between 1788 and 1789, the problem of recall and representation becomes truly enormous. There is no doubt that Equiano was a precocious child but even that fact alone cannot account for his 'excellent' history of his country. I shall therefore suggest that *The Interesting Narrative* is a fiction written in the tradition of Daniel Defoe and that in many respects Equiano, the central character of *The Interesting Narrative*, is as ignorant of the African continent as Defoe's Captain Singleton and Robinson Crusoe.

As we shall see later, apart from the considerable evidence of the obvious influence of contemporary accounts of Africa on Equiano's narrative, it appears that Equiano, in fact, followed the narrative technique of Defoe and in many instances we can detect close verbal parallels in both Defoe and Equiano. A comparison of the title pages of *The Interesting Narrative* and *The Adventures of Robinson Crusoe* yields an interesting result. The main title of Defoe's *Robinson Crusoe* runs thus:

The Life and Strange Surprizing
ADVENTURES OF
ROBINSON
CRUSOE
OF YORK, MARINER
Written by Himself

Now compare this with Equiano's:

THE INTERESTING NARRATIVE
OF
THE LIFE
OF
OLAUDAH EQUIANO
OR
GUSTAVUS VASSA
THE AFRICAN
WRITTEN BY HIMSELF

Thus both title pages give the same essential information about their main characters and in spite of slight verbal alteration, they follow the same format. In the first edition of each book, opposite the title page is a frontispiece with a portrait of the main character. This makes the physical resemblance even more striking. It is true that Defoe adds to the title page a brief summary of the extraordinary adventures of Robinson Crusoe. Equiano does the same thing but in a different fashion. Because *The Interesting Narrative*, unlike *Robinson Crusoe*, is not a continuous story but divided into chapters, Equiano provides head notes which serve as a summary of each chapter. We may observe at this point that the head note to the introductory chapter of *The Interesting Narrative* is in many respects ordinary and stereotyped, the type that adorns the title page of many a volume of eighteenth-century voyage writing. For instance, the title page of *The Life, Adventures and Pyracies of the Famous Captain Singleton* includes the following information:

> Containing an Account of his being set on shore in the Island of Madagascar, his settlement there, with a Description of the place and Inhabitants: of his passage from thence in a Paraguay, to the mainland of *Africa*, with an account of the customs and manners of the people: His great Deliverance from the barbarous Natives and Wild Beasts ...

Equiano follows the same pattern in his head note though his emphasis is understandably different:

> The author's account of his country, and their manners and customs – Administration of justice – embreche – marriage ceremony, and public entertainments – mode of living – Dress – manufactures – buildings – commerce – Agriculture – War and religion – superstition of the natives .... Some hints concerning the origin of the author's countrymen ....

In the eighteenth century all these details would be regarded as necessary preliminaries which inevitably adorn any respectable book on travel in distant places, whether fiction, pseudo-history or true history.

But it is in narrative technique and character presentation that Equiano's debt to Defoe can be best illustrated. Let us concede at the outset that because both Defoe and Equiano used the autobiographical mode of narration, their techniques may tend to be similar. However, the matter is more than a mere question of narration. It involves a whole complex of the paraphernalia of narration such as verisimilitude, context of narration and indeed even verbal mannerisms and implies a conscious echo of an existing pattern of narration. This pattern, we would like to suggest, is that of the popular fiction of Daniel Defoe. True, Equiano does not quote directly from Daniel Defoe but it is inconceivable that he could have read Milton without reading Defoe, considering the popularity of the latter in the eighteenth century.

I have demonstrated in an earlier paper[6] that much of Equiano's autobiography, especially the part dealing with his childhood, is mere fiction woven out of a whole range of travellers' tales. It is possible that Equiano read much of the travel literature on Africa but he could also have got much of his information from Anthony Benezet whose *Short account of that Part of Africa inhabited by the Negroes*[7] became a very popular anti-slavery tract. Indeed it was so popular that it reached its second Philadelphia edition within a year of publication and in 1771 it was substantially enlarged and published as *Some Historical Account of Guinea*.[8] Like its predecessor, *Some Historical Account of Guinea* contains 'the sentiments of several Authors of Note' on the slave trade, particularly those of Granville Sharpe, Montesquieu, the philosopher Francis Hutcheson and the seventeenth-century churchman, Morgan Godwyn.

An extraordinary fact about the reception and criticism of *The Interesting Narrative* is that Equiano's confident 'account of his country' has not been seriously questioned. On the contrary, contemporary reviews like that in *The General and Impartial Review* (July 1789) took especial note of Equiano's 'accounts of the manners of the natives of his own province (Eboe), (which) is interesting and pleasing'. And more recently, Paul Edwards could only detect 'occasional slight echoes of Benezet' in *The Interesting Narrative*. But a careful reading of Benezet's *Historical Account* shows that Equiano is greatly indebted to the volume. His impressive definition of Guinea derives almost verbatim from Benezet's book. Equiano wrote:

> That part of Africa, known by the name of Guinea, to which the trade for slaves is carried on, extends along the coast above 3400 miles, from the Senegal to Angola, and includes a variety of Kingdoms. Of these the most considerable is the Kingdom of Benin, both as to extent of wealth, the

richness and cultivation of the soil, the power of its king and the number and war like disposition of the inhabitants. It is situated nearly under the line, and extends along the coast about 170 miles, but runs back into the interior part of Africa to a distance hitherto I believe unexplored by any traveller and seems terminated at length by the empire of Abyssinia near 1500 miles from its beginning.

(The Interesting Narrative, 1789, I,4)

Observe that the definition begins with a positive and seemingly factual statement and progresses to a somewhat vague and deliberately imprecise speculation. But the really interesting aspect of the passage is that many of the facts and conjectures in it are taken from various parts of Benezet's *Historical Account* and it must be stated that Equiano knew enough to give credit to Benezet who wrote thus about Guinea:

That part of Africa from which the Negroes are sold to be carried into slavery, commonly known by the name of Guinea, extends along the coast three or four thousand miles. Beginning at the river Senegal, situate about 17th degree of north latitude, being the nearest part of Guinea as well to Europe as to North America ... the land of Guinea takes a turn to the eastward, extending that course about fifteen hundred miles, including these several divisions known by the name of *The Grain Coast*, *The Ivory Coast*, *The Gold Coast*, and *The Slave Coast*, with *The Large Kingdom of Benin*. From thence the land runs Southward along the coast about twelve hundred miles, which contains the *Kingdoms of Congo* and *Angola*.

(*Historical Account*, 1772, pp. 6–7)

Equiano thus telescoped the information available to him and indeed, brought in information from p. 35 of the *Historical Account* which he lumped together with information from pp. 6–7 of the same book. For we read on p. 35: 'Next adjoining to the Slave Coast is the Kingdom of Benin, which though it extends but 170 miles on the sea, yet spreads far inland, as to be esteemed the most potent Kingdom in Guinea'.

The first chapter of Equiano's narrative ends with a quotation from Acts Chapter 17, Verse 26. The interesting thing is that the title page of Benezet's *Historical Account* also quotes the words of Acts Chapter 17, Verses 24, 26. Yet another interesting borrowing is the citation of the 329th Act of the Assembly of Barbadoes which Equiano lifted word for word from Benezet. (Cf. *The Interesting Narrative*, pp. 1217–18, with *Historical Account*, pp. 81–2.) Equiano also borrowed from contemporary African writers.[9] It is against this background of extensive and, in some instances, wholesale borrowing, that we shall examine the literary style of Equiano, both as reflecting the general tradition of voyage literature as well as exemplifying the particular influence of Daniel Defoe's fiction. As I have already suggested, I shall examine this aspect in terms of character presentation as well as narrative technique.

The Interesting Narrative can be described as the 'Strange and surprising adventures of Olaudah Equiano' and can bear such title without the least impression of straining after an effect; for that is what, in fact, it really is. Whatever truth may lie behind the adventures of Equiano is lost in the romance of the tale. The sense of high adventure, or the feeling of knowing more than other men or of having experienced what other men may never experience, appears to have defined his narrative strategy. It is true of course that he avows at the beginning of his tale that his motive is not vanity; but that was a common literary trick of the century and both Fielding and Johnson have at different times thought it a silly trick.[10] The really important fact is that, like most Defoe characters, Equiano is a lonely man with all the odds heavily weighted against him, and again, he is resourceful and inventive enough to overcome all odds. Like them, too, he succeeds because he has a will to succeed. Naturally, his experiences are almost always unheard of although they are told with a simplicity that charms us as well as commanding credibility. Finally, most of Defoe's characters are incredibly self-centred, precisely because the hypocrisies of their social system would condemn them to cruel oblivion. They have to fight against the world of man and nature and in spite of all odds, succeed. Equiano shares this psychological need for survival and social recognition with them and throughout The Interesting Narrative, he presents himself as the hero who in spite of very severe social limitations, triumphs over all difficulties. So he endows himself with the qualities of courage, prowess, sheer ability and intelligence, and above all, an indomitable faith in himself.

There is another sense in which Equiano shares with Crusoe, Singleton and Captain Jack, the tradition of Defoe: they are all very well-travelled men of action. They can all recall their adventures in Africa, North America, South America, Europe and Asia. More significantly, perhaps, they have all experienced life at almost every rung of the social ladder. Crusoe's analysis of the three main stations of life in the introductory chapter of The Adventures of Robinson Crusoe is as much a record of his own personal life as a recall of the wise words of his father. It is interesting to note at this point that in terms of personal experience, both Crusoe and Equiano follow a common path and as their tales unfold, we observe a common underlying framework. In the worlds of both characters, we experience a sense of vastness in the field of action and it is this breadth and variety of experience that tend to lend value to their judgement. They are able to make statements of a universal nature because they have 'seen the world' and they are ever comparing and contrasting their experiences in various parts of the world precisely because of their enormous knowledge.

Equiano's experience among the Mosquito Indians is particularly interesting because it bears a close parallel to the experience of Captain Singleton among the Africans; and also, because in his account of his experience, Equiano seems to assume the role of the *civilized* traveller among some barbarous natives. Thus he tells us how, at Cape Gracias a Dios,

> Some native Indians came on board of us ... and we used them well and told them we were come to dwell amongst them, which they seemed pleased at. So the Doctor (Dr Irving) and I, with some others, went with them ashore; and they took us to different places to view the land, in order to choose a place to make a plantation of. We fixed on a spot near a river bank, in a rich soil; and, having got our necessaries out of the sloop, began to clear away the woods, and plant different kinds of vegetables which had quick growth.
> (*The Interesting Narrative* II, 179, cf. I,20–3)

As usual in this narrative, Equiano is in the forefront of the action although it is quite inconceivable that he could have occupied a position of any significance in this venture, and certainly not that of second in command which he seems to suggest. But more germane to the enquiry is Equiano's echo of the traditional sense of wonder expressed by Europeans at the almost spontaneous growth of crops in tropical climates. Captain Singleton made similar observation in his epic of African travel:

> And here we found some *Maize* or *Indian Wheat*, which the Negroe women planted, as we sow seeds in a Garden, and immediately our new Proveditor ordered some of our Negroes to plant it, and it grew up presently, and by watering it often, we had a crop in less than three Months Growth.
> (*Captain Singleton*, p. 162)

Anthony Benezet in his *Historical Account* cites the Dutchman, William Bosman, whose *Accurate Description of Guinea* was first published in 1704 and translated into English in 1705. Bosman was so impressed by the richness of the soil of the Gold Coast that he christened it the true *Cornucopia* and talked of 'well built and populous towns, agreeably enriched with vast quantities of corn, cattle, palm wine and oil. The inhabitants, all applying themselves without distinction to agriculture (*Historical Account*, p. 24). The tradition was thus fairly established and when Equiano asserts that 'Agriculture is our chief employment; and everyone, even the children and women, are engaged in it' (*The Interesting Narrative*, p. 20) we are almost certain that he is here utilizing the tradition of voyage literature in much the same way as Defoe did in his fiction. But while Defoe has long been recognized for what he is – a writer of fiction – the overwhelming evidence of the strong fictional base of *The Interesting Narrative* of Equiano has been ignored.

It is impossible to demonstrate within the limits of an essay how Equiano transfers, wholesale, simple fiction into autobiography through a combination of factors. The first of these is that he is an African and must therefore (presumably) know everything about Africa. Secondly, the field of action is located somewhere in distant places, and in the eighteenth century the temptation to lie about distant places was almost irresistible, since the chances of being found out were slim indeed. Like Defoe's characters, Equiano's education was obtained in the finest of schools – the hard school of life.[11] His range of experience is as rich and varied as that of Robinson Crusoe or Captain Singleton. And like Defoe's characters too, Equiano is always anxious to assure us that his experience is in every sense unusual. Thus he is tempted to use typical Defoe idiom[12] like 'the best ever' and 'the largest ever'. He describes the house and premises of the wealthy widow as 'the finest I ever saw in Africa' (I,64); the ship in which he sailed was 'one night over taken with a terrible gale of wind, greater than I had ever yet experienced' (I,140); 'I never beheld a more awful scene' (I,148).

There are other areas in which Equiano seems to duplicate the experience of Defoe's characters. For instance, like Crusoe, Equiano tends to have a somewhat primitive attitude towards providence, a term which seems to embrace God, Fate and Destiny. We may again recall an incident from *Robinson Crusoe*. The sudden appearance of a footprint on the lonely island has set in motion a whole train of ideas that threatened Crusoe's sane existence. Until

> One Morning early, lying on my Bed, and fill'd with Thought about my Danger from the Appearance of Savages, I found it discompos'd me very much, upon which those Words of the Scripture came into my Thoughts, *call upon me in the Day of Trouble, and I will deliver, and thou shalt glorify me.*
>
> (*Robinson Crusoe*, I,182)

Upon which Crusoe was greatly comforted and was even more reassured when, on picking up the bible, the first passage his eyes fell on was *Wait on the Lord, and be of Good Cheer, and he shall strengthen thy Heart'*.

We can profitably compare the above passage with the following one from Equiano. Our hero has been subjected to ill-treatment by the Captain of *The Indian Queen*, who on one occasion threatened to blow up the ship together with himself and Equiano. Equiano believed that he could have justifiably killed the man but rather he

> prayed for resignation, that his (God's) will might be done; and the following two portions of his Holy word, which occurred to my mind, bouyed up my hope, and kept me from taking the life of this wicked man (Quotes Acts 18.6 and Isaiah 1.10). And thus by the grace of God I was enabled to do (sic). I found him a present help in the time of need ard the Captain's fury began to subside as the night approached (II,209-10)

Both Equiano and Crusoe always magnify their personal danger but they ultimately escape, thanks to the mysterious hand of providence.

As Everett Zimmerman has observed, 'In *Robinson Crusoe*, providence often seems to be a method of interpretation, a theory rather than a force. And on several occasions, events suggest that it may be Crusoe's "fancy".'[13] The observation is even more true of Equiano. We remember how in the very first chapter of his book, Equiano tells us that he was *a particular favourite of heaven* and even, as a child, there was evidence that he was a chosen one. Equiano thus sees his subsequent experience as a fulfilment of his early promise. He remained a particular care of Heaven although it is not clear at what point his African gods merged with the Christian God. When he fell into the Thames, there were 'some watermen who providentially came' to his rescue (I,135-6). And on another occasion, he reports:

> I myself one day fell headlong from the upper deck of the *Etna* down the after-hold, when the ballast was out; and all who saw me fall cried out I was killed: but I received not the least injury. And in the same ship, a man fell from the mast head without being hurt. In these, and in many more instances, I thought I could plainly trace the hand of God, without whose permission a sparrow cannot fall. (I,160; cf. II,177; II,104)

Another incident reported by Equiano has its roots in fiction. It was Oroonoko who, in the novel of that title by Aphra Behn, first proposed to his fellow slaves that they escape from their miserable condition by making their way to the sea and seizing a boat in which to sail back to Africa (although none of them knew how to sail a boat). They were, however, unable to put the plan into action because they were stopped by the local militia before they could get to the sea. Defoe fleshed out this ingenious tale when he made Singleton meet a boat of over 600 black slaves without one single white man (all the slave merchants who, Defoe predictably concluded, must be French and Dutch were presumably massacred). These black slaves were adrift, not knowing where they were or where they were going because they had no knowledge of navigation. Singleton, at the instance of the hypocritical Quaker William, saved and fed them but only to sell them at the next port of call (*Captain Singleton*, pp. 191–9).

It is possible that Equiano was making use of this incident when he tells of what befell the black slaves of the Mosquito shore settlement of Dr Irving:

> I learned that after I left the estate which I managed for this gentleman on the Mosquito Shore, during which the slaves were well fed and comfortable, a white overseer had supplied my place: this man, through inhumanity and ill-judged avarice, beat and cut the poor slaves most unmercifully, and the consequence was, that every one got into a long Puriogua canoe, and endeavoured to escape; but not knowing where to go or how to manage the canoe, they were all drowned. (II,211–12)

It is also possible that Equiano was making use of a popular fiction that grew out of the slave trade. There were numerous cases of slaves attempting to overpower their captors at sea. Such incidents could be stretched just a bit further to relate a situation in which the attempt actually succeeds and thus give slave dealers some justification for the harsh treatment of slaves. Note that Captain Singleton's first reaction to the slaves was to have every one of them murdered and in any case, very few Englishmen could have the sophistry of Quaker William to worry about the murder of barbarous slaves. Observe also that Equiano handles the tale quite differently from either Aphra Behn or Daniel Defoe.

A contemporary reviewer of *The Interesting Narrative* remarked that it appeared just at the right time.[14] Equiano, like Defoe, 'had an adequate sense of the power of PUBLIC OPINION, and of the use to which that opinion might be put'.[15] The ultimate purpose of *The Interesting Narrative* was to lend support to the considerable shift of opinion in favour of the slave. But like Defoe, Equiano's attitude to the problem of slavery was ambiguous. He bought slaves even if they were all his countrymen, as he claimed (II,178). For quite a good part of *The Interesting Narrative* one is left with the impression that Equiano was more concerned with the humane treatment of the slave

than his total liberation and thus shared a common philosophy with
Defoe's Colonel Jack who, against the considered opinion of Adam
Smith and Hume,[16] held that humane treatment of the slave was an
adequate substitute for his freedom. So Defoe set up his model
plantation in which slave labour became productive rather than
uneconomical as both Smith and Hume were later to maintain. And
slaves in Colonel Jack's model plantation were so well cared for that
they dreaded nothing worse than being dismissed from the plantation (*Colonel Jack*, p. 150). Colonel Jack achieved this feat in slave
management through a psychological approach to the problem of
slave labour. This is how he presents his argument:

> They (the slaves) never had any Mercy show'd them; that we (the slave-
> drivers) never try'd them, whether they would be grateful or no; that if
> they did a Fault, they were never spar'd, but punish'd with the utmost
> Cruelty; so that they had no Passion, no Affection to Act upon, but that of
> Fear, which necessarily brought Hatred with it; but that if they were used
> with Compassion, they would serve with Affection, as well as other
> Servants: Nature is the same, and Reason Governs in just Proportions in
> all Creatures; But having never been let to Taste what Mercy is, they know
> not how to act from a Principle of Love. (p. 143, cf. p. 145)

Surprisingly enough, Equiano, in spite of the evidence of cruelty
which he accumulates, appears not only to romanticize the model
planter who is kind to his slaves, but boasts like Defoe's Colonel Jack,
of having actually played the model planter himself.[17] He maintains
that when 'the negroes are treated with lenity and proper care, ...
their lives are prolonged and their masters are profited' (I,208–9). By
1789 when *The Interesting Narrative* was published, the idealized
planter had become a fictional character whose main purpose was to
demonstrate an alternative mode of plantation management.
Equiano's model planters, as we have seen, had made their appearance as early as 1720 in Defoe's Colonel Jack. But Colonel Jack
was a practical, hard-headed young man who sought to maximize the
profit from slave labour through a show of affection. He resolved the
dilemma in which many plantation owners must have often found
themselves and which his master expressed thus:

> It is my Aversion (the cruelty used on slaves), it fills my very soul, with
> Horror; I believe, if I should come by while they were using those Cruelties
> on the poor Creatures, I should either sink down at the Sight of it, or fly
> into a Rage, and kill the fellow that did it; tho' it is done too by my own
> Authority.
>
> (*Colonel Jack*, p. 145)

He probably would have been more convincing had he added that it was all done for his profit. But of course, Colonel Jack's master was not a man of true sensibility. Indeed we may compare his attitude with that of Sir George Ellison, the main character of Sarah Scott's novel of feeling, *The History of Sir George Ellison*.[18] Sir George took the myth of the model planter a stage further, stretching it to its very limits by virtually freeing all his slaves whom he assures thus: 'while you perform your duty, I shall look upon you as free servants, or rather, like my children, for whose well-being, I am anxious and watchful' (I,31). Equiano's Mr King may be less paternal in his relationship with his slaves, but he is no less anxious for their well-being, and it is perhaps significant that Equiano actually describes Mr King as 'a man of feeling' (I,198).

Although we cannot categorically affirm that Equiano was indebted to Defoe, the evidence suggests that Defoe's essays and fiction about Africa substantially influenced Equiano's image of Africa. Before slavery became a subject of public debate and Africa came into fashion, Defoe had doggedly considered the relationship between Africa and England from several angles. Much of the information about Africa in the eighteenth century and some of the fables about Africa were first presented *as facts* by Daniel Defoe. Later in the century, writers drew on Defoe without acknowledging him. The final chapter of Equiano's *The Interesting Narrative* illustrates this situation rather graphically. The last seven pages of the book contain Equiano's theory of a new commercial arrangement which was to emerge between Africa and England after the abolition of the Slave Trade. The ideas expounded in this section of the book have their root in Defoe's writings. For Defoe believed that it was much more profitable to colonize the African continent than to transport Africans across the seas to work in the plantations of America and the West Indies. And he said as much in 1713:

> Some attempts have been made for planting this part of the World with cotton, ginger, sugar, indigo etc. but the mistaken policy of trade among those who fancy they understand it, has put a check to that increase of commerce which is yet reserved for Wiser posterity, till when, we continue foolishly to carry the Negroes to the plants, when we might bring the plants to the Negroes, and make the coast of Africa as ten of the islands, either of Barbadoes or Jamaica.[19]

Theoretically, Defoe's logic cannot be faulted on economic grounds. It would be less expensive to bring the plants to the Negroes and still less so to transport sugar, indigo and cotton from Africa to

Britain. In all this calculation, be it observed, the interest, convenience or safety of the African was not considered. Although we cannot accuse Equiano of similar lack of concern for the African, it is obvious that in the final thrust of his argument, he emphasized the British 'interest and advantage'. His plea was like Defoe's: 'civilize' the African continent and you will have a ready source of raw materials and a ready market for your manufactured goods, 'beyond the reach of imagination' (II,253). His conclusion reads like the above passage from Defoe:

> This I conceive to be a theory founded upon facts, and therefore an infallible one. If the blacks were permitted to remain in their own country, they would double themselves every fifteen years. In proportion to such increase will be the demand for manufactures. Cotton and indigo grow spontaneously in most parts of Africa; a consideration of this is of no small consequence to the manufacturing towns of Great Britain. It opens a most immense, glorious, and a happy prospect in the clothing etc. of a continent ten thousand miles in circumference, and immensely rich in production of every denomination in return for manufactures. (II,253–4)

Thus when they speculate on the nature and direction of the relationship between Great Britain and the African continent, Daniel Defoe and Olaudah Equiano tend to arrive invariably at the same conclusion. Defoe had shown in *Captain Singleton* that the African continent is rich in minerals. Equiano agrees and adds that it is in the interest of Britain to cultivate and civilize the continent. More significantly, perhaps, is the fact that both Defoe and Equiano build their image of Africa on hearsay, pseudo-history and pure fiction.

In conclusion, I would like to re-emphasize my proposition, that much of Equiano's *The Interesting Narrative* is pure fiction and that in technique of narration, the extent of his adventures and the tenor of his experience, Equiano may be said to have used Defoe as his model. His simplicity and apparent naïveté may have led many scholars to ignore the impossibility of his so-called personal experiences.[20] The truly historical aspects of his narrative have been blurred in his attempt to romanticize his past and make a superman of himself. It is impossible to reconcile his self-portrait with what we know of the status of the African in eighteenth-century colonial America and indeed, in eighteenth-century England. The real Gustavus Vassa was truthfully presented by Charles Irving in 1776:

> The bearer, Gustavus Vassa, has served me several years with strict honesty, sobriety and fidelity. I can, therefore, with justice recommend him for these qualifications; and indeed, in every respect, I consider him

an excellent servant. I do hereby certify that he always behaved well and that he is perfectly trust-worthy.

(The Interesting Narrative, II,79)

When Gustavus Vassa rechristened himself Olaudah Equiano he underwent an interesting transformation that is recorded in *The Interesting Narrative of Olaudah Equiano.*

NOTES

1. Olaudah Equiano, *Equiano's travels: his autobiography. The interesting narrative of the life of Olaudah Equiano or Gustavus Vassa the African,* two volumes, London, printed for and sold by the author, 1789. Abridged with new introduction and notes by Paul Edwards, London, Heinemann (AWS 10), 1966; New York, Praeger, 1967.
2. Daniel Defoe, *The Life and Adventures of Robinson Crusoe,* London, reprinted in 1927, Oxford, Basil Blackwell.
3. Daniel Defoe, *The Life, Adventures and Pyracies of the Famous Captain Singleton,* London, Dent, reprinted 1927, Oxford, Basil Blackwell.
4. Daniel Defoe, *Colonel Jack,* London, reprinted 1970, Oxford, Oxford University Press.
5. Samuel Johnson wrote in 1735, 'he who tells nothing exceeding the bounds of probability has a right to demand they should believe him who cannot contradict him'. Johnson's 'Preface' to Jeronymo Lobo's *A voyage to Abyssinia ... with a continuation of the history of Abyssinia down to the beginning of the eighteenth century and fifteen dissertations on various subjects ... by Mr Le Grand From the French* (of Le Grand by Samuel Johnson), London, A. Butterworth and C. Hitch, 1735, p. vii.
6. S. E. Ogude, 'Facts Into Fiction: Equiano's Narrative Reconsidered', in *Research In African Literature,* Vol. 13, No. 1, Spring 1982.
7. *Short Account of that Part of Africa inhabited by the Negroes; with respect the fertility of the country; the good disposition of some of the natives.* Extracted from several authors, Philadelphia, 1762; reprinted London, 1768.
8. Anthony Benezet, *Some Historical Account of Guinea, its situation, produce and the general disposition of its inhabitants.* Philadelphia, Joseph Crukshank, 1771; London, W. Owen, 1772.
9. For example, James Albert Ukawsaw Gronniosaw, *A Narrative of the most remarkable particulars in the Life of James Albert Ukawsaw Gronniosaw,* Bath, 1770. Cf. pp. 16–17 with Equiano Narrative I,106–7; also Gronniosaw p. 31 with Equiano II,71; Equiano II,210 quotes a

couplet from Colley Cibber's *Love's Last Shift or the Fool in Fashion,* London, 1696, which Ignatius Sancho had earlier quoted in Letter XIII. Equiano repeats the mistake in Sancho's quotation:

> He who cannot stem his anger's tide
> Doth a wild horse without a bridle ride.

Cibber actually wrote:

> He that strives not to stem his Anger's tide
> Does a mad Horse without a bridle ride.
>
> (*Love's Last Shift* III. Sc. 1)

10. Johnson was of the opinion that 'No man but a block head ever wrote except for money'. *Boswell's Life of Johnson,* ed. R. W. Chapman, London, Oxford University Press, 1958, p. 731; and Henry Fielding declared that nothing but ' The vanity of knowing more than other men is, perhaps, besides hunger, the only inducement to writing, at least to publishing, at all', *Jonathan Wild and a Voyage to Lisbon,* with Introduction by A. R. Humphreys, and Notes by Douglas Brooks-Davies, London, Melbourne and Toronto, Dent, 1973, p. 187.
11. Brian V. Street, *The Savage in Literature,* London and Boston, Routledge & Kegan Paul, 1975, p. 109.
12. Defoe had a habit of expressing the experience of his characters in superlative terms. For example, Captain Singleton assures us: 'We were now gotten among a prodigious Number of ravenous Inhabitants, the like whereof, 'tis most certain the Eye of Man never saw: for as I firmly believe, that never Man, nor a Body of Men, passed this Desert since the Flood, so I believe there is not the like Collection of fierce, ravenous, and devouring Creatures in the World', *Captain Singleton,* pp. 105–6; see also pp. 148, 165; See also *Robinson Crusoe,* pp. 30, 33.
13. Everett Zimmerman, *Defoe and The Novel,* Berkeley, University of California Press, 1975, p. 37.
14. *Monthly Review,* June 1789, p. 551.
15. *Defoe, The Critical Heritage,* ed. Pat Rogers, London and Boston, Routledge & Kegan Paul, 1972, p. 193.
16. Adam Smith declared in his *Wealth of the Nations,* 1776, I,471: 'The experience of all ages and nations, I believe, demonstrates that work done by slaves, though it appears to cost only their maintenance is in the end, the dearest of any.' and Hume, *Philosophical Works,* ed. T. H. Green and T. H. Grose, 1875, III,390, n.2, avowed that 'from the experience of our planters, slavery is as little advantageous to the master as to the slave where ever hired servants can be procured.'
17. *The Interesting Narrative,* I,210: 'I myself ... managed an estate where, by these attentions, the Negroes were uncommonly healthy and did more work by half than by the common mode of treatment they usually do'.
18. *The History of Sir George Ellison,* London, 1766, I,31.

19. Daniel Defoe, *A General History of Trade*, 1713, 3rd essay, p. 10. See also *A Plan of English Commerce*, 1730, pt. III, Chapter 3, where Defoe anticipates the Victorian idea of colonization.
20. G. I. Jones, 'Olaudah Equiano of the Niger Ibo', in *Africa Remembered: Narratives by West Africans from the Era of the Slave Trade*, Madison, Milwaukee, and London, The University of Wisconsin Press; Ibadan, Ibadan University Press, 1967, pp. 62–3, 66–7.

The Black Pseudo-Autobiographical Novel: Miss Jane Pittman and Houseboy

Bede M. Ssensalo

It is generally agreed that an extremely large proportion of the finest literature from Black authors all over the world has been written in the form of autobiography.[1] The autobiographical mode has continued to flourish as a basic instrument for Black literary expression. Through it the Black author has articulated, defined and responded to the Black experience. Wilfred Cartey, in his *Whispers from a Continent: The Literature of Contemporary Black Africa*, says that 'literary autobiographical expressions ... have become a strong element in recent African literature'.[2] J. A. Emmanuel and T. L. Gross make the same observation when they say that 'like so much of American Negro writing, *Invisible Man* is cast in the form of an autobiographical Odyssey'.[3] Finally, Roger Rosenblatt says that Black literature in America is difficult to classify. Part of this difficulty stems from the fact that it is not purely fiction.

> So much of this literature is autobiographical (*Not Without Laughter, Their Eyes Were Watching God, Go Tell It On the Mountain*), so much of the autobiography, fictional (*Manchild in the Promised Land, Black Boy*), that the genres are largely interchangeable.[4]

The purpose of this study is to identify and establish a new sub-genre within Black fiction: the pseudo-autobiographical novel. This is a fictional narrative in which the imaginary narrator assumes the posture of an actual person writing or narrating his autobiography. Ernest Gaines' *The Autobiography of Miss Jane Pittman*[5] and Ferdinand Oyono's *Houseboy*[6] will be used to demonstrate the manner in which non-fictional (autobiographical) elements are injected into a fictional (novel) form to produce the pseudo-autobiographical novel. Both of these novels contain two sets of characteristics that render them pseudo-autobiographical. The first set typifies the autobiographical style in general: (a) the first person narrative built around a singular character, (b) from the perspective of the first person, and (c) covering a broad span of time. The other set seems to be unique to Black autobiographies, whether written by Africans on the continent or by people of African descent in the diaspora: (a) the tendency on the part of the author to regard his life as representative of the race, (b) the preoccupation with the physical and psychic violence to which Blacks are subjected by whites as a major theme, and (c) the correlation between one's name and one's identity on the one hand and that between one's identity and one's freedom on the other.

The pseudo-autobiographical novel is not to be confused with the autobiographical novel. The latter is simply a novel which, whether written in the first person narrative style or otherwise, presents a character who is a mask of the author and lives within the writer's own experience. This category includes works such as James Joyce's *A Portrait of the Artist as a Young Man*, James Baldwin's *Go Tell it on the Mountain* and Bernard Dadié's *Climbié* among others.

The prime characteristic of the pseudo-autobiographical novel, however, is the author's deliberate attempt to convince the reader that the events described actually occurred. The pseudo-autobiographical novel employs all the elements of the autobiography. It reads as an autobiography and is often presented as such. In Ernest Gaines' book, for example, the word 'autobiography' even occurs in the title. Indeed, unless the reader knows facts to the contrary, there is very little to indicate that such a work is not a verifiable autobiography. Surely this is a deliberate strategy adopted by the author for reasons I will surmise at the conclusion of the paper.

As in all autobiographies, *The Autobiography of Miss Jane Pittman* has one main character. Miss Jane, the narrator, is the central figure around which the story evolves. All the other characters are minor and are seen through her eyes. They are important to the story only to the extent that they illuminate Miss Jane's character. As a consequence, the facts or historical events of the story are related through the context of her experience.

Another link between this novel and the autobiography as a genre is that Miss Jane's tale covers a very significant segment of her life: from the age of five to eight months before her death, one hundred and ten years later. This in itself elevates her story and enhances its significance and validity. Further, since Miss Jane tells her story from memory, the novel acquires an added depth, or what Pascal calls 'the meaning an event acquires when viewed in the perspective of a whole life'.[7] Miss Jane attaches a new meaning to each event in retrospect because, like the autobiographer, she is dealing with a *fait accompli*.

The book is written in the form of a series of tape-recorded interviews of a Black woman who was once a slave. In his attempt to simulate the autobiographical form, Ernest Gaines went out of his way to demonstrate Miss Jane's dependence upon what William Howarth calls an 'essential control' in autobiography,[8] memory. Due to her age, however, many times her memory fails her. The narrative is full of statements to illustrate this point.

> Miss Jane said, 'It might 'a' been July, I'm not too sure, but it was July or August' (when the Confederate soldiers first appeared on her plantation). (*MJP*, p. 3)
>
> 'I can't remember how many buckets (of water) I hauled' (for the soldiers). (*MJP*, p. 4)
>
> 'It was hot. Must have been May or June. Probably June – but I'm not sure' (of the actual time it was when freedom was proclaimed on her plantation). (*MJP*, p. 16)

In fact, in the introduction to the book, the school teacher who 'conducted' the interviews talks about the difficulties caused by the lapses in Miss Jane's memory; at some points she was said to forget everything.

Another strategy Ernest Gaines employed to make his book look like a real autobiography was to model it after a major sub-genre of the Afro-American autobiography, the slave narrative. In the tradition of this mode, the ex-slave would risk recounting his life only after he was safely out of the slave states. Similarly, the fictional Miss Jane tells her story from a position of relative impunity. When she agrees to talk to the school teacher, she is already over a hundred years old. Her life has run its course and is only a few months from its glorious end. The incidents she narrates, including the bold and militant act of drinking from a fountain marked FOR WHITES ONLY, are of no consequence to her future life.

On finds in *Miss Jane Pittman* many other major themes of the slave narrative outlined in Osofsky's essay, 'Puttin' on Ole Massa: The Significance of Slave Narratives'.[9] Like the slaves in the earlier narratives, the characters of this novel either hid their intelligence or paid with their lives. The attitudes of the characters in *Miss Jane Pittman* and of the slaves in the narratives towards religion were similar; namely, a tendency to move away from the white man's interpretation of Christianity towards a quest for some meaningful spiritual guidance. In *Miss Jane Pittman*, Miss Jane's godson, Jimmy, is looked upon by all the other Blacks as the 'One' destined to lead his people to full human rights and equality. Superstition, another characteristic of the slave narrative, is also found in this novel. In the chapter entitled 'Man's Way', Miss Jane consults a witch to ascertain the fate of her husband, a horsebreeder, who she fears will be killed by one particular horse.

The final theme of the slave narrative that Ernest Gaines employs so effectively is that of naming. Most slave narratives make reference to the fact that after the Africans had been brought to the New World against their will, every effort was made to strip them of their language and traditions. In their place they were forced to learn what the slave holders deemed safe for them to learn. To symbolize and to emphasize their westernization, slaves were denied the use of African names and given others. These names were first names only. The slaves were denied a last name, one which is associated with family history, and thus, respectability. Or if the slave had two names, one would be the master's name, either first in possessive form, as Brown's William, or simply, William Brown. Such naming practice symbolized the slave's essential nature: mere property. Upon gaining freedom, therefore, the first thing most ex-slaves did was to name themselves anew. In so doing, the ex-bondsman rejected an identity forced upon him by society and asserted his new-found freedom. The rite of naming was thus a central experience in the life of the ex-slave, symbolizing the act of liberation.

True to the slave narrative mode, *The Autobiography of Miss Jane Pittman* addresses itself to the question of naming. The topic is first mentioned in the first chapter of the novel. During the civil war the Yankees came to Miss Jane's plantation. Her master went into hiding and Miss Jane, then Ticey, was asked by her mistress to give them water to drink. One of the Yankees struck up a conversation with the young girl concerning slavery. By the time the conversation was through, he had convinced Ticey of the evils of slavery (if any convincing was necessary) and had given her another name not associated with slavery – two names in fact: Jane Brown. After being offered respectability (by the only member of society that accepts her) as a human being, Jane, at the age of eleven, was willing to die in defence of what her new name symbolized. 'You little wench, didn't you hear me calling you?' her mistress asked her after the Yankees had left:

> I raised my head high and looked her straight in the face and said: 'You called me Ticey. My name ain't Ticey no more, it's Miss Jane Brown. And Mr Brown say catch him and tell him if you don't like it.'
> My mistress face got red, her eyes got wide, and for about half a minute she just stood there gaping at me. Then she gathered up her dress and started running for the house... My master told two of the other slaves to hold me down. One took my arms, the other one took my legs. My master jecked my dress and gived my mistress the whip and told her to teach me a lesson. Every time she hit me she asked me what my name was. I said Jane Brown. She hit me again what I said my name was. I said Jane Brown. (*MJP*, p. 9)

Miss Jane would have been killed but for the fear of the Yankees coming back and asking about her. Instead, the little girl lost her position in the big house and was put in the field where she 'put up with a lot of trouble to hold on to' her new name for a whole year, until the Proclamation declared freedom for all slaves. Even then she still had to go through one more fight to make sure nobody called himself 'Brown' that was no kin of hers.

After the Proclamation, most of the slaves on Miss Jane's plantation decided to leave the South and head for Ohio. Like Miss Jane, they all thought that they had to change their names to get rid of the last vestige of slavery:

> Then somebody said: 'My new name Abe Washington. Don't call me Buck no more.' We must have been two dozen of us there, and now everybody started changing names like you change hats. Nobody was keeping the same name Old Master had given them. This one would say, 'My new name Cam Lincoln'. That one would say, 'My new name Ace Freeman'. Anoter one, 'My new name Sherman S. Sherman'. 'What that S for?' 'My title.' Another one would say, 'My new name Job'. 'Job what?' 'Just Job.' 'Nigger, this ain't slavery no more. You got to have two names.' 'Job Lincoln, then.' 'Nigger, you ain't no kin to me. I'm Lincoln.' 'I don't care. I'm still Job Lincoln. Want fight?' Another one would say, 'My name Neremiah King'. Another one standing by a tree would say, 'My new name Bill Moses. No more Rufus.'
> And so it continued. (*MJP*, p. 17)

Two other elements unique to the black autobiography are also found in Ernest Gaines' novel. One of these is the theme of violence; the other is the tendency on the part of the author to regard his life as a microcosm of the race. Regarding the first, it seems that one of the functions of black autobiography is to portray in realistic and convincing terms the violence to which Blacks have been subjected and the contradictions and absurdity of racism. Blyden Jackson believes that this statement is equally true of Black fiction: 'all Negro fiction ... tended to protest a single irony, the irony of the way Negroes were mistreated in a country that espoused democracy'.[10] In keeping with this tradition, Gaines has employed the character of Miss Jane as a vehicle for the exposure of the inhumanity and irony of American racism. Her low-key, matter-of-fact reportage neither detracts from nor diminishes the violence and injustice of the facts described. If anything, the author has given Miss Jane a style much more effective in portraying her rage than a more melodramatic stance might have been. While her whole life is one long story of the contradictions and absurdity of American racism, three events, however, are most vivid.

The first one is reported in the chapter entitled 'Massacre'. Here, after the slaves have been declared free men by a proclamation from President Lincoln, some decide to go north to the land of freedom they had sung so much about in their spirituals. But, as fate would have it, scarcely have they left the plantation when they are overtaken by the patrollers and soldiers from the 'Secesh Army'. They are all beaten to death save Miss Jane and little Ned. That this was not an isolated case of White southern violence against Blacks is well illustrated by Miss Jane's words. After seeing all the bodies, including that of Big Laura with the baby in her arms, dead, she said, 'I didn't cry, I couldn't cry. I had seen so much beating and suffering; I had heard about so much cruelty in those 'leven or twelve years of my life I hardly knowed how to cry' (*MJP*. p. 23).

The second incident concerned Miss Jane's barrenness which is discussed in the chapter describing her relationship with Joe Pittman. As a tot, during the days of slavery, she had been whipped in a way that had hurt her reproductive system irreparably. She did not know this until she was an adult. Although this very important incident in her life is dismissed in less than a paragraph, the economy on the part of the author does not in any way diminish the tragedy of the incident. Miss Jane's inability to have children creates in her a diminished sense of self, especially when dealing with men. For a long time she suppresses her emotional response to Joe Pittman because she is afraid that no self-respecting man would want to be involved with a barren woman. After their 'marriage' we learn from Madame Gautire in the chapter entitled 'Man's Way' that Miss Jane's barrenness is probably the chief reason behind Joe Pittman's death. Since he could not impregnate Jane, Joe Pittman has to find other ways to satisfy the natural desire to prove himself a man. Because he could not 'ride' Miss Jane successfully, he took on the job of riding and breaking horses. One day there came on the plantation a horse that was extremely wild. Despite all warnings, Joe Pittman insisted on breaking the horse and it killed him. Throughout the rest of her life, Miss Jane is never to recover from the feelings of guilt stemming from the conviction that it was her barrenness that had driven Joe Pittman to his grave.

The third incident occurs after Joe Pittman's death, when Ned comes back to the South. After learning about Black awareness in the North, he returns to enlighten the Blacks so they can better claim their rights. But the Whites of Colonel Dye's plantation do not want their Blacks to be awakened from the ignorance that helps to keep them in 'their place'. They, in turn, hire Albert Cluveau, Miss Jane's closest White friend, to kill Ned. All the inhumanity of racial hatred is embodied in Albert Cluveau, friendship notwithstanding:

> 'Can you kill my boy?' Miss Jane asked him.
> 'I must do what they tell me,' he said.
> 'Can you kill my boy?' she asked him again.
> 'Yes,' he said. (MJP, p. 105)

And he did.

These three incidents demonstrate a few of the tragedies rampant throughout Miss Jane's long life. Yet it is important to notice that her suffering is a microcosm of the sufferings her race has had to endure over the years. Perhaps Joe Pittman's response to Miss Jane's suggestion that they end their romance because of her barrenness best expresses this sentiment: 'Ain't we all been hurt by slavery?'

The above is indicative of the final element unique to the Black autobiography that Ernest Gaines employs in his novel, the theme of collective consciousness. Inherent in this theme is the assumption on the part of the author that one Black man's life is representative of Black life in general. In the introduction to Miss Jane Pittman, the interviewer, a young white schoolteacher, expresses his belief that the story of this one Black woman will give him some insight into the lives of other Blacks, confident that 'her life's story can help (me) explain things to my students'.

Gaines further demonstrates his skill as a novelist by involving other characters in the interviews, about which the young teacher says:

> I should mention here that even though I have used only Miss Jane's voice throughout the narrative, there were times when others carried the story for her. When she was tired, or when she had forgotten certain things,

someone else would always pick up the narration. Miss Jane would sit there listening until she got ready to talk again. (MJP, pp. vi–vii)

It is natural and plausible that at her age, Miss Jane has lapses of memory or occasionally tires of talking. Aside from adding to the realism of her portrayal, her silences also provide an opportunity for her friends and companions to recount events and experiences that are not only part of Miss Jane's life, but shared by them all. By the end of the project, the young teacher is convinced more than ever that what has been captured on tape is not just Miss Jane's story, but rather the story of a whole race.

Thus, the reader comes away from the novel with the conviction that *The Autobiography of Miss Jane Pittman* is centred not around a solitary heroine but around a people whose collective deeds border upon the heroic. Though Miss Jane is the dominant personality of the narrative, the autobiography itself is that of a people. It recounts the life and death struggles of slaves and freedmen alike. As the novel progresses, all these people, together with Miss Jane, come together in the historic march towards dignity and freedom. That final march in Sampson is only a symbol of the march that has been going on for centuries. As Addison Gayle puts it, Gaines' book is a 'people's novel, one revealing unwritten history and depicting the examples of those who, in refusing to accept reality without question, rebelled against it'.[11]

The foregoing not only demonstrates the manner in which *The Autobiography of Miss Jane Pittman* adheres to the general format of autobiography, but also the manner in which it incorporates the thematic characteristics peculiar to Black autobiography, the slave narrative in particular. Just as *The Autobiography of Miss Jane Pittman* represents a specialized form of the pseudo-autobiography, so the simulated slave narrative, Ferdinand Oyono's *Houseboy* embodies another specialized form of the pseudo-autobiography: the simulated diary. Diaries are usually personal records not meant for the public eye.

In the tradition of the autobiography, they contain narratives written by a single subject from a single perspective over a period of time. If they ever come to the attention of the public they do so posthumously. Consequently, just as Ernest Gaines goes out of his way to present his tale as a true slave narrative, in the same way Ferdinand Oyono goes out of his way to present his tale as a real diary. In keeping with the diary tradition, Oyono's hero-narrator does not survive to recount his own story. Instead, as in *Miss Jane Pittman*, there is a double narrative via an anonymous narrator.

This anonymous narrator happens to be travelling through Spanish Guinea when the tom-tom announces that a 'Frances', a 'Frenchman', meaning a Black person from neighbouring Cameroon, is dying. He immediately heads for the village of M'foula on the other side of the great forest where he finds his compatriot on his deathbed with a pierced lung from a brutal beating. With the death of Toundi-Joseph, the name of the dying man, the narrator comes into possession of two notebooks written in Ewondo, which contain the dead man's story. The narrator translates this into French for publication explaining that he has 'tried to keep the richness of the original language without letting it get in the way of the story itself' (*Houseboy*, p. 5).

The pretext of the supposed translation from Ewondo has the advantage of justifying the lack of idiomatic flexibility in French (or in the English translation) and gives the book the impression of being an authentic translation of a work from a writer who has just learned to read and write and, therefore, possesses only limited literary abilities. Further, in keeping with the pretence of the pseudo-autobiography, the language and style in Toundi's diary are appropriately naïve in accordance with the character and naïvety of the narrator. Sometimes, however, Toundi is portrayed as being intelligent and ambitious. When he uses a word he does not understand, he promises to look it up at the first available opportunity.

As in all autobiographies, Ferdinand Oyono's book is also a one-character story. The events of the novel are depicted through the boyish eyes of the subject and all the other characters are discussed only through the context of his own experience. Furthermore, at the risk of running into stylistic trouble, Oyono expands the time covered by his protagonist's diary so that the book encompasses a very significant segment of the author's life, as in all autobiographies.

As we move from those aspects of Oyono's book that are true of all autobiographies (or diaries) to those unique to the Black autobiography, it is significant to note the source of similarity between African and Afro-American literature. It was earlier argued that in his treatment of the theme of naming, Ernest Gaines was simply following the pattern of the slave narrative. However, the theme of naming also occurs in Ferdinand Oyono's book, although it cannot be traced to the slave narrative or said to be a derivative of the genre. The presence of this theme, therefore, and of the other themes to be discussed in the following pages can only be explained by the similarity of the experience suffered by Black people both in Africa and the new world.

As in America where slaves were stripped of their African names and given those of their masters, Africans in Africa encountered a similar experience during the process of colonization. As explorers renamed the continent in honour of their kings, queens and other heroes, the Africans looked on as the continent took on a European identity. Natural phenomena like rivers, mountains and lakes exchanged their African names for those dispensed by the colonizing powers.

This process of 'finding and civilizing' the continent included the people as well as the natural resources. After being told of their 'pagan' nature, they were persuaded and sometimes threatened into an acceptance of Christianity. Colonial civilization brought with it new tags for the African, euphemistically referred to as 'Christian names'.

It is against such a background that the reader must appreciate the significance of the names of Oyono's protagonist in *Houseboy*. At birth, Oyono's hero was given two African names: Toundi Ondoua. On the eve of his initiation, however, in the aftermath of a verbal fight with his father, Toundi runs away from his family and joins the French Catholic missionary school at Dangan. There he is baptized in the Catholic faith and given the name Joseph. By this act, Toundi acquires a new identity, one that strips him of his African roots and makes him a pseudo-Frenchman. Like the anonymous narrator reporting the diary, Toundi refers to himself as a Frenchman. He embraces Father Gilbert as his father. At Saint Peter's Catholic Mission, Toundi declares 'Everything I am I owe to Father Gilbert' (*Houseboy*, p. 14). And what is he? In place of the manhood he would have achieved had he stayed at home and gone through the initiation ceremonies, Toundi accepts the role of a permanent child, a White man's boy, 'a boy who can read and write, serve Mass, lay a table, sweep out his (Father Gilbert's) room and make his bed' (p. 15). This surely is not the picture of an African boy. It is more like the picture of a Catholic western boy. Toundi's new name, Joseph, corresponds to this new identity admirably well.

After the accidental death of Father Gilbert, Toundi is removed to the Residence where he becomes the 'boy' of the local Commandant. His pride in his new assignment and his continued identification with a foreign culture is expressed in his diary. He writes, 'I shall be the chief European's boy. The dog of the King is the King of dogs'

(*Houseboy*, p. 20). Whenever asked his name, instead of answering Toundi Ondoua, he would reply, 'Joseph, the Commandant's boy' (p. 25).

Thus the name 'Joseph' serves the same function in this novel that the slave names do in the slave narratives. It symbolizes the distance between Toundi and the other African workers at the Residence, the extent to which he is attached to his French masters, and the fact that he has fully accepted the role they have assigned him. In the slave narratives the slave names are symbolic of the slave's status. As soon as this status changes and a slave becomes free, the first thing he does is to rid himself of the master's name to symbolize his new freedom. Toundi's adoption of the name Joseph, however, symbolizes his quasi-slave status. He never frees himself from his bondage, so he dies Joseph, the Commandant's boy.

The amount of attention Oyono pays to the theme of violence seems to make it the major subject of the novel. Oyono seems to agree with Kofi Awoonor who argues that the French, unlike the British, inflicted upon their colonial subjects a senseless type of brutality that defies explanation. At the Catholic mission, while going through Father Gilbert's diary, Toundi stumbles across a note that reminds him of the kick he received from Father Gilbert for mimicking him: 'I felt my bottom burning all over again' (*Houseboy*, p. 9). Toundi usually understates things and for him to have said that much is an indication to the reader that it must have been quite a kick.

On his very first day of work at the Residence after Father Gilbert's death, he receives a dosage of his new master's power:

From the sitting room, his sharp voice came demanding a beer. As I ran to serve him my cap rolled across the floor to his feet. In a flash I saw his eyes grow as small as a cat's eyes in the sun. I was turning to go to the refrigerator when he pointed to the cap at his foot. I was nearly dead with fear.
 'Are you going to pick it up?'
 'In a moment, Sir!'
 'What are you waiting for?'
 'I will bring you your beer first, Sir.'
 'But ...' Then he said gently, 'Take your time'.
 I took a step towards him when I came back towards the refrigerator. I could feel the Commandant near me, the smell of him getting stronger and stronger.
 'Pick up your cap.'
 Feebly I bent to pick it up. The Commandant grabbed me by the hair, swung me round and peered into my eyes.
 'I am not a monster ... but I wouldn't like to disappoint you!'

With that he shot out a kick to my shins that sent me sprawling under the table. The Commandant's kick was even more painful than the kick of the late Father Gilbert. He seemed pleased with his effort. (p. 23)

As a house boy, Toundi found himself an eye-witness to Madame Decazy's affair with Moreau, the prison director, which makes him an embarrassment to the Commandant and his wife. Consequently they frame him for complicity in a theft and send him to Moreau who finds the perfect excuse to torture him in a very brutal manner.

> I vomited blood. My body has let me down. There is a shooting pain through my chest like a hook caught me in my lungs ... I felt cold. Even in the strong sun, my teeth chattered. A numb weariness filled me. I felt light, a thousand pains of bellows quickened my breathing. My thoughts came to a stop. (p. 117)

Many of the other Africans in Toundi's diary are also portrayed as being victims of the French colonialist's brutal whims. One afternoon, for example, Madame Decazy gives Toundi a note to take to her lover, Monsieur Moreau. He finds him in the process of punishing two Africans suspected of stealing from a White man, Monsieur Janopoulos. The brutality and lack of human feeling with which they mete out the accused's punishment almost surpasses the treatment of the slaves in America:

> With the help of a constable he was giving them a flogging in front of M. Janopoulos. They were stripped to the waist and handcuffed. There was a rope round their necks, tied to the pole in the Flogging Yard, so that they couldn't turn their necks towards the blows.
>
> It was terrible. The hippopotamus-hide whip tore up their flesh. Every time they groaned it went through my bowels. M. Moreau with his hair down over his face and his shirt sleeves rolled up was setting about them so violently that I wondered, in agony of mind, if they would come out of it alive. Chewing on his cigar M. Janopoulous released his dog. It mouthed about the heels of the prisoners and tore at their trousers.
>
> 'Confess, you thieves,' shouted M. Moreau. 'Give them the butt of your rifle, Ndjangoula.'
>
> The huge Sara ran up, presented his weapon and brought down the butt on the suspects.
>
> 'Not on the head, Ndjangoula, they've got hard heads. In the kidneys.'
>
> Ndjangoula brought the butt down on their kidneys. They went down, got up and then went down again under another violent blow to the kidneys. (pp. 75–6)

Toundi's summary of the situation is indicative of the colonialists' attitudes towards the people they had supposedly come to administer justice to: 'Janopoulos was laughing. M. Moreau panted for breath. The prisoners had lost consciousness' (p. 76). These three sentences demonstrate Ferdinand Oyono's economy of language as well as the control he uses in the expression of his anger and rage.

This type of physical assault was not the only type of abuse that Toundi and the other Africans receive at the hands of the French colonialists. Their pride is also assaulted. Although he breaks into ecstasy when he first meets the Commandant's wife, she ironically does not think of him even as a human being. When Toundi confides to her that he has not married because he cannot afford to support a wife and children in the manner and style of the Whites, she accuses him of having 'delusions of grandeur'. 'You must be serious. Everyone has their position in life. You are a houseboy. My husband is a commandant. Nothing can be done about it' (p. 56).

Kofi Awoonor correctly points out that this 'sweet' paternalism is far more brutal than the open hostility and physical violence Toundi suffers everyday from the Commandant.[12] It reminds one of the same psychological atrocities that the slave narrators and post-slavery autobiographers encountered. In his Narrative,[13] for example, Frederick Douglass says that his command from his master was far more painful than all the whippings he had received so far. Richard Wright in *Black Boy* states how one lady for whom he had been working for some days jeered at him when he told her that he was planning to become a writer. 'You'll never be a writer. ... Who on earth put such ideas into your nigger head?'[14] This woman's assault hurt Richard Wright so much that, as hard as it was for Blacks to get jobs, he decided to quit. Maya Angelou recounts the same experience in her autobiography. During her graduation a local White politician tells Angelou and her class that the Black man's capability to rise up the social scale is limited to the field of sports. Like the White people that Angelou, Richard Wright and Frederick Douglass encounter, the Commandant and his wife have established limits beyond which Toundi dare not step.

The laundryman complains of the same psychological attack on his personality to which Toundi is subjected. He, a man, is made to wash Madame's soiled linen and sanitary towels as if she has no shame. Baklu's attempt to blame this type of behaviour on culturally different worlds is no help. 'There are two worlds ... ours is a world of respect and mystery and magic. Their world brings everything into the daylight, even the things that weren't meant to be' (p. 81). The big question still remains. '"What are we to these whites?" asked the cook. "Everyone I have ever worked for has handed over these things to the laundryman as if he wasn't a man at all ... these women have no shame"' (p. 81).

All in all, the theme of violence to the Black man's body and psyche that is so central to the slave narratives and the other autobiographical writings is also the main topic of Oyono's *Houseboy*. The novel attacks and ridicules the racial prejudice and brutality suffered by Africans at the hands of the colonialists. Of particular importance is the colonialist attitude that the African is not quite a human being and every attempt must be made to deprive him of his basic humanity and/or manliness. The African is always referred to in animal terms and when his humanity is conceded it is only as 'boy'.

Unlike *Miss Jane Pittman*'s narrative, Toundi's diary is not reflective. Toundi records the events of each day without stopping to interpret their significance. Not until moments before his death does it occur to him that the treatment he has received is shared by other Africans. It is argued, however, that although Toundi may not have seen himself in this light, his creator did. In other words, Oyono meant to portray his hero not as an individual but as a type.

> Our hero, Toundi, is himself the symbol of that misguided Africa (sic) who ran without thought to the European invader in search of sustenance and an excitingly newer way of life which was to degenerate into a bad dream for him.... Toundi is the young African entranced and ensnared from his village into the European world.

Seen in this light, *Houseboy* becomes a witty understatement of a big, significant issue to which scores of African writers have addressed themselves: the folly of the African who hopes to find happiness and contentment in the material world of the European.

This brings us to the theme of greed which is very important in Oyono's novel. According to Awoonor, if Africa had not been greedy it would not have sold itself to the Europeans and subjected itself to the latter's material greed which superseded all moral and other considerations. Toundi's troubles started with his greed. The dispute between him and his father at the beginning of the novel came about because on the eve of his initiation he ran off in pursuit of the lumps of sugar the White man threw to the Black kids, 'like throwing corn to chickens' (p. 10). The scuffle which ensues leads the young man to run away from home. Of all the places he could go to, including those of his relatives, Toundi chooses to go to that of the White man, because 'I just wanted to get close to the white man ... (who) gave little black boys sugar lumps' (p. 9). At the Catholic Mission and at the Residence greed for the white man's way of life continues to be the sole motive for his actions. The very first night at the Catholic Mission, Father Gilbert gives him the leavings off his plate and Toundi finds them 'strange and delicious' (p. 13). Later on he says that an old woman prepared food for all the African workers at the mission. But 'we prefer the leavings from the priest's meals' (p. 14). It is because Toundi aspires to live as a White man that he learns reading, writing, French and eventually decides to write a diary. His ambition to advance and improve himself leads him to study his new world closely – too closely, in fact. Earlier his mother had warned him, 'Toundi, what will your greediness bring you to ... ?' (p. 14) Years later, away in Spanish Guinea on his deathbed, these words haunt him. He finally admits that his greed has brought him to his tragic end.

It is also on his deathbed that for the first time he makes a connection between his own suffering and that of the other Africans, and between his life and theirs. 'What are we blackmen who are called French?' (p. 4) Toundi's story, therefore, is a collective story like that of the authors of the slave narratives or the autobiographers both real and fictional discussed above. His is the embodiment of his continent's folly; a blind running after the promises of the White man's material benefits which, when seen in their proper perspective, prove to be nothing more substantial than 'lumps of sugar' to the African.

Why is the autobiographical form so appealing to the Black writers discussed here? What can be done through the pseudo-autobiography that cannot be done as effectively in a straight fictional mode? In an attempt to answer these questions, I found that a writer resorts to the pseudo-autobiographical mode for the same reasons that one writes an autobiography.

First, in terms of time, the autobiographical mode imposes a sequential chronology in accordance with the character's life span. In so doing, it provides a controlled perspective, setting up a constant psyche for interpretation of experience which may be followed more easily by the reader. Usually this element does not come so naturally in the fictional mode, even if written in the first person narrative style. In the regular fictional mode the reader normally has to follow the story and come up with his own conclusions unless the author 'assists'. In the pseudo-autobiography, just as in the regular autobiography, the reader is presented with a set of values and interpretations by the fictional autobiographer which serve as a springboard for the reader's interpretations and conclusions.

Secondly, in terms of tone and/or attitude, the autobiographical mode provides one of the most suitable forms for the expression of hope, which has been one of the cornerstones of the Black man's experience. In his book, *Black Drama*, Loften Mitchell tells the story of a Miss Jane Pittman-like character named Alice Payton Brown. Miss Brown was born a slave. She repeatedly describes her days during slavery as being terrible. 'It was a cruel era in America's history.' She says:

> They made us like animals. Sometimes when the old man Sam and his family had finished eating, we slaves would sneak into the house and just about knock one another down, snatching the crumbs from the table ... We was just dirt, just dirt. When colored folks died, they dragged 'em off to a corner of the plantation and dumped 'em in the ground.[15]

Yet she never gave up hope that she would be free and at the age of fourteen Miss Brown *was* freed. She lived to be 113 years old! Of her old age Mother Brown, as she was commonly referred to, used to say, 'I'm doing fine.... Really making up for them bad days. If I'd a let the devil talk me into giving up hope a long time ago, I wouldn't be around here now, enjoying these days.'[16]

The hope that characterizes Mother Brown's existence has been the strongest motivation for all Black people. During the years of slavery, Blacks cried out in their Spirituals for deliverance, longing to cross the Jordan into the promised land. Africans during the days of colonialism – and even now in South Africa – sang the same song of hope for a better day. Martin Luther King's famous speech 'I have a dream' perhaps best expresses this sentiment. In all cases total freedom has always been in sight, no matter how dimly at times.

In most Black autobiographies hope is expressed for the future by virtue of survival and endurance. In the pseudo-autobiographies discussed above, this same element can be discerned. These books present similar responses to the Black man's experience. The slave era is represented by Toundi in *Houseboy*. It is characterized by the Black man's total acceptance of the White man's world, either because there is no other choice or because of total ignorance. In either case the slave's devotion to his master goes unrewarded. In the case of Toundi, the imagined benefits of serving as 'the king's dog' are not worthy of mention. What is important is the fact that his blind devotion to his masters leads him not to security and well-being, but instead to destruction.

Miss Jane Pittman embodies the spirit of the truly proud and defiant. Her acceptance of death after her long life puts her beyond the threat of retribution. She leads the march against the Jim Crow laws in the hope that this action will prevent her successors from going through the same humiliating experiences she has endured. After years of quietly accepting the racist indignities and physical abuse which have so characterized her life, she decides to act in sheer defiance.

Furthermore, the events in a pseudo-autobiography need little corroboration by other characters or authorities because they are presented by the person who lived them. This is the advantage the autobiographer possesses over the novelist. Closely connected with this is the fact that in the pseudo-autobiography realism is created through the use of the first person account of events. This is especially true of those experiences of the narrator which are based on historic facts that are well known and accepted. Dramatic tension and suspense are decreased and uncertainty removed because the reader knows that the narrator must survive each crisis in order to be able to record. Such is the case with regard to most of the events described in both *Houseboy* and *Miss Jane Pittman*.

The pseudo-autobiography, taking over from where the Black autobiography leaves off, represents the attempt of Black writers to establish within the realm of fiction a realistic, sensitive, and dynamic recreation of the Black experience with emotions and events that transcend the stereotyped images often depicted in White literature and media. The pseudo-autobiography as a genre satisfies a need to validate an experience in a form that is less subject to question than most fictional forms.

NOTES

1. James Olney, *Tell Me Africa*, New Jersey, Princeton University Press, 1973, p. 7 and p. 271.
2. Wilfred Cartey, *Whispers from a Continent: The Literature of Contemporary Black Africa*, New York, Random House, 1969, p. 3; London, Heinemann, 1971.
3. J. A. Emmanuel and T. L. Gross, *Dark Symphony: Negro Literature in America*, New York, Free Press, 1968, p. 251.
4. Roger Rosenblatt, *Black Fiction*, Cambridge, Mass., Harvard University Press, 1974, p. 11.
5. Ernest Gaines, *The Autobiography of Miss Jane Pittman*, New York, Bantam, 1971. In further extracts, *MJP – The Autobiography of Miss Jane Pittman*.

110 Miss Jane Pittman *and* Houseboy

6. Ferdinand Oyono, *Houseboy*, Nairobi, Heinemann (AWS 29), 1966. Hereafter all quotations are taken from the reset edition of 1975.
7. Roy Pascal, *Design and Truth in Autobiography*, Cambridge, Mass., Harvard University Press, 1960, p. 17.
8. William L. Howarth, 'Some Principles of Autobiography,' in *New Literary History*, Vol. 5, 1974, p. 364.
9. Gilbert Osofsky, 'Puttin' on Ole Massa: The Significance of Slave Narratives,' an introduction to his *Puttin' on Ole Massa*, New York, Harper and Row, 1969, pp. 9–44.
10. Blyden Jackson, *The Waiting Years: Essays on American Negro Literature*, Baton Rouge, Louisiana State University Press, 1976, p. 24.
11. Addison Gayle, Jr, *The Way of the World: The Black Novel in America*, New York, Doubleday, 1975, p. 357.
12. Kofi Awoonor, *The Breast of the Earth*, Garden City, Doubleday, 1976, p. 294.
13. Frederick Douglas, 'Narrative of the Life ...', Boston, 1845 and Cambridge, Mass., 1960.
14. Richard Wright, *Black Boy*, New York, Harper and Row, 1966, p. 162; London, Longman, 1970.
15. Loften Mitchell, *Black Drama*, San Francisco. Leswing Press, 1967, p. 21.
16. ibid, pp. 21–2.

Trans-Saharan Views: Mutually Negative Portrayals

Kole Omotoso

Writing in a recent issue of *Magallat al-Thaqafat al-Sudaniyyah* (Journal of Sudanese Culture),[1] Dr Marwan Hamid al-Rashid of the Literature department at the University of Khartoum in the Sudan expressed surprise at the bitterness with which Ayi Kwei Armah portrays Arabs in his fourth novel, *Two Thousand Seasons*.[2]

> The reader (of Armah's novel; specifically Sudanese and/or Arab here) unfamiliar with the previous writings of Ayi Kwei Armah, finds himself confronted by a unique experience at least in the area of literature, whereby this Ghanaian writer, African like us (Sudanese? Arabs?), in the last quarter of the twentieth century, describes the 'entry' of Muslim Arabs into the continent of Africa in the most ugly epithets. He considers their (Arab) history in terms of barbarism and illegal seizure of lands, their easy capitulation to women, their abandonment to sensual enjoyment and their selling in slave markets of men who were born free. The novel says that all this was done in the name of the 'god of the Desert'. After this Armah turns to the invasion of Africa by Christian European imperialism.

Al-Rashid believes that the European reader would find little to arouse his resentment in Armah's presentation since he is already familiar with anti-European literature by colonials.

> But as for the Muslim Arab reader, with particular reference to the political and social conditions for which his country is condemned, he may face difficulty in accepting this type of angry attack against his ancestors and their history especially from a writer with whom they

would agree and share identical feelings of the danger that European economic and political supremacy poses for the world. The consequences of such a danger can be seen in the way European civilization has transformed the character of and diffused the cultural communal and religious heritage of Africa.

It may be that Armah is the only African writer who deals with Arab–Islamic intrusion into Africa with such negative damaging criticism. He equates this Arab–Islamic intrusion into Africa with Christian Europe's imperialist invasion (of Africa).

Without attempting to understand the reasons for Ayi Kwei Armah's negative portrayal of Arabs in his novel – and Armah is not the only African writer who has, or who is doing this – Dr al-Rashid goes into the defence of Arabs.

There are naturally, African writers who celebrate their Islamic heritage in their books and who are proud of this heritage. Furthermore, some of them insist that the mixing of Islamic heritage with ancient African heritage had saved them from being swamped by Western thought.

The general thrust of al-Rashid's pre-occupation is to mediate between Ayi Kwei Armah and his potential Arab reader.

This note is an attempt to raise certain questions as well as to provide information which may assist in understanding those questions. Why is it necessary for Dr al-Rashid to generalize about Ayi Kwei Armah's specific carpeting of the Arab role in African history? Are Armah and other African writers – for example, Yambo Ouologuem, author of *Bound to Violence* – fair (historically, politically) in their portrayal of Arabs? Are there counters to this negative portrayal – that is: are there contemporary Arab writers, who portray Africans in their fiction?

Within the Third World today the Arabs consider themselves the only way out of the conflict between East and West, capitalism and socialism. If countries of the Third World, especially those within the continent of Africa, refuse to accept this proffered Arab leadership of the Third World, it is the fault of western colonialism which has painted a picture of the Arab presence in Africa as one of horrendous slave raids into and settlement in the continent. In the last six years, several Arab countries as well as (particularly since 1973) various Arab institutions have organized seminars and symposia dedicated to the changing of this view of Afro-Arab relations. Two volumes of essays (in Arabic) entitled *Arab–African Connections*,[3] were recently published by ALECSO (Arab League Educational, Cultural and

Scientific Organization) against the background of continued Arab efforts to present their own version of their presence in the continent of Africa.

The first volume, published in 1977, presents its case in a short, four-page introduction. This case is that the continued weakness of Afro-Arab relations is consequent upon the politics of European colonialism and neo-colonialism. Weakness is seen in issues related to politics, economics and culture. European colonialism presents African history, prior to Europe's encounter with the continent, as the continent's pre-history. The Arabs insist that that pre-history has a properly-written record in Arabic, documenting Afro-Arab contacts during a period of twelve centuries. What these Arab scholars do not say – and this is the general feature of all the essays in these two volumes – is that the Arabs themselves refer to the period of African history prior to their contact with the continent as the 'Period of Ignorance' ('asr al-Jahiliyyah)! And the introduction continues its argument by suggesting that European colonialism has been able to achieve a large measure of 'distortion' as a result of the loss or complete disregard of Arab records on Arab civilization in Africa. There is also the 'fact' that all the available source materials for studying the history of the Arabs in Africa exist only in European historical records. Arab and African researchers should be aware of this situation when they approach this subject.

Having given this presentation, the introduction goes on to provide summations of the ten essays of the first volume: Arab–African contacts prior to Europe's voyages of discovery, Portuguese colonization and its effects on Arab–African contacts, the role of Britain and Germany in the break-up of the Sultanate of Zanzibar, Arabs and Africans in the face of German colonization and its effects on Arabism and Islam in Africa, and French colonization and Arab culture in North Africa and the influence of the French on Islamic potentials in West Africa.

There are three major themes that may be extracted from these ten essays by eight contemporary Arab scholars. First, there is the much regretted absence of material in Arabic on the history of Arabs in Africa. As a result of this, scholars are therefore forced to utilize Roman, Greek, German, English, French and Portuguese sources. While they seem to regret this dependence on European records, the scholars willingly quote any snatches of material seen as complimentary to the Arabs. For instance, at the beginning of the sixth essay – 'The break-up of Egyptian Imperialism in Africa' – Sir Samuel Baker is quoted approvingly in connection with his statement that only

Egypt could bring the light of civilization to the Nile Valley and the rest of Africa.

The second theme, conspicuous because of its absence, is the fact that all the scholars ignore Africa's pre-Arab history! Their concern, it would seem, is with Europe's interruption of the arabization of Africa, an interruption which changed the writing of some African languages from Arabic script to Roman script and the culture from Islamic to European. With regard to the issue of scripts, Arab historians tend to forget that Somalia, a member of the Arab League, changed its script from Arabic to Roman only a few years ago.

The third theme has to do with the view taken of slavery and the slave trade. Much space is given to the non-issue of a comparison of Arab slave-trading activities in Africa with those of the Europeans. European historians, we are told, seem to imply that slave trading was the only Arab economic activity. The scholars assert that Arabs traded in gold and ivory as well as slaves and while there were collecting centres for gold and ivory, there were none for slaves, which indicates its low priority in Arab trading activities. Furthermore, we are asked to believe that Arab settlements in Africa were established without conflicts with the existing African populations. Apparently the Arabs brought cities into Africa, besides introducing certain agricultural crops until then unknown to Africans. And we are told that the Arab settlements were not set up for military purposes, although it is well known that these settlements led to the establishment of Arab hegemony over the local African populations. Thus by the time the first essay comes face to face with the questions which all the essayists clearly have at the back of their minds – can Arab activities on the East African coast be termed colonialism? – the answer is an obvious no. Yet, for scholars arguing almost exclusively on the basis of material which they have earlier accepted as prejudicial to their case, it is, to say the least, a bold conclusion. It is almost unbelievable that the Arab occupation of North Africa is referred to as *fath* (conquest) in Arab historical records; that African slaves worked in salt mines owned by Arabs in the Sahara; dived for pearls for Arabs in the Persian Gulf; restored marshlands for sugar plantation purposes in southern Iraq and served as soldiers in Arab armies from as far back as 833 AD. The condition of the slaves in southern Iraq was so inhuman that the slaves revolted and set up their own kingdom which resisted the soldiers of the Abbasid caliphs for thirteen years. This incident is usually referred to in Arab history as the 'Revolt of the Zanj' (Blacks). It is impossible to believe that these scholars are dealing with the same slave trade which is calculated to have taken away fourteen million Africans during twelve centuries of Arab slaving activity in Africa.

The 1978 volume, while mopping up some of the area already covered by the 1977 volume, brings the record up to the contemporary situation. The introduction rightly points out the fact that the Arab World (a sixth continent?) has 73 per cent of its land area within the continent of Africa and as much as 67 per cent of its population. Thus to an extent the Arab World shares a common boundary confine with Africa. But more important to both Arabs and Africans is the shared colonial experience, the shared exploitation by capitalism and the shared racial oppression of Africans in southern Africa and the Arabs in Palestine. Furthermore, western neo-colonialism continues to destabilize both areas through the old system of divide-and-rule. The introduction ends by stating that since we are now in an age of dialogue, it would be surprising if African and Arab countries did not get together for a dialogue.

There are eleven essays in the second volume. The first essay deals with Arab–African connections in ancient times; the second deals with the development and growth of Arab–African contacts during the Middle Ages; the third essay discusses the destruction of these contacts during the period of European colonialism. The remaining essays deal with the various economic, cultural and political co-operative ventures between Arab and African countries. In this regard emphasis is laid on the one-to-one co-operation which has existed between Arab and African countries since the historic meeting of the Organization of African Unity in 1973 in Algiers, the meeting that led to African states breaking diplomatic relations with Israel. The final two essays, which occupy the greater part of this volume, deal with the coverage of African issues in the Arab press such as the Congo Crisis, the Nigerian Civil War and the liberation of the former Portuguese colonies in Africa. The last essay details existing agreements facilitating economic and cultural co-operation which have been signed by Arab and African countries. The long bibliography at the end of this volume, over six hundred entries, shows that over two-thirds of the sources for these essays are of European origin.

There is no denying that all countries, whether ex-colonial or under neo-colonial influences, must unite to fight neo-colonialism and exploitation. Arab scholars are intensely concerned with this issue, as if it was in itself a sufficient basis for co-operation even among Arab countries. A 'scrambled' history of African–Arab contacts thus constitutes the intellectual buttress of this much-needed co-operation. This argument has been carried to a ridiculous extent in the suggestion at the Sharjah Symposium on 'The Future of Afro-Arab Relations', in December 1976, that Arab countries should endow a chair of history in African universities and that this chair of history should be named after Tippu Tip (Muhammed bin Sayed – 'A gangster of the most brutal kind'), a slave trader in East Africa in the second half of the nineteenth century. Unfortunately, Arab contemporary literature does not encourage anything as bright as these essayists would approve.

Thuqub fi al-thaub al-Aswad[4] (Blemishes in the Black Robe) is a short novel (258 pages in Arabic) by Ihsan Abdul Qudus, who died in 1978. Ihsan Abdul Qudus was one of the most (financially) successful Egyptian writers. He generally wrote about women and love in imitation of European tear-jerker novels for adolescents. *Blemishes in the Black Robe* was written after a visit to Dakar in 1966 during the First Negro Festival of the Arts. It is the story of an African bush girl and a Lebanese youth of Lebanese–African descent. The story is based in Bamako, capital of Mali. An Arab psychiatrist needs a holiday after a short conference in the United States of America and Africa is recommended for him as the best place to go. He arrives in Bamako to find that he cannot run away from the demands of his profession. An Arab family demands that he help them to restore the reason of their son who has fallen in love with an African girl from the village. Not only does this son go into the woods to participate in wild African dances and ceremonies, he also speaks their language. Working with professional dexterity, the psychiatrist is able to restore the reason of the boy and the family are forever grateful to him.

The novel was published in 1977. One glaring difference in the mutually negative portrayals that Arabs and Africans give of each other is that while African authors write only of the Arab élite and their debaucheries in Black Africa, Arab authors do not invest characters in Black Africa with any form of dignity or heroic status that they can respect. The tourist psychiatrist meets no African of equal education, erudition or qualifications; in contrast, whilst the African writer is prepared to recognize an Arab élite, whatever he may think of it, he too ignores the general mass of Arab people and therefore presumes that Arabs have no humanity. In Ihsan Abdul al-Qudus' novel, the characters from the past are big, fat, half-naked chiefs (in the manner of Batouala), forever presiding over cannibal initiation ceremonies, night orgies accompanied by the sound of wild drumming and witch-hunting (a classic description of this is to be found in *King Solomon's Mines* by Rider Haggard). The African characters from the present are servants, cooks and all those whose life is one of exploitation and oppression. They live without any strong belief in themselves, and they live completely for the Arab whites for whom they work.

It would seem that the Arab writer, in his portrayal of African characters, has taken his cue from modern writings of Europeans and Americans. The African writer's reaction to the Arabs has been identical to his reaction to Europeans. It is often forgotten by both sides that while the Arabs colonized and settled in many parts of Africa they today are themselves the victims of European and American colonialism, imperialism and neo-colonialism. On this basis Arabs and Africans need to fight together to win freedom. But co-operation can only be based on a mutual acceptance of and respect for each other. This is not as yet reflected in the imaginative literature of Arabs or Africans.

NOTES

1. *Magallat al-Thaqafalt al-Sudaniyyah* (Journal of Sudanese Studies), Ministry of Culture and Information, Khartoum, no. 11, August 1979.
2. Ayi Kwei Armah, *Two Thousand Seasons*, Nairobi, East African Publishing House, 1973; London, Heinemann (AWS 218), 1979.
3. *Arab–African Connections*, Cairo, Arab League Educational, Cultural and Scientific Organization (ALECSO), two volumes, 1977, 1978.
4. Ihsan Abdul al-Qudus, *Thuqub fi al-thaub al-Aswad* (Blemishes in the Black Robe), Cairo, 1977.

The Backward Glance: Lamming's *Season of Adventure* and Williams' *Other Leopards*

Funso Aiyejina

> But his wife looked back...
> and she became a pillar of salt.
>
> (Genesis 19, v.26)

Despite the many centuries of separation between the New World African and his African ancestry, a number of African cultural traits continue to survive in the New World, the religious being the most enduring. In places such as Brazil, Cuba, Haiti, Jamaica, Puerto Rico, Surinam, Trinidad and Tobago, the United States and Venezuela, transplanted African deities have been preserved and reinterpreted to suit the spirit of these new environments. Consequently, many West Indian writers have attempted to comprehend Africa and the African by looking at the ramifications of these religious survivals. This has been attempted by Sylvia Wynter (*The Hills of Hebron*), Andrew Salkey (*A Quality of Violence*), Orlando Patterson (*Children of Sisyphus*), Derek Walcott (*O Babylon!*) and George Lamming (*Season of Adventure*). Lamming's *Season of Adventure* is, however, the most comprehensive and the most perceptive of all.

In *Season of Adventure*,[1] Lamming uses the practice of *vodum* (voodoo) to make statements about the existence of a virile image of Africa in the thought and behaviour patterns of Afro-West Indians, especially those who belong to the peasant class. He goes on to demonstrate that this image is an obligatory factor in any significant assessment of the Afro-West Indian psyche and in any consideration of the concept of the past as a source of replenishment in the process of moulding the consciousness of the present.

In a response to V. S. Naipaul's claim that Africa has been forgotten in the West Indies and that 'films about African tribesmen excite derisive West Indian laughter', Lamming affirms that 'it is precisely because Africa has not been forgotten that the West Indian embarrassment takes the form of derisive laughter'.[2] He goes on to cite the example of Calypso, the basic folk rhythm of the Caribbean and its African origin as further refutation of Naipaul's theory of amnesia. He concludes that it is the 'treacherous foundations' of West Indian education which have perpetuated a negative image of Africa in the West Indies and that this has, in turn, led to a limited presence of a positive concept of Africa there. 'The concept of Africa, reinforced by some familiarity with its history,' he declares, 'has not percolated through the vital layers of the West Indian consciousness. Until this happens, no one can say what is the true meaning of Africa for the West Indian people and their intellectual classes'.[3]

Season of Adventure is, in a way, an imaginative projection of the 'true meaning of Africa for the West Indian people and their intellectual classes'. The novel opens with echoes of two distinctly folk idioms – the steel drum and the religious ceremony of the Souls – both of which recall continental African religious practices. The steel drums and their music recall the African drums whose music is used as the 'intensive language of transition and its communicant means, the catalyst and solvent of its regenerative hoard'.[4] The ceremony of the Souls on which the novel is based is a *vodum* religious ceremony practised in Haiti by 'peasants who have retained a racial, a historic, desire to worship their original gods'.[5] The Haitian peasants regard this ceremony as a solemn communication in the process of which they hear the secrets of the Dead at first hand. During the ceremony, the Dead return to offer, through the medium of the Priest, a full and honest report on their relation with the living. The African antecedent of the ceremony of the Souls is the Masquerade Cult (the Cult of the Ancestors) which manifests in concrete and imagistic terms the African rendezvous with the past.

In San Cristobal, the recently independent fictional West Indian island on which *Season of Adventure* is set, all signs of the past and the living links with aboriginal civilizations are denigrated by the small ruling middle-class élite, who perpetuate an educational system which displays a fear of any affirmation of ancestral heritage as a tool for shaping a revolutionary future. Members of this élite group are enthralled by foreign values and systems; they shy away from their African and slave pasts and the need to use these for creating a viable alternative to their inherited colonial power structure. The only survivors of their systematic deracination of the past in this island are the ceremony of the Souls and the steel drums. Fola, the middle-class mulatto heroine of the novel, is taken by Charlot, her European teacher of History to the *tonelle* (shrine) to witness a ceremony of the Souls. As Fola watches the women dance feverishly, she, in a moment of inspiration/possession, recognizes the ancestral link between her and the worshippers, between her West Indian island and Africa. She is shaken out of her middle-class entombment and becomes aware of the need to take the all important backward glance into her and her society's past in order to possess the future:

> The facts were unreal until she looked again at the faces of the women. They had lost control over their passions. The bodies seemed to stretch beyond this moment of dance. Perhaps the gods were there waiting for the dance to prove their presence in the *tonelle*. The child's eyes revealed some terrible future.... The dance was a kind of prophecy. Fola knew that something was about to happen, something her imagination could not tell. (*SOA*, p. 29)

That 'something' turns out to be her obsessional pre-occupation with the quest for self-comprehension/discovery – a season of adventure. She joins the other characters in the search for 'who work on who to give you life.... Which man you may call father however it happen, which woman you can call mother whatever her past position' (*SOA*, p. 147): an obsession with the need to have 'a sense of one's past, the need to know what happened' (*SOA*, p. 128). *Season of Adventure* is, ultimately, about the 'fearful encounter' with the forgotten and neglected self/Africa in the West Indies. The Forest Reserve Boys find that with the aid of the steel drums and their music, they are able to stir awake dormant memories and reach out to their ancestral origins because they have not been blinded to the past by the hoax of success as has happened with the ruling/ruining élite. Through Fola's search for her father whose identity her middle-class mother has kept a secret, Lamming conveys the re-creative possibility in her and her society's search for a link with their past and ancestry as a counter to the lies about Africa that are peddled by Europe:

> She was alive to the change which was taking shape within her; alive to the passion which would let her give new meanings to her past; alive to the power which ordered her to choose some future for herself. (*SOA*, p. 247)

Even in the case of the members of San Cristobal's middle-class who refuse to acknowledge the potency of the past, the past continually haunts them in the guise of the suppressed figure of Fola's father, and concretizes itself in the mysterious death of Raymond (the Chief of Police through whom the government suppresses ancestral activities) who is thought to have been murdered by Fola's mysterious father. Even when it is later known that Powell, one of the Forest Reserve Boys, is the assassin, he still emerges as the vehicle through which the past manifests itself. Similarly, the Forest Reserve, with its peculiar steel drum music and its *tonelle*, operates as the point of entry for the African heritage in this fictional West Indian island.

The events that follow in the wake of the murder of Raymond demonstrate the vitality and virility of the African past in San Cristobal and, by implication, the New World. By banning and desecrating the steel drum and harassing the priests of the *tonelle*, the government had hoped to sever all communion between the island's peasants and their African past and forestall their use of such a communion as a unifying factor among them. When the shock of the government's blasphemy wears off, however, it triggers off the anger of the inhabitants of the Forest Reserve. They eventually convert this anger into a revolutionary fervour and embark on a defiant and triumphant mass revolt/parade which culminates in the collapse of the repressive government and ushers in the alternative and progressive government of Dr Kofi James-Williams Baako.

The new direction taken by the island finds expression in the multiple culture signalled by the range of tunes played by the Forest Reserve Boys on their triumphant parade, by Fola's now-manifest father, and by the montage of the new leader's names – a montage that parallels the island's cultural and historical evolution: Kofi for the new awareness of Africa, James-Williams for the Anglo-American connections, and Baako for the island's subterranean African heritage. This new and historically logical social and political awareness is one that has always been articulated by the syncretic nature of the religion of the *tonelle* where Erzulie, an African goddess, harmoniously co-exists with the Christian Virgin Mary, and the saints live in an easy alliance with the gods of *tonelle*. The examples of the Forest Reserve Boys, of Fola, and of the multi-dimensional nature of the African-influenced religion of the *tonelle* are indications that the backward glance by the West Indies/the New World need not result in a one-culture nationalism.

While Lamming's Africa in *Season of Adventure* is an implied and subterranean phenomenon, Denis Williams' *Other Leopards*[6] focuses on actual Africa with specific emphasis on the problem of independence within the colonial political units created by the colonial masters of Africa. Denis Williams spent the decade of 1957–67 divided equally between teaching art history in East Africa and West Africa, and the Johkara of this novel bears some resemblance to the Democratic Republic of the Sudan whose Napatan and Meroitic sites he had visited and studied while in East Africa. The religious tensions in this fictional African state also recall the Christian/Muslim dichotomy to be found in many African states.

Lionel Lobo Froad, the Afro-West Indian protagonist of *Other Leopards* is as schizophrenic ('a man plagued by ... two names ...: Lionel, the who I was, dealing with Lobo, the who I continually felt I ought to become.') as the African setting in which he is situated ('Not quite sub-Sahara, but then not quite desert; not Equatorial black, not Mediterranean white. Mulatto' (*OL*, pl 19)). His attempts to comprehend his environment may thus be seen as an externalization of his efforts at reconciling the competing aspects of his cultural dualism. In an attempt to establish his Africanness and the contributions of his African ancestors to civilization, Froad, with the promptings of Hughie, his white boss, literally descends into the past, into the relics that are the only surviving physical evidence of his and his people's evolution from time past into time present and time future; like Fola, he becomes possessed by this past.

As Froad rummages among the ruins of the pyramids, a whole construct of history emerges to conjure up the grandeur and secrets of the ancient city of Meroë. Froad's prying among the ruins affirms the need for the crucial confrontation with the anonymous rubble of a past that forms the index of his and his people's history. The picture that emerges is, however, neither anonymous nor is it static; the ruins are activated and endowed with their past and present lives so as to suggest Africa's historical progression from the pre-colonial era through colonialism to an independent state that is replete with colonial trappings. Williams' description of siesta time in Kutam, the capital of Johkara, demonstrates this quality of his art:

> Siesta. The whole country flat on its back. The streets lay like dead zebras ... High up, astride his camel, General Craig inspected the distances outside the palace gates from the depths of an imperial shadow; gazed back into the gory old days....
>
> Past the Post Office, Pugin-style Gothic. Victorian Gothic, Victorian Regency, New Brutalism: Kutam ... There were the pavements dotted with rust-coloured rags inside which people slept. There were the usual grease-spots of semi-nude mechanics, performing a languorous and approximate engineering on the guts of ancient soule lorries and decrepit taxicabs. These assaulted the donkey-men with indolent superiority. They were superior: they walked with the century. (*OL*, p. 83)

The all-pervading ineptitude and poverty in Africa, the numerous reminders of her past colonial subjugation (the domineering and camel-riding bronze statue of General Craig), the 'New Brutalism' of imported values (lorries) over traditional ones (donkeys) and the overall sub-standard state of the society come alive in the above slice of Kutam.

Perhaps by far the most revealing relic is the statue of Queen Amanishakete. When Froad confronts this vessel of his ancestry, he finds in her beauty and brutality evidence of the paradoxes of power and the African past he seeks to repossess; his romantic picture of pre-colonial Africa as a haven of love and care is shattered by the emptiness and the 'spreading hate and love' that emanate from it. The queen comes across as an older version of the modern-day African leaders who conceive of themselves in grand images but are impotent in finding solutions to the problems of the continent.

Williams' portrayal of Johkara also highlights the extent to which the arbitrary political units created in Africa are mere collections of strange bedfellows whose historical animosities are manifested in their contemporary relationships. For as long as these units were ruled by foreign powers, ethnic and other forms of internal rivalries remained subdued. But with independence and the transfer of power to the indigenous population, a new attitude to power often emerges, with various interest groups, often based on ethno-religious lines, struggling for political supremacy. In independent Johkara, the political contest is between the Arab–Islamic North (the base of the ruling élite) and the Negroid-mainly Christian South. These internal divisions within Johkara and the problem of the Arab and Black African faces of Africa are vividly re-enacted during the visit of the black Prime Minister of Noba to the Arab-ruled Johkara. The prime minister's speech about African unity is mere rhetoric and the 'uninterrupted mechanical unity' of the cheering crowd merely serves to bring the 'Arab and Africans once more face to face' (OL, p. 21) without any genuine wish for friendship, especially as the first meeting had culminated in the trans-Saharan slave trade. In addition to the split of the country between the Crescent and the Cross, Johkara also has to contend with other influences from America, Europe and the Far East.

In a Johkara that is racially, religiously and ideologically fragmented into antagonistic factions, demands are made upon Froad by the major interest groups. Hassan and Mohammed, advocates of pan Arab–Islamism and scorners of pan-Africanism, see Froad as the ideal propaganda tool for persuading the southerners to accept assimilation into the Arab–Islamic mainstream culture, since he belongs to a minority black group that has become absorbed into the mainstream culture of the West. On the other hand, the chief, a Christian missionary and a fellow Afro-Guyanese who has spent thirty years preaching the gospel in Africa, calls upon him as a Christian 'negro' to cast his lot with the Christian South and help in liberating its people from the clutches of the Arab–Islamic North. The chief argues that the only way forward for the southerners and humanity is the acceptance of Christianity.

Froad sees through the utilitarian and narrow-minded interpretations of history by both camps. Eventually, he agrees to propagate Mohammed's philosophy of the 'inevitability of environment' and the need for the minority to fizzle into the mainstream culture. But his decision is dictated by a selfish motive: he needs the money that Mohammed is going to pay him for writing the propaganda article on the eve of a national election. Froad calls the article 'A Eunuch in the Desert' and argues that the African is impotent to fashion his own future, and thus the sudanic African must break with his futile tradition and embrace the Arab–Islamic framework in the same way that the New World African has broken away from Africa and created a new and better life for himself within the context of Euro-America. The irony of this argument is obvious: if the New World African has dissociated himself from Africa, what is Lobo doing in Africa trying to dislodge Lionel? Froad is the real eunuch: 'a bastard's indifferent to father and mother, both; possesses the naked instant, bare of past and future' (*OL*, p. 99).

On the national level, the crisis of confidence and the enthno-religious conflicts culminate in a nation-wide strike of the scavengers, most of whom are from the South. With the excuse of trying to restore law and order, the military stages a *coup d'état*. But, on the evidence of Hassan, one of the leaders of the *coup* – and as it has become evident in actual experiences in Africa – the military is there to perpetuate the same mistakes of past regimes, especially in the drive to impose Arab–Islamism on the South: 'Now the military were in power they meant to deal very sternly ... with matters affecting Islamic tradition in Johkara: the African threat had to be faced' (*OL*, p. 202).

Out of the ruins of Froad's dream of Africa, following his confrontations with the tensions and paradoxes of his ancestry, he emerges as a universal man creating a luminous presence from the shadows and relics of the past and says, with confidence, 'I'd tell you who I am since now I know. I am a man hunting and running; neither infra nor supra' (*OL*, p. 221). At the end of the road, towards 'the nameless yearning for origins that besets most of us' (OL, p. 91), Froad discovers that at the heart of the African mirage, there is no water; and he is thrown back into his 'instants which had no contour, to the void of my perennial present' (OL, p. 155).

For both Fola and Froad, the backward glance culminates in self-discovery and self-awareness and, taken together, their experiences of Africa reveal three basic and inter-related ways of seeing Africa and the African in the West Indies. The West Indian may relate to Africa and the African as (a) an ancestor figure, (b) an *alter-ego* and (c) a compatriot in man's struggle within time and space. In *Season of Adventure*, ancestral Africa manifests itself and emerges as the informing factor in the radical re-awakening of Fola but the statements which this leads to are of contemporary relevance to both the West Indies and Africa. Similarly, Froad in *Other Leopards* confronts ancestral Africa through the ruins of the pyramids and the eloquent statue of Queen Amanishakete, and his African *alter-ego* and compatriot through the citizens of Johkara, especially Mojo Kua ('the true original thing, pure African ... never been sold, never been a slave ... got a name ... and a tribe' (OL, p. 74)) who challenges Froad to define himself. It is this challenge that prompts Froad to embark on the task of appraising his Africanness or non-Africanness.

Both Lamming and Williams, by investing their treatment of the African past with contemporary relevance, show that they are aware of the dangers inherent in treating the past and whatever gestures emanate from it as a flashpoint for escapist indulgence. Both novelists are also agreed on the fact that, for the sensitive and willing New World African, the backward glance, though a traumatic venture, need not result in a pillar of salt but in self-discovery and self-awareness.

NOTES

1. George Lamming, *Season of Adventure*, London, Allison and Busby Ltd, 1979. First published by Michael Joseph, London, 1960. Both editions carry the same pagination. In further extracts, SOA – *Season of Adventure*.
2. See George Lamming, *The Pleasures of Exile*, London, Michael Joseph, 1960; Alison and Busby Ltd, 1984, p. 225 for an account of the debate.

3. George Lamming, 'Caribbean Literature: The Black Rock of Africa', in *African Forum*, Vol. 1, No. 4, p. 32.
4. Wole Soyinka, *Myth, Literature and the African World*, London, Cambridge University Press, 1974, p. 36.
5. George Lamming, *The Pleasures of Exile*, op. cit., p. 9.
6. Denis Williams, *Other Leopards*, London, Hutchinson New Authors, 1963. Heinemann, Caribbean Writers Series, 1983. In further extracts, OL – *Other Leopards*.

Charles Dickens and the Zulus

Bernth Lindfors

In March 1853, A. T. Caldecott, a prominent merchant of Pietermaritzburg, accompanied by his son C. H. Caldecott, arrived in London with a troupe of thirteen Zulus – eleven men, one woman and a child – who were to be presented in a theatrical exhibition so 'that the English public should be gratified with a sight of the interesting savages, by whom he was surrounded in the fertile and flourishing colony of Natal'.[1]

The Zulus became one of the most popular shows in London during the summer of that year. Caldecott, a canny businessman, had spared no expense in mounting the exhibition. He had rented St George's Gallery (formerly known as the Chinese Museum) at Hyde Park Corner for the performances and had hired Charles Marshall, one of the most highly regarded painters and set designers of his day, to paint authentic scenery which could be changed mechanically to suit the time, place and action depicted – a rather recent innovation in stage technology.[2] Two months were spent preparing the troupe for the first performance on the evening of 16 May, and daily advertisements were placed in leading papers and journals throughout the exhibition's three-month run in London.

These efforts paid off handsomely. When the show opened, performances were given every evening at eight o'clock and Wednesday and Friday afternoons at three o'clock. By 1 June, a third matinee had been added, and three weeks later there were afternoon and evening performances daily. To provide background information on the Zulus and Natal, Caldecott's son wrote a thirty-two page pamphlet entitled *Descriptive History of the Zulu Kafirs, Their Customs and Their Country, with Illustrations*, which was sold for sixpence during performances at the Gallery. But even this was not enough to satisfy London's appetite for so unusual an attraction. On 25 July, The Times carried an announcement by Caldecott that

> In consequence of the increasing interest excited by this extraordinary and pleasing EXHIBITION, arrangements have been made to meet the public wishes, by which visitors will be allowed to see and converse with this interesting tribe daily from 11 to 1 o'clock, during the remaining period of their performance in London.[3]

Before the troupe left in mid August to tour France, Germany and possibly some of the English provinces, a second pamphlet on them had been published which reprinted several enthusiastic reviews of their performances and provided more information on the sanguinary history of the Zulus under 'warlike and ambitious' Essenzingercona (Senzangakhona), 'terrible' and 'despotic' Chaka, 'cruel and treacherous' Dingarn (Dingaan), and 'their present king, Panda, [who] is to a considerable extent imbued with civilization, [having] got the good sense to prefer trading to fighting'.[4]

What helped to make the Zulu exhibition more popular than other ethnographic displays was the fact that it was an extremely dramatic performance, not a static sideshow. The performers acted out incidents said to be typical of Zulu life and did so with great fervour. The advertisement placed in The Times on the day the show opened stated that the exhibition would illustrate 'in an extensive and unexampled manner this wild and interesting tribe of savages in their domestic habits, their nuptial ceremonies, the charm song, finding the witch, hunting tramp, preparation for war, and territorial conflicts'.[5] To explain some of the scenes, Caldecott's son served as interpreter and master of ceremonies, lecturing briefly on Zulu customs and traditions before they were enacted on the stage.

The earliest review of the 'Caffres at Hyde-Park-Corner' (as they came to be called), appeared in The Times two days after the première. It is worth quoting in full because it is typical of the response of British theatre critics to this novel entertainment:

> Although there have been several attempts to render Caffre life familiar to the English public through the medium of exhibitions, nothing in this way has been done so completely or on so large a scale as the new exhibition opened on Monday evening in the rooms formerly occupied by the Chinese museum. Eleven Zulu men, with a woman and a child, are assembled into a company, and instead of performing one or two commonplace feats, may be said to go through the whole drama of Caffre life, while a series of scenes, painted by Mr Charles Marshall, gives an air of

reality to the living pictures. Now the Caffres are at their meal, feeding themselves with enormous spoons, and expressing their satisfaction by a wild chant, under the inspiration of which they bump themselves along without rising in a sort of circular dance. Now the witchfinder commences his operations to discover the culprit whose magic has brought sickness into the tribe, and becomes perfectly rabid through the effect of his own incantations. Now there is a wedding ceremony, now a hunt, now a military expedition, all with characteristic dances; and the whole ends with a general conflict between rival tribes. The songs and dances are, as may be expected, monotonous in the extreme, and without the bill it would be difficult to distinguish the expression of love from the gesture of martial defiance. Nevertheless, as a picture of manners, nothing can be more complete; and not the least remarkable part of the exhibition is the perfect training of the wild artists. They seem utterly to lose all sense of their present position, and, inspired by the situations in which they are placed, appear to take Mr Marshall's scenes for their actual abode in the vicinity of Port Natal. If 11 English actors could be found so completely to lose themselves in the characters they assumed, histrionic art would be in a state truly magnificent.[6]

Other reviewers singled out many of the same features of the exhibition for comment – the excellent scenery, the impressive physical appearance of the Zulus, the spirited and uninhibited acting. A columnist in *The Athenaeum*, after noting how the physiognomy of the Zulus differed from that of West African Negroes, went on to say,

Most of the men have a fine muscular developement [sic], and they exhibit considerable strength in some of their exhibitions on the stage. One thing is very striking in those performances, – that is, the almost perfect dramatic effect with which these wild men play their parts.[7]

The reviewer for *The Spectator* was equally impressed with the 'considerable dramatic propriety' of the performances but found several of the scenes highly amusing:

The Zulus – fine well-formed men, of fleshy frames but attenuated legs – get up the quarrel, and discuss the chances of war, with a great appearance of being in earnest about it all. In this point, and in its lifelike character, to which the accessories contribute, the exhibition transcends all others we have witnessed of the kind. The charm-song and the proceedings of the witchfinder or 'smeller out' were especially expressive and forcible in their pantomime. As for the noises – the howls, yells, hoots, and whoops, the snuffling, wheezing, bubbling, grovelling, and stamping – they form a concert to whose savagery we cannot attempt to do justice.[8]

The Illustrated Weekly News initially described the exhibition as a 'picturesque drama [consisting of] a series of scenes which charm by their spirit and *vraisemblance*' and often excite laughter by depicting incidents 'more amusing than anything in a farce',[9] but in its next issue printed a sketch of one of the scenes in the show, gave brief biographical details of several of the performers, and elaborated on what it had found particularly entertaining:

> After a supper of meal, of which the Kaffirs partake with their large wooden spoons, an extraordinary song and dance are performed, in which each performer moves about on his haunches, grunting and snorting the while like a pair of asthmatic bellows ... but no description can give an idea of the cries and shouts – now comic, now terrible – by which the Kaffirs express their emotions. The scene illustrative of the preliminaries of marriage and the bridal festivities might leave one in doubt which was the bridegroom, did not that interesting savage announce his enviable situation by screams of ecstacy which convulse the audience.
>
> The Zulus must be naturally good actors; for a performance more natural and less like acting is seldom if ever seen upon any stage.[10]

The 'Zulu Kafir Exhibition' was obviously good theatre and deserved to become a smash hit.

On 26 May, after the show had been on for a week and a half and the first rave reviews had appeared, Charles Dickens went to see it, inviting his friend John Leech to accompany him.[11] Dickens may have been in need of relaxation for he was terribly overworked at the time. Not only was he writing the final chapters of *Bleak House* in monthly instalments and the middle chapters of *A Child's History of England*, but in addition he was quite busy editing *Household Words*, a popular weekly journal he had launched in 1850. As might be expected in such circumstances, the Zulu turned out to be more than mere transitory entertainment for him; they became grist for his prolific mill. Shortly after witnessing their performance, he wrote a humorous essay entitled 'The Noble Savage' which appeared in the 11 June issue of *Household Words*. Though he made reference to such peoples as the 'Ojibbeway' Indians and the Bushmen who had been on display in London earlier, he focused his attention primarily on Caldecott's Zulus, using them as hilarious examples of the ignobility of uncivilized man. The essay has been called 'one of the most effective philippics of our language',[12] and there can be no doubt that Dickens, with his incomparable flair for comic exaggeration, achieved his aim of debunking the Romantic myth of the 'noble savage', but today this piece of Dickens' writing is seldom commented on by scholars or teachers of Victorian literature, possibly because the views expressed in it are embarrassing and offensive to a contemporary sensibility.

Here is how the onslaught begins:

> To come to the point at once, I beg to say that I have not the least belief in the Noble Savage. I consider him a prodigious nuisance, and an enormous superstition. His calling rum fire-water, and me a pale face, wholly fail to reconcile me to him. I don't care what he calls me. I call him a savage, and I call a savage a something highly desirable to be civilised off the face of the earth. I think a mere gent (which I take to be the lowest form of civilisation) better than a howling, whistling, clucking, stamping, jumping, tearing savage. It is all one to me, whether he sticks a fishbone through his visage, or bits of trees through the lobes of his ears, or birds' feathers in his head; whether he flattens his hair between two boards, or spreads his nose over the breadth of his face, or drags his lower lip down by great weights, or blackens his teeth, or knocks them out, or paints one cheek red and another blue, or tattoos himself, or oils himself, or rubs his body with fat, or crimps it with knives. Yielding to whichsoever of these agreeable eccentricities, he is a savage – cruel, false, thievish, murderous; addicted more or less to grease, entrails, and beastly customs; a wild animal with the questionable gift of boasting; a conceited, tiresome, bloodthirsty, monotonous humbug.[13]

From here Dickens goes on to grumble about the way some people whimper over the savage 'with maudlin admiration' and pretend that 'the tenor of his swinish life' is preferable to 'the blemishes of civilisation'. He cites the 'miserable jigs' of the Ojibways and the 'horrid' pantomimes of the Bushmen as evidence of the degenerate nature of such peoples, and then reinforces his argument by taking a long look at the Zulus.

> There is at present a party of Zulu Kaffirs exhibiting at the St George's Gallery, Hyde Park Corner, London. These noble savages are represented in a most agreeable manner; they are seen in an elegant theatre, fitted with appropriate scenery of great beauty, and they are described in a very sensible and unpretending lecture, delivered with a modesty which is quite a pattern to all similar exponents. Though extremely ugly, they are much better shaped than such of their predecessors as I have referred to; and they are rather picturesque to the eye, though far from odoriferous to the nose. What a visitor left to his own interpretings and imaginings might suppose these noblemen to be about, when they give vent to that pantomimic expression which is quite settled to be the natural gift of the noble savage, I cannot possibly conceive; for it is so much too luminous for my personal civilisation that it conveys no idea to my mind beyond a general stamping, ramping, and raving, remarkable (as everything in savage life is) for its dire uniformity. But let us – with the interpreter's

assistance, of which I for one stand so much in need – see what the noble savage does in Zulu Kaffirland.

It is apparent that Dickens relied heavily on the ethnographic information supplied in young Caldecott's lecture, but he supplemented what he heard with his own observations of the Zulus in action. It is interesting to compare the descriptions of Zulu life and customs in Caldecott's later pamphlet (which presumably grew out of his lecture) with Dickens' version of how these wild creatures conducted their affairs. The accounts were often quite similar, though Dickens had a tendency to stress graphic details and toss in amusing asides to his readers.

For instance, young Caldecott, after describing the land, racial background and material culture of the Zulus, devoted one entire chapter of his booklet to Zulu 'Laws and Government' and another to 'Zulu Characteristics'. Since he based his remarks on Nathaniel Isaacs' *Travels and Adventures in Eastern Africa, Descriptive of the Zoolus, Their Manners, Customs, with a Sketch of Natal* (1836), it is perhaps best to begin with Isaacs' account and to observe how this was transmuted via Caldecott into vintage Dickens. Isaacs regarded the Zulus as 'the most extraordinary people in existence' and 'zoolacratical government' as

> the most incomprehensible government with which any known nation on the face of the earth is conversant ... Its outline, however, may be said to be perfectly simple – namely, despotic.... It is monarchical, it is true; but apparently neither hereditary nor elective, the succession depending on the murder of the existing monarch, which usually takes place when he begins to exhibit either of those two signs of age – wrinkles or grey hairs. In this case, the criminal who performs the bloody deed, or directs its execution, is perhaps a son or some other member of the royal family. When the throne has become vacant by the sacrifice of the monarch, it usually happens that civil disputes settle the succession.... When the monarch is firmly seated on his throne – which is seldom or never accomplished without, as it were, wading through blood to it – he becomes an absolute king, or 'inquose'. His name then becomes sacred, and adoration is paid to it.... The power of the monarch is indeed not only despotic, but even atrocious; for he can command indiscriminate massacres by his nod.... (His warriors) are a morose, sullen, savage set of monsters, fit only for deeds of darkness and for the devastations of war; and these are their sole occupations.[14]

As for religion, Isaacs says simply, '(The Zulus) have none' and 'are unquestionably the most superstitious creatures on the face of the earth'.[15]

Dickens and the Zulus 133

That young Caldecott followed Isaacs very closely, at times even slavishly, can be seen quite plainly in his description of Zulu government as most nearly resembling 'a perfect despotism':

> The king is absolute; there is no liberty of the subject; a nod from the monarch consigns any one to death, no matter whether guilty or innocent. At the command of his ruler a father must murder his own unoffending child, brother must slay brother, or a husband destroy his wife. Appeal is death to the appealer. It is a monarchical government, but apparently neither hereditary nor elective. The succession depends on the murder of the existing sovereign, which usually takes place when he begins to exhibit the signs of age. The criminal who performs the deed, or directs it, is usually the son, or some other member of the royal family. When the throne has become vacant by the sacrifice of the monarch, a dispute and some additional murders settle the succession.... When the king becomes firmly seated on the throne, he is called an 'Inkosa'. His name then becomes sacred, and adoration is paid to it. (DH, p. 19)

In his chapter on 'Zulu Characteristics' young Caldecott also asserted that:

> In his present savage state (the Zulu) has very little idea of morality and none whatever of religion. Behind his agreeable outward bearing, he conceals the most vindictive feelings, and a capacity for perpetrating the most atrocious cruelty. Impulsive, emotional, and excitable even to frenzy, he makes no effort to control his impulses, nor at any time reasons upon the abstract justice of his deeds. (DH, pp. 21–2)

Dickens compressed all this information into a brief paragraph which conveyed the essence of what he had learned from Caldecott about Zulu law, government and character:

> The noble savage sets a king to reign over him, to whom he submits his life and limbs without a murmur or question, and whose whole life is passed chin deep in a lake of blood; but who, after killing incessantly, is in his turn killed by his relations and friends, the moment a gray hair appears on his head. All the noble savage's wars with his fellow-savages (and he takes no pleasure in anything else) are wars of extermination – which is the best thing I know of him, and the most comfortable to my mind when I look at him. He has no moral feelings of any kind, sort, or description; and his 'mission' may be summed up as simply diabolical.

Dickens then went on to poke fun at the way in which Zulu marriages were contracted. Here his description seems to be based as much on the performance he saw as on the lecture he heard. Young Caldecott's written account also appears to owe a great deal to personal observation, though portions of it were taken directly from his two primary sources, Isaacs' *Travels* and Captain Allen F. Gardiner's *Narrative of a Journey to the Zoolu Country in South Africa* (1836). Here is how Caldecott introduces the subject of marriage:

> A Zulu marriage festival is a very noisy and animated affair. Preliminary matters having been gone through, the bridegroom, in company with his friends, seats himself, and waits the arrival of the bride, who comes escorted by the people of her tribe. She is tastefully attired; her hair being decorated with feathers, in imitation of a coronet, and her skin well oiled and polished for the occasion. Rows of beads in varied colours are suspended round her neck, and she brings many strings of beads with her. The overture is as often made by the women as the men. The bride's father usually sends a cow with her as a present. When she arrives in the presence of her future husband, she and her attendants perform a dance, accompanied with as large an amount of noise as they can conveniently get up for the occasion. It is the aim of the lady, on this occasion, to appear as agile as possible in the presence of the bridegroom's friends, and that which she may lack in grace she compensates for in expertness. The ballet being finished, and all present being satisfied with the lady's performance, her friends proceed to settle the important business of how much she is worth. They value her at six cows. Her lover offers three: the offer is rejected. Very much clattering and haranguing takes place, but at length the bargain is struck at the price originally demanded; and the bridegroom is made a happy man by the gain of a wife and the loss of his six cows. (*DH*, p. 25)

Dickens turns this 'very noisy and animated affair' into a raucous unmusical comedy in which the bridal barter and 'ballet' are pictured as uninhibited haggling punctuated by ear-splitting ejaculations and frenzied foot-stomping.

> If he wants a wife he appears before the kennel of the gentleman whom he has selected for his father-in-law, attended by a party of male friends of a very strong flavour, who screech and whistle and stamp an offer of so many cows for the young lady's hand. The chosen father-in-law – also supported by high-flavoured party of male friends – screeches, whistles, and yells (being seated on the ground, he can't stamp) that there never was such a daughter in the market as his daughter, and that he must have six more cows. The son-in-law and his select circle of backers, screech, whistle, stamp, and yell in reply, that they will give three more cows. The father-in-law (an old deluder, overpaid at the beginning) accepts four, and rises to bind the bargain. The whole party, the young lady included, then falling into epileptic convulsions, and screeching, whistling, stamping, and yelling together – and nobody taking any notice of the young lady

(whose charms are not to be thought of without a shudder) – the noble savage is considered married, and his friends make demoniacal leaps at him by way of congratulation.

Dickens gets even more dramatic when describing Zulu witchcraft, a subject calculated to amuse a Victorian public sceptical of the efficacy of any form of non-European divination. Young Caldecott, who shared this prejudice with his London audience, may have helped to shape Dickens' negative attitude towards Zulu sorcery, but it is apparent that the spirited enactment of a witch hunt by Caldecott's troupe made a very powerful impression on him, one which he tried to replicate for others in onomatopoeic prose. Before looking at Dickens' account, however, let us see how young Caldecott presented this custom, which he frankly regarded as 'singularly absurd':

> The Zulus believe illness to be always the result of witchcraft. When any of their tribe are taken ill, the services of the *Inyanger* or witch-finder are called into requisition, to *nooker* or smell out the *Umtugartie* or witch, who has caused the illness of the invalid. They abhor the tiger-cat, or *Imparker*, as they call it, and believe it to be as necessary a companion to the witch of the Zulu, as a black cat is thought by some people, to be indispensable to the witches of more civilized nations. The witch-finder, or *Inyanger*, makes his appearance, attired very demoniacally in shaggy strips of fur; all the people seat themselves before him. He dances in their presence, flinging himself about in the wildest manner imaginable; then smells the ground, and eventually pouncing upon one of the party present, declares him to be the person who has bewitched the sick man. The *Inyanger's* assertion is unhesitatingly believed, and the denounced individual is at once hustled away by his neighbours, and beaten to death with their knob-kerrees. It is almost needless to add that these *Inyangers* are the vilest imposters. (*DH*, pp. 27–8)

Dickens substitutes a grizzly bear for the leopard (or 'tiger-cat' as it was called in South Africa then) and spells phonetically all the Zulu words introduced by young Caldecott, but otherwise his account is fairly faithful to the substance and tone of his source. It differs mainly in its dramatic immediacy and hilarious sound effects.

> When the noble savage finds himself a little unwell, and mentions the circumstance to his friends, it is immediately perceived that he is under the influence of witchcraft. A learned personage, called an Inyanger or Witch Doctor, is immediately sent for to Nooker the Umtargartie, or smell out the witch. The male inhabitants of the kraal being seated on the ground, the learned doctor, got up like a grizzly bear, appears, and

administers a dance of a most terrific nature, during the exhibition of which remedy he incessantly gnashes his teeth, and howls: 'I am the original physician to Nooker the Umtargartie. Yow yow yow! No connexion with any other establishment. Till till till! All other Umtargarties are feigned Umtargarties, Boroo Boroo! but I perceive here a genuine and real Umtargartie, Hoosh Hoosh Hoosh! in whose blood I, the original Inyanger and Nookerer, Blizzerum Boo! will wash these bear's claws of mine. O yow yow yow!' All this time the learned physician is looking out among the attentive faces for some unfortunate man who owes him a cow, or who has given him any small offence, or against whom, without offence, he has conceived a spite. Him he never fails to Nooker as the Umtargartie, and he is instantly killed. In the absence of such an individual, the usual practice is to Nooker the quietest and most gentlemanly person in company. But the nookering is invariably followed on the spot by the butchering.

Dickens' next subject was the Zulu 'Praiser' whom young Caldecott described as a 'Poet-laureate' and a

> most uncouth-looking individual, dressed in the skin of a leopard, or a tiger-cat, the head of the animal forming his own head for the nonce, and his occupation being to utter, through the leopard's mouth, and in very deep-toned words, the attributes and excellencies of his super-excellent monarch. The more he disregards the laws of punctuation in performing his duty, the better he acquits himself. We subjoin a portion of his eulogy, printing the epithets as they are spoken, without any intervening pauses – 'Thou who are as high as the mountains thou noble elephant thou black one thou who art as high as the heavens thou who art the bird who eats other birds thou who art the great cow and the peace maker!' &c. &c. &c. (*DH*, p. 27)

Dickens anglicizes the praise-song and throws in a few more animals unknown in the African sub-continent but again captures the vigour and spectacle of the Zulu performance at Hyde Park Corner.

> There suddenly rushes in a poet, retained for the purpose, called a Praiser. This literary gentleman wears a leopard's head over his own, and a dress of tigers' tails; he has the appearance of having come express on his hind legs from the Zoological Gardens; and he incontinently strikes up the chief's praises, plunging and tearing all the while. There is a frantic wickedness in this brute's manner of worrying the air, and gnashing out 'O what a delightful chief he is! O what a delicious quantity of blood he sheds! O how majestically he laps it up! O how charmingly cruel he is! O how he tears the flesh of his enemies and crunches the bones! O how like the tiger and the leopard and the wolf and the bear he is! O, row row row row, how fond I am of him!' – which might tempt the Society of Friends to charge at a hand-gallop into the Swartz-Kop location and exterminate the whole kraal.

The last example Dickens gives of the culture of this uncultured people is their colourful preparation for battle. A war song had been performed as part of the show at St George's Gallery, and Dickens, as usual, based his description of the custom on both what he had seen and what he had heard from young Caldecott, whose booklet put it this way:

> War is the principal business of a Zulu Kafir. Before going to battle the king calls a council of his chief men. He appears among them arrayed in a mantle of tigers' tails, and with an attendant behind him holding a shield above his head. The particulars of the projected campaign are detailed, and one warrior after another steps forward to give his advice. Though in the presence of his monarch, he does not speak coolly, nor conduct himself with modesty, but utters his opinions with a howl, emphasizes them with a jump, and bangs his shield with his assegai to enforce their justness, and the strength of his own convictions. When, at length, the place of action is determined upon, the warriors rush off at once to where the conflict is to take place, singing with savage glee their war song on the way. (DH, pp. 28-9)

Now here is Dickens expanding on the subject:

> When war is afoot among the noble savages — which is always — the chief holds a council to ascertain whether it is the opinion of his brothers and friends in general that the enemy shall be exterminated. On this occasion, after the performance of an Umsebeuza, or war song — which is exactly like all the other songs — the chief makes a speech to his brothers and friends, arranged in single file. No particular order is observed during the delivery of this address, but every gentleman who finds himself excited by the subject, instead of crying 'Hear, Hear!' as is the custom with us, darts from the rank and tramples out the life, or crushes the skull, or mashes the face, or scoops out the eyes, or breaks the limbs, or performs a whirlwind of atrocities on the body, of an imaginary enemy. Several gentlemen becoming thus excited at once, and pounding away without the least regard to the orator, that illustrious person is rather in the position of an orator in an Irish House of Commons. But, several of these scenes of savage life bear a strong generic resemblance to an Irish election, and I think would be extremely well received and understood at Cork.

Dickens followed this up with a paragraph playfully suggesting other parallels between the ceremonies of the noble savage and the practices of civilized man in Europe, but he returned to his main theme in his concluding statement:

> My position is, that if we have anything to learn from the Noble Savage, it is what to avoid. His virtues are a fable; his happiness is a delusion; his

nobility, nonsense ... and the world will be all the better when his place knows him no more.

Although it sometimes appears so in this essay, Dickens was not really recommending genocide. He was very much the Victorian pragmatist striving to puncture an inflated Romantic conception of the dignity of 'primitive' peoples. The Zulu were simply a convenient case in point, a group so far removed from Europe in custom and culture that they could easily be held up as examples of an underdeveloped race obviously in need of moral improvement and mental refinement. Dickens did not suggest that such peoples be exterminated; rather, he wanted them 'civilised off the face of the earth'. He believed in cultural, not literal, genocide.

Yet it is interesting to note with what contempt Zulu customs, traditions, and institutions were viewed by the London audiences who saw this troupe perform. The performers obviously overstepped the boundaries of Victorian decorum when they sang and danced, but their antics presumably would not have provoked so much hilarity among spectators with cultural traditions more closely akin to those of the performers themselves. Underlying the reaction of Dickens and other English viewers was a broad streak of undisguised racism, a belief that the Zulu were morally and mentally inferior to Europeans. The numerous comments on their smell, their bizarre modes of dress (and undress), their noises, their monotonous songs, rabid incantations, and wild-demoniacal dances, betray an arrogant assumption that the Zulu were overgrown children of nature who had not yet developed the inhibitions, self-discipline and manners that distinguish more civilized folk. They were savages pure and simple, primitives in the raw.

Of course, one cannot really blame the Victorians for being so ethnocentric. Nineteenth-century Europe, with its numerous civil and international wars, was not exactly a showcase of ethnic tolerance, and inadequate opportunities for meaningful face-to-face cultural contact with representatives of the non-western world hindered Europeans from learning much about the human beings who inhabited the rest of the globe. There were no documentary films or television specials then to bring more accurate images of foreign peoples to the drawing rooms of London. The Zulus were therefore merely a spectacle, a carnival act consciously designed to play up their 'abnormalities' – i.e., their radical deviation from European norms of dress and behaviour. It would be ethnocentric of us to expect audiences who saw them more than 130 years ago to react

Dickens and the Zulus 139

with a more modern sensibility and to come away from such a performance with a richer understanding and appreciation of Zulu culture.[16]

Indeed, one wonders if this would be possible in Europe or America even today. There is strong evidence to suggest that it would not. If we examine public reactions to more recent black South African performances in London and New York – shows such as the jazz opera *King Kong* (1961), the musical adaptation of Macbeth, *Umabatha* (1972), and the long-running song-and-dance hit *Ipi-Tombi* (1975) – we hear remarkable echoes of those antiquated Victorian attitudes.[17] Moreover, if we immerse ourselves in contemporary popular culture, we find commercial films, network television and other mass media continuing to project images of Africa and Africans that deliberately emphasize the exotic at the expense of the ordinary. We are far more likely to see resurrections of Tarzan than revelations of Tanzania. So powerful an ethnocentric compulsion to discover savages at every bend of the river, to define the 'Dark Continent' as the benighted antithesis of the enlightened West, reveals that Dickens is not dead yet.

NOTES

1. C. H. Caldecott, *Descriptive History of the Zulu Kafirs, Their Customs and Their Country, with Illustrations*, London, John Mitchell, 1853, pp. 4–5. In further extracts, *DH* – *Descriptive History of the Zulu Kafirs*.
2. See the entry on Marshall in the *Dictionary of National Biography*, Vol. 36, London, Smith, Elder and Co., 1893, pp. 235–6.
3. *Times*, 25 July 1853, p. 1.
4. *Final Close of the St George's Gallery, Hyde Park Corner, Piccadilly. Zulu Kafirs. Last Few Days in London.* London, 1853. This pamphlet reprinted reviews from the *The Morning Chronicle*, 25 July 1853; *The Morning Post*, 15 June 1853; and *The Times*, 18 May 1853.
5. *The Times*, 16 May 1853, p. 4.
6. *The Times*, 18 May 1853, p. 8.
7. *The Athenaeum*, 28 May 1853, p. 650.
8. *The Spectator*, 21 May 1853, p. 485.
9. *The Illustrated London News*, 21 May 1853, p. 399.
10. *The Illustrated London News*, 28 May 1853, p. 409.
11. Letter to John Leech, 23 May 1853, in *The Letters of Charles Dickens*, ed. Walter Dexter. Vol. 2, Bloomsbury, Nonesuch Press, 1938, pp. 462–3.

12. W. Walter Crotch, *The Touchstone of Dickens*, London, Chapman and Hall, 1920, p. 85.
13. 'The Noble Savage,' in *Household Words*, 11 June 1853, pp. 337–9. All quotations are taken from this source. The essay later appeared in Dickens' *Reprinted Pieces and the Lazy Tour of Two Idle Apprentices*, London, Macmillan, 1925, pp. 197–202.
14. Nathaniel Isaacs, *Travels and Adventures in Eastern Africa, Descriptive of the Zoolus, Their Manners, Customs, with a Sketch of Natal*, London, Edward Churton, 1836; reprinted in one vol., Cape Town, Struik, 1970, pp. 294–6.
15. ibid., pp. 297–8.
16. It is interesting to compare the English reaction to the Zulus with the Zulu reaction to the English. See my *A Zulu View of Victorian London*, Pasadena, Munger Africana Library, 1979, for an account of the outside world given to a group of Zulu elders by one of these performers shortly after his return to Natal.
17. I discuss this in 'Indigenous Performance in Alien Communities', in *Individual and Community in Commonwealth Literature*, ed. Daniel Massa, Msida, Malta University Press, 1979, pp. 20–7.

Reviews

Wole Soyinka, *Aké: The Years of Childhood*, London, Rex Collings, 1981; New York, Random House, 1982, 230 pp.

To enter the world of *Aké: The Years of Childhood*, is to enter an enchanted world, Senghor's 'Kingdom of Childhood', sometimes charmingly re-created by the adult Soyinka in some of his best prose to date. One of the most charming features of the work is the image of the boy which comes across – a precocious, mischievous but clever boy who is only too ready to become physically aggressive in an expression of an as yet unreached manhood: a denial of his inevitable youthful weakness. Another element is the child's perspective from which people, things and events are seen and described. Soyinka is able to convey a child's sense of the magic and wonder of life – wonder at the incomprehensible world around him as in the early recapitulations (pp. 1–5), and the magic world of imagined demons and spirits, or 'creatures', which people the world of children. Most charming and amusing of all is the child's sense of himself which Soyinka the narrator, through his tongue-in-cheek prose, evokes admirably. This sense of self is very meaningful and serious for the child while it is only quixotic to adults. Hence the general indulgence of the boy, although this is partly due to his being male and a firstborn son. Going to school, being choosy of women when he hasn't even reached puberty, his concern with his 'wife', Mrs Odufuwa – all these incidents come across humorously from the child's perspective so acutely presented in the older Soyinka's mocking tone.

Such passages in the work are best when the older Soyinka's personal view does not intervene, as it does in the later Ogboni scenes. These later scenes sound like the view of the older Soyinka in

The Interpreters and recent works. Did Soyinka always hold a view of the Ogboni as cruel and awe-inspiring? Does he now carry into adulthood a childhood impression of these societal judicial executives? I think it is a sensational and typically western approach to underscore and reiterate only the awe-inspiring aspects of what are positive and real roles in Egba traditional administrative structures.

The child's sense of phenomena as disjointed, disparate and incomplete is well conveyed in such scenes as his father's inexplicable and frenetic taking of photographs; the little Soyinka's mystification over mythical words like 'Temperature' and 'Birthday'; or over concepts like 'Change'. Soyinka conveys well how loved adults appear mythical to children: for instance, Bishop Ajayi Crowther, his mother, ('Wild Christian'), his retiring father and of course Daodu, who was a real myth in his lifetime in Yoruba country. As he is depicted in Aké, Daodu reminds one of the Forest Father in *A Dance of the Forests*, in the way he strolls, ruminative and brooding, in the school compound, from time to time coming out with brief, wisdom-laden statements *telling the incapable and non-plussed women at their meeting what to do* (p. 178).

My initial reaction was a cry of 'Male chauvinism again!' But in an interview with Cousin Koye of the book, now Professor Ransome-Kuti (University of Lagos), he confirms that the Revd Ransome-Kuti was very involved with his wife's activities, read through many of her articles and saw to it that they were flown by special courier to London to appear in *The Daily Worker*. Despite the Revd Ransome-Kuti's supportiveness, however, it cannot be that the women at the meeting table in *Aké* were completely lost and unable to know what to do.

In fact, histories of the time confirm my initial objection to Soyinka's depiction of the women's activities and Mrs Kuti's role. Mrs Funmilayo Ransome-Kuti was a very politically conscious, sophisticated and able woman. She would have been quite able to guide her group at a meeting. A daughter of educated and wealthy parents, she had studied in England from 1919 to 1923 in the heyday of the British suffragette movement and had been influenced by it. She returned to Nigeria an admirer of Mahatma Gandhi, a confirmed socialist, anti-colonialist and radical feminist. Ironically – but maybe wisely – she used the colonial officers and administrative bodies in Nigeria against her local political enemies, the Alake and the Sole Native Authority of Abeokuta. Mrs Kuti and the women in her group were quite capable of initiating ideas and action.

The child tells his story, particularly in the portion relating to his pranks, in the collective 'we' which is typical of children – in particular, Yoruba children. The 'we' expresses the strong peer-group sense which is installed early in the life of many Yoruba children. In addition, they nearly always play in groups. But significantly, none of these other children enters into the work or emerges as perceptible and active characters, to the reader's disappointment. Only the little Soyinka is visible. The other children in the book like Tinu, Femi or the Abiku appear briefly here and there but only as foils, stills or emblematic figures like the Abiku. Significantly, the child-narrator also sees the cousins and wards as 'cousins' and 'strays'. From whose viewpoint is this? In fact, one of the fictive problems of *Aké* is that of narrative voice – is it the man-child or the older Soyinka who is speaking? The best parts are when the older Soyinka's narrative voice effectively and eloquently emerges from the vision of the manchild's. In seeing his mother's wards as 'strays', was he estranged from those children and the experience of living with them even in his childhood? Is it a failure of the child to understand the sociological reality of which he is a part, where children normally stay as wards of adults? Despite the narrative 'we', there is a striking sense of alienation from family and other children in the narration. Do we see here the beginnings of the fascination with the 'loner' complex which would later yield a whole section of poems on 'the lone figure' in *Idanre and other Poems*?

Soyinka succeeds in recreating the past from a child's perspective by his handling of focus – in an almost cinematic but verbal and structural way. It is best exemplified by the first chapter, in particular in the evocation of Bishop Ajayi Crowther (pp. 4–5). In Soyinka's past work, these characteristic techniques, employed in *The Interpreters*, and to our chagrin, in *A Dance of The Forests* and in parts of *Idanre* have aroused the cry of 'obscurity' and 'difficulty' among his readers. But in *Aké* these techniques are perfectly suited to the handling of a child's incomplete, imaginative and often surrealist view of life. But while we enjoy the charming, scenic evocation in chapter ten of the parsonage, the old city and the old market at night and the child's memory of the foods and smells, written in vintage prose (which for me is the best portion of the work), some questions about focus and perspective also arise. Did Soyinka always see his parents as 'Essay' and 'Wild Christian'? Surely it is the older Soyinka now who dares to be so familiar and teasing? Did he think of them in those names then or is it an emotional, adult Soyinka now projecting backwards and forwards? There is the complex vision of a child speaking at times from his own perspective, being slapped around by someone he calls 'Wild Christian'. Also, the recreations of the women's uprising and the dialogues – Kemberi's speeches, for instance – read like pure adult Soyinka. It is the adult Soyinka at work and emergent from behind the child, recreating the speeches and the scenes as something new and his own; in fact, as something totally different from actuality. At such points, the reader is so conscious of Soyinka the dramatist at work that an uncomfortable feeling of being manipulated is aroused. One might be charmed by the recognition of familiar Soyinka but the pleasure deriving from this play of writing might be soured by the historical distortion such scenes represent.

The child in Aké is portrayed as sensitive (as in his reaction to his sister's death) and naturally loving of justice. Was this love of justice natural or environmental? And we may ask how much of the image of the child in Aké is really a recreation of oneself in the image one has of oneself which, I suppose, autobiography can be. For the autobiography, not being a documentary (and that in itself cannot be complete) gives us the memory, which is an edited, selected, and reworked version of facts and events, battered by time, not as they actually happened. Memory fictionalizes. And since memory does this, one wonders how useful Aké will be to the social historian as the blurb writer claims, considering the high level of fictionalization and incorrect historical ordering in the work. Perhaps the social historian may get some of the feel of the period, but what can he make of the actual, historical events? Very little of these appear except in tiny reverberations, and one which occurs in Aké in some notable proportion – the Women's Movement – is chronologically and factually confused and obscured.

The protest against the Sole Native Authority System and the taxation of women which spread to other areas of the Western Region took place between 1947 and 1952. Soyinka was thirteen in 1947. Must he not have gone to his secondary school, the Government College, Ibadan (GCI) by then, considering how early he started school? Soyinka was at the Government College, Ibadan, from January 1946 to May 1951 according to two of his school alumni, Professor Olumuyiwa Awe of the Physics Department, Ibadan and Arts Director Dapo Adelugba of the Theatre Arts Department. In a longer interview with Professor Awe who was also Soyinka's classmate, Professor Awe said Wole was always very vocal and irrepressible, and resisted all injustices from seniors, prefects and bigger boys in his own class. He was also very full of his Aké life in his conversations with his schoolmates. If he went to the Government College in 1946 and the Women's Movement was in 1947 and after, the closing sections of the book (pp. 222–30) must be out of order chronologically. Mrs Kuti is presented as talking to him about going to Government College after the crises. He himself claims to have been taking entry exams 'during the turmoil' (p. 222). But during the turmoil, he must have been in Form Two already. When was he acting as courier? According to Nina Mba, there were two forty-eight-hour vigils in 1947, one from November 29 to 30 the other from December 8 to 10. We are not sure which one of these Soyinka is describing in Aké. In addition, there were five-hourly street demonstrations, as on 28 April 1948, where looting and violence were virtually absent. Soyinka was fourteen in 1948. Surely he must have gone to GCI by then? Autpa-Parlour, the king's favourite wife is reported in histories of the period to have been rough-handled by members of the Women's Union in 1948.

Perhaps the greatest historical disservice Soyinka does the Women's Movement is to portray it as an unplanned, impulsive, gut reaction to contemporary maladministration. The movement was in fact highly organized. The Abeokuta Women's Union had printed *The Constitution, Rules and Regulations for the Women's Union of Abeokuta* (Abeokuta, Bosere Press, 1948). So organized was the union which had diversified to include women trade unions, common interest associations, and traditional chiefs, that it hired an accountant to prepare a detailed report of the Sole Native Authority's expenditure to make their case against that authority. A copy of the report, planned for presentation to the British colonial administration, is to be found among the Ransome-Kuti papers at the University of Ibadan. The movement was politically modern and considered. Its actions did not derive from a rash of spontaneous speeches from women such as Kemberi in Aké. The movement used modern methods: petitions, propaganda, the legal process and the press – letters to the editor, articles and press conferences – as well as marches, demonstrations and vigils. Mrs Kuti herself, in her political sophistication not only confronted both the 'native' authority and the colonial administration but also played one group against the other, manipulating the confused and guilt-ridden liberal humanist consciences of the colonial administrators in Nigeria at the same time as she was putting international pressure on the colonial 'home' administration in Britain. She had made personal and political friends in the British Labour Party and the Women's International Democratic Federation. She publicized her ideas and movement in Europe in an article in *The Daily Worker* (18 August 1947).

It could be argued that a child could not know all this. Precocious as he was, he would have received some intimations. My concern is with the adult artist's responsibility in an autobiography or any writing left for posterity, and that writing's effect on those who read it. And this particular artist admits his concern with 'self-retrieval'.

One defence can be made: that this is what he remembers – alas! He remembers that the women could not put their ideas together, chatting like weaverbirds around a table until Forest Father comes strolling by. Essay, for his part, was marionetting – or more contemporaneously, tele-guiding Wild Christian with his notes from a distance (p. 186). That is *all* that he remembers of *how* the movement functioned. But since the adult Soyinka is also present in other parts of the book, the adult self could have intervened to give a positive and more correct rendering of the women's doings. Well then, it is necessary to publicize the information above for all lovers of *Aké* who may not read African history! One significance of the Soyinka version of the Women's Movement in Abeokuta is the revelation that the roots of his male-chauvinist rendering of society and human endeavour are long and deep. *Aké* is also useful textual material for feminists to demonstrate how adoringly and like a little god an African *male* child is raised, leading to some of the calloused attitudes of adult male supremacy which obtain in Yoruba society.

To respond to the blurbwriter's claim that *Aké* reveals a 'little-known' kind of childhood, it can be said that this kind of childhood is in fact standard or stereotypical of the colonial world. Family life in *Aké* is typical, not only in Nigeria but in the Third World, of the people of 'the good Book' – the Church and the missionary school. There exists a common culture among such people across the imperial globe; to wit, the culture of a preoccupation with the Christian faith, of endless prayers, strictness in discipline and sequestration from the local cultural life as with Obi Okonkwo's father in Achebe's *No Longer At Ease*. Often it was the mother who was somehow more in touch with the local culture as a teacher, churchworker or trader. Also typical of this colonial Christian family type was its role as a cultural intermediary as exemplified in the cultural angst of Daodu in *Aké*. Certainly, Christianized African readers, even Third World ones, know this kind of childhood. But who is the blurbwriter writing for?

The question of who is writing for whom brings us appropriately to the question of the audience of *Aké*, and consequently to the issue of style. The prose is of high quality, subtly interlaced at points with wit and humour which occasionally broaden into admirable and hilarious slapstick, as in the scene of the schoolboys and the stolen chicken. From time to time, however, Nigerianisms slip in; unconscious usages not perhaps intentional and certainly not artistically functional. But this is the bane of all writers who live in a second-language situation where local un-English renderings slip into the writer's prose; as for example when the narrator says, 'Wild Christian replied him' (p. 209). None the less, the prose is generally so sensitive and moving as to become poetry, yet such poetic moments are controlled and brief 'like match-flare in wind's breath'. Nowhere in this finely-written work do you find a purpleness of prose, or overwriting.

But these Yoruba intrusions re-open the issues of perspective in the context of the writer's audience. Who and what are these intrusions for? It seems that Soyinka as a second-language writer is forced to be Janus-faced, as is the fate of any such writer riding two emotional horses, talking to two audiences, talking from two mouths in two or several voices (like a Tutuolan character). For the Yoruba reader, these intrusions naturally trigger the pleasure of a recognition of the familiar – writing style, social situation and humour. But for the foreign reader? One is forced to consider why the Yoruba renderings are deemed necessary.

I question why Soyinka does not write in Yoruba and have the work translated if the impulse to 'go Yoruba' at dramatic, crucial or intensely descriptive points is so strong. Is the writer thinking in Yoruba and writing in English, or thinking and writing in English but breaking into Yoruba at points where English emotionally fails him? Or is he thinking and writing in English but using Yoruba at dramatic points for colour? There are other possible permutations, and they all add up to serious problems in the poetic of African writing for all who write in a foreign language.

Significant in this question of audience are the moments when the narrator's voice is obviously directed to a foreign audience – in some detailed and unnecessary description of the familiar and in some stylistically mannered paragraphs. These particular techniques are clearly not meant for the average Nigerian or African reader (whom we cannot stop to identify now) not because such readers are genetically inferior but because reading tastes and habits are simply not sophisticated enough. This is a simple sociological point.

The enchanted world of *Aké* does get boring. I felt bogged down with too much detail and the trivia of family living. At such times, the reader may feel lost. The obvious narcissism in the whole work, a narcissism which seems to be its whole purpose, also repels in a world of inconsequentialities and insignificant anecdotes. But the book is invaluable for the light it sheds on the sources of some of Soyinka's characters, motifs and later concerns. One recognizes the sources of poems like 'Abiku' and 'A First Death-Day'; scenes in *The Interpreters* and *A Dance of the Forests* (in the forest creatures, though Fagunwa and others may have contributed something to the play also); Wild Christian and Amope; the old women in the market and *Madmen and Specialists*; the escaping Ogboni, the miming girls and Iyaloja herself in *Death and The King's Horseman*. And so on for us cattle-egret critics who trail the writer-cows. It is regrettable that the autobiography says nothing concrete about the formative reading of the little Soyinka – the specific titles of books he read. Since the work harps on Soyinka's concern with books from an early stage and his voracity for them, it would have been appropriate and useful to be told the titles, particularly if the presentation of self and the self's education (in the etymological sense of 'e-ducare': 'a leading out') is one of the objectives of the work. Certainly, we cattle-egrets are interested in the nature of the books which perhaps formed the older man and writer.

Despite all my objections and the issues taken up in this essay, I feel that *Aké* is, on the whole, a rewarding and sometimes charming literary experience – an enchanted world of childhood.

'Molara Ogundipe-Leslie

Alan Paton, *Ah, But Your Land is Beautiful*, London, Jonathan Cape; Cape Town, David Philip, 1981; New York, Scribner, 1982, 271 pp.

This courageous work traces the first seven years of the period of peaceable opposition to the National Party epoch of government in South Africa. Paton is a staunch campaigner from within against a legal system which he sees from a double point of view. As a South African he recognizes the internal consistency of the programme of legislation, but as a descendant of the tradition of liberal emancipation on a world scale which has its origins in the work of Equiano and Wilberforce, he exposes the absurdity and folly of the programme and its adherents. The photograph on the back cover is a portrait of Paton, a man with three expressions in one, the whimsical satirist, the benign observer, and the man of a virtually Calvinist dedication to survival in the face of an implacable judgement. Two further volumes are promised, and so this is the start of a trilogy. When completed, it will provide a fine internal view of the internal panorama of defeat and embitterment which modern South Africa has become.

There are many pointers in this book towards the crises of the ensuing two decades, each punctuated by Sharpeville and Soweto. The current state of armed conflict is clearly implied as well, but Paton remains enigmatic in his attitude to this state of affairs. Clearly he feels that it is the inevitable consequence of the failure of the Liberal Party, but he goes further than that, since the white man's hunger for land and his relentless opportunism in obtaining it are the underlying cause. This emerges clearly from the glimpses of history which appear in passing. Nevertheless, the plea for the abolition of the entire miscarriage of law upon which the edifice rests is not accompanied by any endorsement of future policies. Paton is Tolstoian rather than Dostoevskian in his approach to his country's ailments. The underlying causes are shown and a remedy is implied, and there is a burning faith in a transformation of the spirit, but there is no transfigured vision of vice and degradation as paths towards a new life.

As a central dramatic event, the drafting, adoption and public repudiation of the Freedom Charter is portrayed with less conviction than the negative episodes, among which the principal incident is the suicide of a head of a government department named Fischer, who is trapped with a black female decoy and arrested under the Immorality Act. Rightly, Paton points to the post-Union legislation which formed the curtain raiser to the notorious Acts of the 1950s, as the sources of modern legislative outrages. He thus avoids the popular fad of impugning the Afrikaners, but focuses instead on the general run of settler attitudes, both English-orientated and Afrikaner, which have conspired to produce the intellectual and social miasma. If there is hope, he suggests, it lies with the critical attitude which all sections of the population can generate from within, and not in the bright ideas brought in by fresh but essentially alien minds from outside. Another fad, the impugning of Lutuli, is deftly avoided, and this central figure makes a suitably heroic appearance. His successors and their varying roles must surely pose the most difficult task for the chronicler of the ensuing decades, and Paton's courage in dealing with these subjects will undoubtedly be challenged in the rest of the trilogy.

The great events of the decade before 1960 are all present: the Group Areas Act, the Bantu Education Act, the Immorality Act, the bus boycott, the Black Sash vigils, the first treason trial. Paton lingers with grim fondness over these vanished landmarks. The foul-mouthed male and female figures in the foreground of public meetings and secret correspondence appear in grotesque sobriety, without caricature, together with their reckless public consequences, bullets, private bombings, decapitations, and policemen variously servile, hectoring, devious, plaintive, or mercilessly brutal. Five crises form the narrative core around which a scattering of observers present their subjective views or objective narrations. They involve an Indian girl, a black campaigner, a coloured railway official, an English-speaking educationist, and an Afrikaner politician; that is, a sample from each major racial group in the country. As literature, the product of this approach is decidedly arid, an aerial view with all the virtues and defects of the genre. Verbal magic, metaphorical transformation of experience, abundant philosophizing and visionary ecstasy, the stock in trade of one branch of modern fiction, has never been Paton's forte. Instead, he pursues the narrower path of reporting and staccato résumé, the historiography of crime writing and journalist fiction. As befits an Indian girl, the heroine Prem Bodasingh is unrelentingly 'beautiful', as Esther Summerson without blemish until a would-be assassin's bullet disfigures her face; Lutuli is dignified, and the Afrikaner government official whose letters to his aunt supply the Fischer narrative, himself absurdly named Van Onselen, is of an oxlike naïvety. These stereotypes limit the scope of emotional sympathy; they are vessels bearing uneasily the burden of momentous history which passes through their veins, heads and hands.

This is Paton's most ambitious attempt in fiction so far, lacking apocalyptic vision yet moving in its presentation of lived and suffered history. *Cry, the Beloved Country* put modern South African literature on the world map. Here, the map of South Africa itself has been unrolled by one of its most poignantly discerning analysts. The rest of the trilogy will be eagerly awaited.

Christopher Heywood

R. Sarif Easmon, *The Feud and Other Stories*, London, Longman, 1981, 294 pp.

R. Sarif Easmon, who is sometimes a doctor in Freetown, reveals himself in his collection of short stories titled *The Feud* to be an excellent general practitioner and a skilful heart specialist. Already recognized as a novelist and playwright, he has clearly added to his literary reputation with these twelve works in another fictional genre. The stories themselves demonstrate considerable variety, ranging from several short realistic vignettes to longer fantasies and melodramas (using that term in a descriptive and not a pejorative sense). What chiefly binds the stories together so that they do not seem to be just pictures of West African life drawn at random is the tone and voice of their telling, which is generally warm and cosmopolitan, and their almost constant focusing on problems of the heart. Even in the tales that concern political and social matters the heart, the passions, seem to dominate over intellectual considerations.

The strengths of the stories are many. Is it the writer or the doctor who so keenly observes of one character that 'The sun etched out his ribs on his naked chest like a bunch of bananas. His wasted flesh lay on his frame like the remnants of a feast disease had left for death to clear away'? No matter, for here as well as elsewhere a careful dissector of humanity and a compelling storyteller operates to supply insights into the terrible, wonderful nature of the species.

Even in his more romantic stories, Easmon is capable of phrasing that catches the eye and lets you know that if not a master artist then at least a highly skilled craftsman is at work. In the title story, filled with passion, revenge, despicable villainy, blighted young love, and long smouldering hatred enough for a novel, Easmon describes a freshly sharpened stake that will shortly be plunged into a young man's heart: 'How curiously sweet and fragrant the raw wood smelled in the night'. The sentence shocks the reader with its agonizing inappropriateness and yet absolute rightness to the scene. Just before the moment of death, the murder weapon itself reminds us of the simple sweetness of life.

Elsewhere, in *Under the Flamboyante Tree*, a secondary character speaks 'in the raised voice of those who are slightly deaf but can't believe it', and thus springs into a reality the reader can recognize, though only as a minor actor in the tragic events that will occur. In *For Love of Thérèse* a young African businessman, not a failure but no great success either, laughs 'with a deeply cynical laugh' and speaks bitterly about his lack of achievement 'with a shrug of the shoulder, which he had inherited as a cultural cast-off from the French'. That shrug recaptures and communicates so much history – a simple, revealing gesture, the tip of a cultural iceberg that implies generations of Gallic domination of the mercantile tropics. In *The Black Madonna*, that twilight zone of the past which is still real time but is just about to drift into myth – the Swahili *sasa* time before it blends into *zamini* – is expressed in the simple description of 'half-naked little boys and girls, who are now not in the memory of their own grandchildren'. Again the phrase carries with it a slight shock confronting us with the image of little children playing who are now so long gone from history that they are beyond recollection. Many of the stories are placed in colonial or even pre-colonial days, and these seem quite as real as the contemporary stories – some of which are in fact quite fantastic and unreal, though not necessarily untrue. If this time trickery sounds portentous and terribly serious, I should add that Easmon is nearly always simple and economic in his narratives, and often humorous, as in *Last Night in Paris* when the story's protagonist Kandeh discovers the bond linking him with other English-speaking westerners vacationing in Paris: they are all being gulled. 'Kandeh felt ... a blood bond uniting him with these new friends: the bond of a brood of chickens aware they were being plucked to keep the pot of French tourism boiling.'

Occasionally the descriptive language falters into conventionality, as in the ghost story *First Night in Paris* when we are told of the mystified husband's 'hair standing on end'. Hair does prickle up stiff sometimes when you are scared, but I do not believe Henry James or Edgar Allan Poe would have written that it literally stood on end. (Well, perhaps Poe might have, but then for all his greatness he always was a bit vulgar in his effects.) A far more serious problem with the language occurs when Easmon translates West African speech into English. The issue has continued to vex African writers and western writers who employ African materials, and though individual artists have worked out their own methods for dealing with the dilemma there is not yet (and probably never will be) a satisfactory technique for all to feel comfortable with. The problem is not unique to African literature but surfaces whenever fictional material is translated from one language to another. Many western readers still feel most comfortable with Constance Garnett's translations of the Russian masters, despite their creaking and (I am told by experts) often inaccurate Victorianisms, because the translations are part of a fictional fabric whose patterns and designs seem by now natural to us through our familiarity with them in the great nineteenth century British novels. But no accepted mode for re-creating African speech appears to exist that both communicates accurately the spirit of an African tongue and differentiates within a tribal language such matters as region and class and intellect.

In the very first story, The Feud, when the heroine is seized by rampaging soldiers from an enemy tribe, she yells 'let me go, you brute!' The young Susu girl is aristocratic, and therefore 'brute' might be the strongest term she could summon in her shock and anger, but I doubt it. She is speaking Susu and the word in the story is presumably a translation of a Susu term which perhaps translates into 'brute', and yet many readers will associate the term with English swashbuckling or gothic fiction and the arrogant but well-bred ladies that fill its pages. I mention the example at some length because it suggests Easmon's problem. A few pages later, another woman, not a Susu but a Yalie, calls the heroine a 'saucy one', and still later says of her 'Ain't we cocky!' Certainly the Yalie or Susu have words approximating 'brute' or 'saucy' or 'ain't' or 'cocky', but I do not think these terms can be used in English without hauling along with them all kinds of cultural burdens (or gifts). To slip in such locutions discreetly would probably reduce their obtrusiveness, but in the context of Easmon's fiction they stand out boldly. But what are his alternatives? He employs from time to time indigenous words and phrases and ordinarily supplies for them their English meaning in parenthesis or by anglicized variations. Such a technique clearly has its limits, however.

The short story at its best is an intense form and the language of the short story is a delicate matter. The words in a short story are spotlighted in a way that is not always the case in longer fictive modes. When we are told in The Feud that a certain festival 'was the red-letter day in a Susu woman's life', it may be that the confluence of cultures the phrase confronts us with in 'red-letter day' and 'Susu woman' is more linguistically disturbing than is desirable to the author. Surely it would be patronizing and ethnocentric to assume that tribal etiquette precludes the ritual gesture of what is called in English a 'curtsey', but what image does Easmon present the reader with when he says that his heroine's slave in The Feud 'made a hurried curtsey'? I raise the point more for discussion than for criticism. Why should not African writers who write in English have at their command the entire English language – and yet can they invariably divest words of their cultural freight? Certainly African women curtsied, bent their bodies before authority, but did they 'make a curtsey' in the same cultural sense that those sixteenth, seventeenth and eighteenth century ladies did before their social betters? In *The Black Madonna* a crowd of Susu in the colonial period are described as engaging in a 'brouhaha'. If one were translating *The Hunchback of Notre Dame*, could one write that the Paris rabble crowded into the church square were having a brouhaha?

To his credit, Easmon employs his wide linguistic and cultural background consistently. It would be death to him as a writer if he simply incorporated piecemeal aspects of his exceptionally varied intellectual heritage into his fiction, but he does not. In the back of all the stories there is ultimately the same narrator, the same world view, the same highly sophisticated, empathetic, slightly cynical person. He has been accused of that most terrible of vices – not being African enough in his writing – but he writes from his own African and world experience as he must if he is to be natural and true to his world, which is a big one. So it is not surprising to see him describe a pretty Susu girl as being 'as elegant as a figure in a Watteau painting – if Watteau had painted such scenes as Gauguin saw in the tropics'. As long as he does not impose his sensibility upon his characters, whose worlds are narrower than his, I believe he is justified in setting the stage of his character's actions within the greater theatre of his own observations. There are even some interesting ironic effects to be gained from this practice.

The cosmopolitanism of his outlook is reflected in the variety of his stories. *The Feud* is a highly condensed tale of revenge that many another writer might have stretched into a lush, bosomy epic. Realistic in its analysis of harboured hatred, melodramatic in the neatness of its violent working out, the story, like nearly all those in the volume, grips the reader's attention early and holds on to it. *Koya* is a very simple vignette, showing how the humiliation of a proud young girl who is but a kernel of a woman provides a twist to her life that she will always be affected by. It is a quiet initiation tale focusing not upon a tribal rite but upon a small social interaction that is, however, charged with psychological implications. *The Black Madonna* reminded me of some of Nathaniel Hawthorne's stories of sexual obsession and guilt. It tells how a beautiful, innocent young African woman is redeemed by the very act of love that damns the priest who is for a time drawn from his God towards her.

The First Night in Paris is a modern ghost story rare among the others in this collection, since it concerns two young, charming, and totally likeable people. The Last Night in Paris features the same newlywed couple who have a very realistic and comic confrontation not with a ghost as in their first adventure, but with a Parisian sharpster. For Love of Thérèse is a more sombre love or lust story about the rewards of infidelity, which are either destruction or a kind of glorification, depending upon how the ironic, enigmatic ending is interpreted. Perhaps the price of adultery is also the prize. The Mad Woman is a funny story that takes apart just as much as a comic short story should, a young, self-satisfied doctor and a foolish-wise old woman. Michael Woode, District Commissioner is Easmon's strongest anti-colonial story, depicting how a spiritually blind Englishman becomes physically blind through his own ethnocentric and overweening pride. Though perhaps overly long (the story appears to end before the writing about it does) this fairly familiar tale possesses compensatory virtues. To a westerner such as myself, it is refreshing to read an indictment of colonialism that is coupled with an awareness that not all colonials are as ethically obtuse as the infamous Briton at the conclusion of Things Fall Apart. The story's blend of fantasy, guilt-induced hallucination, and what may be real, spiritual forces really operating, is exceptionally well handled, and again reminiscent (though not imitative) of Hawthorne.

Under the Flamboyante Tree is a novella rather than a short story, about young love and how destructive it can unknowingly, perhaps even innocently be. Although its ending seems a bit convenient and more like a doctor's autopsy than the shattering of an idyll, Easmon almost achieves an impossible task in the story: that of making two beautiful post-Shakespearean, post-adolescent lovers real and likeable. Not the least of Dr Easmon's skills is his talent for recapturing woman's beauty, incidentally.

Heart of a Judge again drops into the colonial period and mixes fantasy with fact until one can only faintly discern one from the other. Even in this brief work, Easmon manages both to skewer the arrogance of colonialism and suggest that not all wise English justices were complete fools (unless I have been myself fooled by the story's tricks). No. 2 to Maia's Tailor seems one of the weaker stories. Its headstrong female protagonist is supposed to show up the shallowness and venality of her pre-selected husband by rejecting him for a more common lover, but in doing so she also demonstrates her silliness, and I could not be certain that this was how Dr Easmon intended her character to be read. If so, the story is very cynical and muddled; and if not cynical, simply muddled. Disenchantment is a far more serious treatment of unfaithfulness, although its plot seems conventional to a person such as myself who has seen scores of old Warner Brothers films about husbands or wives cracking up under the pressures of living in the provinces or conversely redeeming themselves in some quiet, heroic fashion. Still, the story will probably hook most readers, because there is a simplicity and honesty and plenty of realistic detail in its retelling, and were it a movie, though I have seen its like before, I would probably (silently) cheer at its conclusion, where the people who should lose are vanquished, and the good people who should win, triumph. Additionally, the story contains numerous, small, delightful social observations, such as when we are told 'It did not flatter him that she did not even turn around on the stool to look him in the face. She was addressing herself to his reflection in the glass: as though she could only endure him at second hand.'

Though I have mentioned some faults in The Feud – mainly of occasional language lapses and perhaps too great a reliance upon familiar situations – I would conclude that the book is eminently successful. We generally read only selected short stories of the masters and forget how bad the best can be sometimes in individual works. As a collection, The Feud is a strong book, and in its skill and variety is certainly one of the best produced by an African writer in many years. I note that apparently almost none of the stories was previously printed in magazines. This is a shame, for a short story writer needs immediate, periodic response to his work. Moreover, a writer needs to be able to aim at a fairly precise audience in order to direct his skills most creatively. In America (the country whose short story market I know best) there once existed a variety of magazines from the glossiest of slicks to the grubbiest of pulps. The market is constricted now, but different magazines still cater to different audiences, to the disparate intellectual needs of variously educated audiences. I sense that this situation does not exist for Dr Easmon, and that a mature, traditional writer such as he has limited opportunities to publish short fiction regularly. This is unfortunate because both he and his audience are thus deprived of an ongoing relationship that would benefit both. In a tough league, that of the short story, he has well succeeded in The Feud, and he should be given more opportunities to succeed again.

Jack B. Moore

Andrew Ekwuru, *Songs of Steel*, London, Thomas Nelson, 1980, 160 pp.

This first novel, originally published by Rex Collings in 1979, is number 1 in a new series of African and Black literature which, together with Longman's 'Drumbeats', has come to challenge the near-monopoly of Heinemann's 'African Writers Series' in the field. Under the collective name 'Panafrican Library' it has already brought together, apart from Andrew Ekwuru's *Songs of Steel* and his second novel, *Going to Storm*, such classics as Wole Soyinka's *Season of Anomy*, Richard Wright's *Black Boy* and Es'kia Mphahlele's *Chirundu*.

Literature on the Biafran War written by Nigerians is once more on the increase. This marks a significant change, since a sizeable proportion of the treatment the war received in the early and mid seventies, either tangentially or centrally, was by non-Nigerians: the Kenyan, Ali Mazrui (*The Trial of Christopher Okigbo*, 1971), the Frenchman, Olivier Todd (*L'année du crabe*, 1972), the Irishman, Vincent Lawrence (*An End to Flight*, 1973), the Englishman, Frederick Forsyth (*The Dogs of War*, 1974), and the German, Klaus Stephan (*Ein feiner Patriot*, 1976) to mention just a few. A renewed interest in this subject-matter is evidenced by a veteran like Cyprian Ekwensi, who has produced two novels on the civil war and its aftermath (*Survive the Peace*, 1976; *Divided We Stand*, 1980), an author of the middle generation like Isidore Okpewho (*The Last Duty*, 1976, and a fledgling writer like Andrew Ekwuru with his *Songs of Steel* (1979). At the same time the soldiers and soldier-politicians who grabbed the levers of power in a crisis-ridden Nigeria have come to the fore with their own accounts of the dramatic events, among them Nigeria's former Head of State, General Olusegun Obasanjo (*My Command*, 1979), the retired Commander of the Biafran Army, Alexander A. Madiebo (*The Nigerian Revolution and the Biafran War*, 1980), and most brilliantly, the only survivor of the heroic trio Nzeogwu-Ifeajuna-Ademoyega that masterminded the overthrow of the First Republic in January 1966, Adewale Ademoyega (*Why We Struck; The Story of the First Nigerian Coup*, 1981).

Songs of Steel is an honourable and memorable novel, although in structure, texture and hasty characterization it shows the mark of

158 Reviews

being a first attempt. However, much of this is compensated for by a striking freshness of tone and a social vision in which cruelty and violence are placed in a wider context of human passion.

It is a novel without an individual hero. The protagonists are the inhabitants of 'the twin-villages' tucked away in the safety of the dense forests off the Okigwe-Umuahia axis. But it turns out to be a safety more presumed than real when the federal war machine moves inexorably towards the Igbo heartland.

Among the villagers the Dibia family stands out. Madam Dibia is the only one who has remained in the village. Her three children now return home from a pogrom-ridden northern Nigeria one after another: first her youngest daughter Abigail, whose husband was murdered by Muslim fanatics in the first massacres, then her daughter Martha with her mutilated but still able-bodied husband Job, and finally, arriving in his own lorry in the grand manner of a prosperous Igbo trader, her son Simon with his Hausa wife, Issa. After the stark horror of the pivotal introductory scene at the railway station with its trainload of maimed and subdued refugees, Simon supplies some comic relief by ululating like an imam at the crack of dawn as a profession of his Muslim faith, much to the amazement of his Christian fellow villagers. His wife goes the opposite way, accepting the Igbo name, Ekeoma, and eagerly attending Christian scripture readings, which gain in intensity as the danger of war becomes ever more imminent.

In fact the eighteen chapters of the book are neatly balanced between the pre-war period starting from the northern massacres in 1966 on the one hand, and from the actual war period from July 1967 to January 1970 on the other, although these dates have to be extrapolated by the reader. The writer strictly adheres to a traditional village chronology not determined by the western calendar but by the change of the seasons and, later on, by the events of the war as they affect the community.

The period from the opening scene of the novel to the outbreak of hostilities, short as it might be in terms of calendar months, is rich in incident, geared to establishing new patterns of social living and economic participation of the refugees. Job, the refugee from Zaria, repossesses his late father's decaying homestead with neighbourly help, although not all help thus rendered is selfless. The roguish and miserly farmer Afouku exploits him, just as he has previously taken advantage of his brother-in-law, Simon, by pawning his son Ariwa to him, a stratagem he had repeatedly adopted with other people before:

'You done promise you no sell me again,' the boy protested. 'Why you wan sell me, Papa?'

'Cause we hungry and one foolish man with money done return for our village,' said his father.

'Don't sell me to him,' pleaded his son. 'Make me go his house and tief his things and money for you.'

'Tief?' his father sounded appalled by his son's request. 'When you come from outside, you can tief only small things from him house. But if you live with him, if you follow him about, you can tief plenty. Not so?' (p. 19)

The new community about to be born in the crucible of persecution — and the village here is but a microcosm of the arising Biafran nation — is thus one of saints and sinners, of the straight and the warped. Its future is shrouded in a pall of uncertainty, and the diviner invited for consultation by the Dibia family predicts 'iron thunder of great magnitude', advising them to plant *eke*, or 'fate trees', which are said to sustain the pain and suffering to come in their stead.

But the cataclysm of the war sweeps away such traditional safeguards. Martha, the elder sister, is foully murdered by the invading army, despite her fate tree, and her husband Job dies along with her.

For Simon Dibia, the hour of revenge has now come. The irresponsible roving trader, with a string of concubines in his various ports of call, had made a vow: 'I will fight my wife's people, if a single member of our family is hurt or killed in this madness' (p. 95). At first shell-shocked by an artillery barrage on the village, he snaps out of it when a sympathetic federal officer, Captain Damisa, slaps him back into reality. Together they prepare the murdered couple for burial:

Damisa took one look at the dead man's face and exclaimed:

'*Wayo* Allah! He was the boss of the Post and Telegraphic Department in Zaria. My brother was his assistant!'

Simon looked malevolently at Damisa. 'Send a message! By Allah, send a message to him! Tell him that Allah's will has been done. Tell him Job is at last dead. He can now become the boss and go and celebrate!'

Simon went to where Martha lay. He drew back his gown away from her body. Without waiting for Damisa's assistance, he lifted his sister down from the bed and towards the washing mat where the buckets of water stood.

'Easy! Easy!' warned Damisa as he helped to lift Martha.

'No one can hurt her in death! I love her! I won't hurt her! She will suffer no more!' said Simon....

They washed and prepared Martha for burial.

'She was a beautiful woman,' said Damisa admiring Martha lying beside her husband.

'Some people derive pleasure from praising those who are dead. Others appreciate the wonderful work of Allah while they are with us, alive and breathing. All that you are admiring is now mere memory. Sleep, sister. Nobody will hurt you again.' Simon's voice shook with the depth of his feelings. He wiped his eyes with his skull cap. Captain Damisa removed his cap and wiped his eyes also, both men suffering as they buried the couple. (pp. 106–7)

Rather inconsistently (but there are a few more such motivational flaws in the novel), the troops under the command of the tough disciplinarian, Captain Damisa, go on happily shooting civilians and blowing them up with hand-grenades. In retaliation the villagers counter-attack after a fortifying church service in the forest, where the symbol of Njoku, the farm god, is enthroned beside the gun and the bible, and people drop their Christian names. Wielding matchetes and cassava-peeling knives, they massacre the invaders. Their leader is Simon, now baptized Kwashiorkor-Boy, who is to become Biafra's dreaded guerrilla leader, carrying out his daring operations deep in enemy-held territory. His men kill Captain Damisa in an ambush. The senselessness of war. The sheer horror.

There comes a moment in the course of any war when the common soldier, or even enlightened officer, realizes that he has been misled, that those at the helm of affairs in his country should never have allowed this war to start in the first place. As Brecht put it:

When men march off to war many do not know
That their enemy is marching at their head.
The voice which gives them their orders
Is the voice of the enemy.
He who speaks of enemies
Himself is the enemy. (Trans. Christopher Middleton)

This mood is intimated in *Songs of Steel*. Nigerian and Biafran soldiers in one earthy episode communicate from trench to trench, calling each other 'Rebel' and 'Vandal' in a teasing manner and exchanging confidential information on the next day's fighting in a coded language. The Federals even loan arms to the Biafrans to enable them to put up an impressive fight when the Nigerian OC comes down from Enugu for inspection:

'Hello, Sergeant-Major!'
'Hello, Captain!' returned the Biafran. 'You get some Kwashiorkor pills?'
'We get some. Come today,' revealed the Nigerian. 'You get Biafran whisky? This damned Scotch whisky no good any more for me. Taste like damned rotten juice wey comot from sugar-cane!'

'Yes,' confirmed the Biafran. 'You get cigarettes? I die for them. I want good ones. No "wee-wee", you understand?'

'You Biafran man clever too much. I smoke pure ones too! Don't want to go crazy and die in this stupid war!'

'Very wise of you! Send your consignment!' ...

The opposing soldiers met near a mound which marked the neutral ground to exchange their gifts. They shook hands and returned to their defensive lines. The Nigerian officer came out of his trench:

'Hello, Utaka!' He was now very friendly, calling the Biafran by his first name.

'Hello, Ali!' returned the Biafran.

'Tomorrow my men go sing too much. My masa de come inspect our position,' warned the Nigerian.

'Okay for me! But tell him not to push your men or they no go come for my birthday party on Saturday,' cautioned the Biafran officer.

'Allah the wise!' the Nigerian was incredulous. 'We must come! I done promise you dat!' He turned to shout into the jungle, 'My masa come and lick my yarsh! Damned fool!' (pp. 123-4)

But despite these pacifist interludes the war continues. In a futile search for food to save their children, the women of the twin-villages, led by Abigail, set out on a long march which becomes ever more delirious and hallucinating. With the Biafran enclave shrinking on all sides they are fated to return to their point of departure in a circular movement. Meanwhile, the federal army, in a highly effective scene, advances for the final assault on the enclave in anticipation of 'the dreaded, savage, dying kicks of Biafra' (p. 154).

The narrative in the novel moves at an appropriate pace, leisurely in the first half, when the rural community tries to cope with the influx of refugees and integrate them into its own rhythm of life, and accelerating to a feverish *staccato* as the villagers are drawn into the cataclysmic events of the war. The narrative development is sustained by dialogue befitting the characters involved, or rather revealing them. Speech patterns range from the sententiousness of the school teacher to the racy idiom of the fighting-man. While the style of the novel at its best is terse and laconic, it occasionally lapses into sloppiness and bathos. On the ideological side, the root causes of the war are discussed in a rather simplistic fashion (pp. 33-4), and one has the uneasy feeling that too much truculent hero worship has gone into the characterization of brother and sister, Simon and Abigail. The young woman, after opting to snuff out the life of her first-born son by an act of euthanasia, also grinds the larynx of a wounded Egyptian 'genocide' pilot underfoot into the Biafran dust: a paroxysm of revenge. In their own anatomy of war, other writers the world over – Gabriel Chevalier in *La Peur*, Theodor Plievier in *Stalingrad*, Norman Mailer in *The Naked and the Dead*, Jerzy Kosinski in *The Painted Bird*, and, nearer home, Ifeanyi Aniebo in *The Anonymity of Sacrifice* – have more compassionately placed pity above terror and fear above defiance.

Willfried Feuser

James Gibbs, ed., *Critical Perspectives on Wole Soyinka*, Washington DC, Three Continents Press, 1980; London, Heinemann, 1981, 274 pp.

We must indeed be grateful for this collection of reviews and critical essays on Wole Soyinka's work to date. Some of the articles have long been familiar to his admirers, while a few of the shorter reviews may have escaped all but the most assiduous. In a large number of cases, however, it is not always easy for newer students and fans to lay hands on the individual publications, and here we have a very comprehensive and balanced selection, covering background material, textual interpretation (including controversy), genre study, and staging, plus an excellent selected bibliography of some twenty pages which includes both primary and secondary sources. For my own part, I could have done without *The Early Writings of Wole Soyinka* by Bernth Lindfors as it adds little or nothing to our knowledge of either the author or his mature works. Juvenilia is always and only juvenilia.

It is not possible to discuss each and every item in the collection, but at least the highpoints of critical perception can be noted. Abiola Irele's article on tradition and the Yoruba writer, which establishes a distinctive literary tradition and world view in the works of Fagunwa, Tutuola, and Soyinka, is indeed masterful, and D. S. Izevbaye's interpretive essays on *The Road* and *Death and the King's Horseman* are illuminating. Annemarie Heywood on the staging of the plays is acutely sensitive to their dramatic modes and conceptions, and she quite rightly focuses our attention on the purely theatrical context of scene, costume, acting style, pace, music, and song in which the literary text must be cast before it can be brought to life. D. I. Nwoga's discussion of *Idanre, and other poems*, in which he discovers its poetic method to be one of revelation, is certainly the most ambitious of the pieces on poetry and offers second-order speculation about the nature of the poet's creative imagination. Of the essays on Soyinka's prose, the hitherto unpublished piece on *The Interpreters* by Mark Kinkead-Weekes is particularly interesting, in that its object is to disprove the prevailing contention that the novel is incoherent and obscure. His thesis is that Soyinka is attempting 'to criticize the facile critics who see the symptoms outside themselves, but cannot diagnose the disease that includes them, along with those they presume to criticize'. (p. 237) He is very convincing.

On the other hand, I am not so ready to agree with Anne B. Davis' assertion in *The Dramatic Theory of Wole Soyinka* that the playwright's reformulation of terms amounts to a startlingly new theoretical premise. Stripped of its jargon, the argument contends that drama induces members of the audience to exchange their individuality for a sense of communality through identification with culturally defined behaviour on stage, and that they then create for themselves 'a new sense of identification based on a renewed awareness of communal values and beliefs'. (p. 148) But so it has always been, however one uses terms such as 'ritual', 'myth', 'social reality', etc. The essay is carefully considered and closely argued, but more foam than wave seems to have been generated.

In a similar vein, the introduction written by the editor makes some rather artificial distinctions. Soyinka, we are told, is to be presented from five different points of view; as Yoruba, academic, man of the theatre, political activist, and writer. The résumé of his education, theatre work, and political activity is much appreciated, yet much of the total information provided is a function of his role as artist. Given a subdivision of five persons in the one man, it is reasonable to expect some inside information on his teaching interests, areas of research, production (direction) methods, acting styles, organizational abilities, and political philosophy. We are not so much interested in his Yoruba identity as in its effect on his work and thought, and everything could have been subsumed under one heading.

There are also one or two editorial problems to be noted. The question of Professor Soyinka's second appointment at the University of Ife, for example, is a matter of record. The date and exact title of the chair, both as originally offered and on assumption of duties in Ife, can easily be verified. Whatever confusion exists arises from conflicting assertions on book jackets. Another complaint must be made concerning the copyediting, and it is not just a question of the typographical errors abounding – which they do – but also of whole sentences which defy grammatical analysis and inconsistencies in the bibliography. The fact that many of the essays are photostatically reproduced from the originals causes some diversity among the notes, and a few of the articles were not well edited in the first place. Surely it would have been better to revise where necessary and reset the notes so that at least all internal references are cited (which is not now the case), and cited consistently. It would also have been advisable to allow authors to revise their essays if they wished, as some may have been produced under pressure or badly mauled in the course of publication. It is hard to believe that Gerald Moore, for example, should choose to persist in the initial assumption that 'the chief about to die takes the young bride intended for his son' (p. 126). The taint of incest is not even hinted at in the text, nor is it necessary to exaggerate the carnal weakness which collaborates with the District Officer's intervention to bring about the tragic fall of the King's Horseman.

Richard Taylor

P. A. Egejuru, *Black Writers: White Audience. A Critical Approach to African Literature*, New York, Exposition Press, 1978, 255 pp.

Black Writers: White Audience is the revised version of a doctoral dissertation in comparative African literature submitted to the University of California, Los Angeles. Its central argument, which is defended through the detailed analyses of the pronouncements and works of some seven writers can be summarized and simply stated as follows: the use of European languages and literary traditions by African writers does not derive basically, as is commonly assumed, from historical circumstances. It is rather a result of the fact that they are writing principally for a European audience which they are eager to please, and by which they crave to be understood and appreciated.

The author writes: 'A brief survey I made among the African elite shows that the African writer today is largely addressing a non-African audience' (p. 19).

While acknowledging the fact that Africa's historical past plays a role in her writers' choice of the language of the ex-colonial master, among other things, to explore their experience, Dr Egejuru none the less attempts to show that the resultant duality in the nature of their creative works (an African content and a non-African medium of expression) is nothing they deeply regret. Given their assumed audience, her implicit contention is that these writers would still have opted for European languages, even if they had been literate in theirs. Indeed, she quotes Senghor's reply, to those who reprimand him for using French to express his African sensibility, to substantiate her point: 'nous n'avons pas choisi. Et s'il avait fallu choisir, nous aurions choisi le français' (p. 55) (we did not choose. But if we had had to, we would have chosen French). According to the author therefore, it is not the choice of language that determines the audience, it is the audience aimed at, that dictates the choice of language. She continues: 'By writing in European languages, African writers cannot escape being read by Europeans.... But the issue is not the fact of "other readers" but the pre-awareness that they must be catered to' (p. 14).

Black Writers: White Audience is thus an attempt to bring to light this 'pre-awareness' of the important and strategic presence of the other; one whose existence is strenuously denied by most of the writers interviewed by the author. To prove her point, Dr Egejuru marshals three types of arguments. These can be characterized as the argument (a) from choice and handling of language (b) from choice of genre (c) from choice and handling of subject matter.

Now, although the present reviewer wholly accepts the point that there are, in African literature, elements that show the pre-awareness of a foreign audience, he thinks the argument from choice of language, outlined above, is the least convincing in *Black Writers: White Audience*. To posit an analogy, as the author does, between the case of Samuel Beckett and Joseph Conrad on the one hand and African writers on the other, and to conclude that in both instances 'the language choice was significantly dictated by an assumed audience' (p. 14), is to gloss over substantial points often raised by the African writers themselves. The first of these is that the use of European languages creates a wider African audience; that African writers, unlike Conrad and Beckett, are often not literate in their languages; and finally that modernity which is also an integral part of the African experience comes in a foreign language.

While, as has been said already, on the insistence of her interviewees, Dr Egejuru concedes the point, albeit contradictorily, that historical necessity does influence the choice of language (pp. 56–7), she is more unequivocal in her assertion that the *way* the language is used – if not its choice as a medium of expression – is indicative of the pressures of the audience, composed here of publishers and readers. Thus because in some of the poems of Senghor she analyses (*Epître à la Princesse, Rêve de jeune fille, Neige sur Paris*, etc.) there is, in her mind, no discernible African influence on the language, she concludes:

> The point here is that Senghor's writing is mostly controlled by his French language and culture and by extension his French audience. Judging from his language, he could not have had an African audience in mind when he wrote such poems. (p. 63)

Conversely, the author sees the various attempts by Anglophone writers like Soyinka and Achebe to africanize their English as an indication not only of the greater flexibility of that language, but of their keener awareness of their local public. With the exception of Sembène Ousmane and Ahmadou Kourouma this awareness, according to her, is not evinced by Francophone writers.

But here again, the student of African literature cannot help but experience a sense of unease at the way in which Dr Egejuru reduces the complex phenomenon of registers of language and of speech patterns in a work of literature to a single explanation: the audience. It is true, to take her example, that the French in that section of *Epître à la Princesse* she quotes is very conventional, or 'pure', to use her adjective. But then could this conventional style not also be attributed to the obvious fact that the subject of the portion quoted (the poet's evocation of his loved one, the Marchioness Daniel de Betteville, and of memories of their pleasant past in Paris) has nothing specifically African about it, and therefore does not necessitate an africanization of the language? Where the spirit of the poem or the angle of vision from which its theme is treated is unmistakably African, as in *Neige sur Paris* (another poem referred to by the author as being totally European), the poet does not fail to inject into his 'pure' French an authentically African image borrowed from his pastoral background. Thus in lines 18 and 19, he identifies the Saras, a Chadian people, with the palmyra trees of the African forest, to suggest their tall and distinguished physique:

J'oublie ...
Les mains blanches qui abattirent la forêt de rôniers qui dominait
l'Afrique, au centre de l'Afrique
Droits et durs, les Saras beaux comme les premiers hommes qui sortirent
de vos mains brunes.   (Senghor, Poèmes, Paris Seuil, 1964, p. 22)

I forget....
The white hands that felled the forest of palmyra trees that dominated
Africa,
That felled the Saras, erect and firm in the heart of Africa, beautiful like
the first men that were created by your brown hands.

By making the 'palmyras' and the 'Saras' the object of the verb 'felled', the poet is also evoking in a concrete way the brutal insensitivity of those 'white hands', referred to obsessively elsewhere in the poem, for whom trees and people were objects to be destroyed at will, to make way for 'civilization'. It could be argued further, as Dr Abiola Irele has done, that the very form of this poem could be traced to the tradition of African praise poetry (Abiola Irele, ed., *Selected Poems of Leopold Sedar Senghor*, London, Cambridge University Press, 1977, pp. 29–36).

One is not suggesting, of course, that there is always such a harmonious integration of language, form and theme in the poetry of Senghor, let alone – to take a totally different example of a writer whose French Dr Egejuru describes as pure – in the fiction of Cheik Hamidou Kane. It is certainly correct to say that the characters in the latter's *Ambiguous Adventure* speak rather incredibly, in spite of their non-literacy, a French whose exaltedness is indistinguishable from that of existentialist philosophers. But is this enough reason to rush to the conclusion that the author could not have had an African audience in mind? (p. 70) Why cannot this be explained instead in terms of Kane's incomplete mastery of the art of the novel, of his inability (unlike Sembène Ousmane) to differentiate his characters through their language; in short, to make them speak in character?

Conversely, could it be said in all logic that simply because Senghor's *Chaka* or Achebe's *Arrow of God* are replete with African images, proverbs, speech-patterns and so on, that these authors *necessarily* show an awareness of a local audience? In the case of *Chaka*, which Dr Egejuru correctly chooses as one of the few Senghor pieces to be genuinely African in form and content, the obverse is more readily the truth. African though it might be in expression and theme, *Chaka* is a poetic defence of the great Zulu warrior against western charges of tyranny and bloodthirstiness. Indeed, it is conceived in the form of a dialogue between the dying warrior and his real audience, the West, represented in the poem by the White Voice. It is clear from what precedes that the relationship between language and audience in individual works of African literature, not to speak of the vast corpus of writings from Black Africa, is far more complex and subtle than *Black Writers: White Audience* allows for.

This rigidity with which Dr Egejuru approaches her subject also does her a great disservice in her handling of what we described as 'the argument from choice of genre'. This is her explanation for the African writers' predilection for that other European invention – the novel:

> By choosing the novel rather than the theatre, for instance, the African writer announces his preferred audience – the bourgeoisie, composed of European bourgeoisie and the western-educated African elite. This choice eliminates the African masses, most of whom do not understand the foreign languages and are not familiar with the novel genre. (p. 15)

The first observation that could be made here is that it is not the choice of a foreign language or an unfamiliar genre that eliminates the 'masses'. It is rather the use of writing in societies whose cultures are still eminently oral. To write a novel in an African language will not automatically enable the masses to have access to it, as this presupposes a level of literacy that is simply not widespread at the moment. Secondly one wonders why the choice of the novel cannot be explained equally validly by, among other factors (a) its relative accessibility to the writer, (b) the communicative, functional and referential nature of its language which is more in consonance with the didactic intentions of most African writers, and (c) finally the greater possibility it offers because of its sheer length and complexity to explore a broader canvas of the experience of societies in transition.

Black Writers: White Audience is, however, very convincing in Chapter 4. There, the author argues persuasively that many of the themes in early African novels were meant to teach a foreign audience the vitality of traditional African cultures or the shortcomings of colonialism. The author's point that the insertion of anthropological glosses, the use of expressions like 'In Africa ...', the tendency to show Africa in a relationship of contrast with the West, and the inclusion of a glossary of African terms are all devices to cater for a non-local audience is incontrovertible. Her analyses of *Things Fall Apart* and the *Radiance of the King* as quasi-epic novels – using George Lukacs' philosophical definition as opposed to the formal definition of the epic – are provocative. On the whole, Dr Egejuru writes perceptively about those individual texts on which she focuses attention. Her inclusion of the not-so-well-known French African authors Nazi Boni and Ahmadou Kourouma is a welcome and refreshing change from the often-cited Oyono, Beti, etc. In spite of its single-explanation approach to the issue of language, genre and theme in African literature, *Black Writers: White Audience* is a lively contribution to a debate begun in the 1940s, on the Francophone side by writers like Léonard Sainville, revived in 1966 by critics such as Mohamadou Kane ('L'Écrivain africain et son public', in *Présence Africaine*, 58, 1966, pp. 8–31) and continued today by Roger Mercier, ('La Littérature négro-africaine et son public', in *Revue de Littérature Comparée*, 3 and 4, 1974, pp. 338–407).

John Conteh-Morgan

Michael Etherton, *The Development of African Drama*, London, Hutchinson; New York, Africana, 1982, 368 pp.

Michael Etherton has written a thoroughly interesting and worthwhile book which should be welcomed by all students of African drama. I think it is worth greeting this book at the outset quite positively as the author disarmingly spends moments of honest anguish worrying away at the dilemma facing all of us concerned about the drama of Africa – namely whether writing about it is the proper approach, and whether the encouragement of its study via the critical text is justified and whether indeed we are studying the right or the real thing. It is a dilemma that the book does not resolve, but it does face it, and the reader will be alerted to the dangers of assuming that a fundamental approach to African drama can be formed merely in the study or the classroom. There is an inevitable conflict between what the book advocates, both politically and artistically, and what it represents. Etherton argues strongly for the study of the materials of African theatre that are not 'centred on a written text' and supports his argument both by drawing our attention to developments in 'popular' and 'people's' theatre and by speculating about the possible development of drama in the years ahead. His closing comments conceive of a movement towards 'the "incomplete" play: the play which is continually undermined by the revelation of new contradictions in each performance. People's consciousness thus continues to articulate a new reality'. In other words, plays in the laboratory of life, not the library.

But the book does not neglect the central plays that form the basis of most people's knowledge of African drama, and indeed it is in these individual essays and analyses that much of the best of the book lies. There are thoughtful and helpful studies of *Ozidi, Ẹ̀dá, The Gods Are Not to Blame, The Island, Ovonramwen Nogbaisi, Kinjeketile, The Trial of Dedan Kimathi, Anowa, Madmen and Specialists*, and (particularly useful) *A Dance of the Forests* amongst the 'classics', but also references to and detailed descriptions of a large number of other plays and theatre happenings, some published, others performed, from the continent. Etherton's own travels and contacts in Africa have provided a wider range of theatre resource material than most other studies offer, and one of the book's virtues, therefore, is the breadth of information offered and the questions raised. Thus we can consider the established and the checkable (Soyinka, Ngugi) alongside the work of lesser-known playwrights such as the Zambian Kabwe Kasoma, and complete unknowns — Nigeria's 'Segun Oyekunle. Etherton may be using, in his terms, a doubtful medium — the critical text — to deal with a subject that he wishes to remove from such elitist approaches, but his lively and challenging questioning and his willingness to range beyond the familiar and the secure and to insist on attention being paid to plays of various kinds and from many circumstances, must stimulate his readers to consider his fundamental argument. His comprehensive approach to the study of drama is indicated by his observation that:

> If much tradition-based critical analysis of African drama is limited by focusing exclusively on the artistic product and omitting its social and economic organization from the discussion, so too are a number of sociological and anthropological studies of African societies severely limited by their exclusion of the plastic and performing arts from their analyses.

He stresses, importantly, the *function* of drama in African society and explores the hazards faced by theatre workers in the continent today where, he suggests, 'western colonialism and neo-colonialism has created a serious disjunction within the process of cultural development. Ruling elites criticize western acculturation whilst proceeding apace with it. This paradoxical situation serves to create a profound cultural uncertainty'. Etherton asks us to study the drama, then, in the total context of the organizational, economic and social structures of the society from which it grows.

The book will have its critics both for its own 'uncertainty' and for its tendency to develop its argument in spasms (and indeed for such odd decisions as that to include a glossary of very western stage terms which seem to work against the general principles Etherton asserts). But I regard its frankness as its virtue, and there are substantial achievements to applaud. The chapter on theatre and development is, for instance, timely and persuasive. The case for live theatre in developmental (educational? propagandist?) work as opposed to film, television and radio, is well made; in Etherton's words it is 'a medium of... present... communication. More than any other medium it can allow an immediate dialogue to take place. Listeners can themselves become speakers'. The notes and references to individual chapters and the bibliography are substantial and informative, and make an important contribution to the usefulness of the book to students and teachers.

Michael Etherton, as I have indicated, allows himself a final speculative paragraph. Perhaps I may, therefore, be permitted a final indulgence. He draws attention to Ama Ata Aidoo's play *Anowa*, describing it as 'one of the most profound African plays to have been written so far'. I would place it even more firmly in the body of the contemporary drama, believing it to be a rare piece, and one of the most disturbing plays of our time. Etherton observes that the play is 'not popular, even amongst students, particularly men, who insist that Anowa herself is a witch and needs to be slapped'. He argues that there is a much greater depth of contemporary and relevant meaning in the play, which poses the question 'how can we enjoy a wealth which means the certain impoverishment of others?' The agents of wealth and the creators of impoverishment are identified as 'international capitalism' and other mysterious collaborators, the traditional villains who may be blamed with a gesture that matters are out of our hands. Without for a moment disputing this, can we not believe that the play advances beyond this cliché to an even more positive statement? As with Soyinka in *A Dance of the Forests*, it seems to me that Ama Ata Aidoo has offered a direct challenge to present-day Africa – namely that the act of regeneration, social, political, moral, spiritual – is one requiring first the acceptance of one's own share of responsibility for the world we live in. The political statement of *Anowa* seems to be much more directed at the new politicians of Africa than to the shabby agents of imperialism.

This is where Ama Ata Aidoo stands with Soyinka and Ngugi. No wonder, as Etherton says, that 'African governments have become much more nervous about theatre than any of the other arts' and African theatre, developed along the lines Etherton advocates, can continue to make a positive contribution to the health and energy of society — however hard it is slapped.

Martin Banham

Bruce King, ed., *West Indian Literature*, London, Macmillan, 1979; Hamden, Conn., Shoe String Press, 1980, 247 pp.

> The thing which has been colonized becomes man during the same process by which it frees itself.
>
> (Frantz Fanon, *The Wretched of the Earth*)

This collection of critical essays covers the whole range of West Indian literature from the early novel, *Becka's Buckra Baby* (1904) by Tom Redcam (anagram of Thomas Henry MacDermot), to Mervyn Morris's volume of poetry, *Shadowboxing* (1979). It uses the selective survey approach in two distinct but partly interlocking sections.

The first section, which forms a solid baseline occupying more than one-third of the book, comprises a synthetizing introduction by the editor and a chapter on the socio-historical background by Rhonda Cobham, as well as four chronological segments of West Indian literature culminating in 'Since 1960: Some Highlights' by Edward Baugh. This is followed by the more voluminous second section made up of in-depth studies on individual authors. Since their selection in itself defines the volume to a considerable extent, we list them here in full: 'Edgar Mittelholzer' by Michael Gilles; 'Samuel Selvon' by Michel Fabre; 'George Lamming' by Ian Munro, who teaches Commonwealth literature at Wuhan University in the People's Republic of China; 'Derek Walcott' by his fellow poet, Mervyn Morris; 'V. S. Naipaul' by Bruce King; 'Wilson Harris' by Hena Maes-Jelinek; 'Jean Rhys' by Cheryl M. L. Dash, and 'Edward Brathwaite' by J. Michael Dash, to whom we owe the English-language edition of Jacques Roumain's *Gouverneurs de la rosée* (Governors of the Dew) in Heinemann's Caribbean Writers Series. Torn between the conflicting claims of class, colour and individual artistic consciousness, the West Indian writer is engaged in a continual process of redefinition and self-exploration. In some cases, he uses Africa as his reference point, as does Edward Kamau Brathwaite in his 'New World Trilogy', *The Arrivants*. V. S. Reid sets his novel *The Leopard* (1958) in Africa, more precisely in Kenya during the Mau Mau rebellion: 'It is an important first in West Indian fiction, that the West Indian's relationship to Africa be pursued on a level other than that of African survivals in the Caribbean' (p. 67). Mongo Beti, the only African writer in the 1950s to have treated the Mau Mau war in fictional form (namely, in his short story *Sans haine et sans amour*, in *Présence Africaine* (1953), tries to adhere to the conventions of psychological realism. On the other hand, Reid, whose hero Nebu reverses the European penetration of Africa in his encounter with the white settler's wife, hovers throughout in the realm of political allegory, free from any realistic constraints. This has prompted the grand old man of Pan-Africanism and veteran novelist C. L. R. James of Trinidad to remark somewhat humorously:

> Vic Reid of Jamaica is the only West Indian novelist who lives in the West Indies. That presumably is why he sets his scene in Africa. An African who knows the West Indies well assures me that there is nothing African about Reid's story. It is the West Indies in African dress. Whatever it is, the novel is a *tour-de-force*. African or West Indian, it reduces the human problems of under-developed countries to a common denominator.
> (*The Black Jacobins*, 2nd ed., New York, Vintage Books, p. 413)

Despite Reid's and Brathwaite's African experiments and the treatment of Afro-Caribbean cult forms in novels as far apart in time as *Hamel, the Obeah Man* (anon. 1827), Claude McKay's *Banana Bottom* (1933) and Andrew Salkey's *A Quality of Violence* (1959), followed by George Lamming's *Season of Adventure* (1960) and Orlando Patterson's evocation of the Rastafarians in *The Children of Sisyphus* (1964), the emphasis in West Indian literature would seem to shift progressively to creolization and the growth of a new, more complex identity nurtured by multifarious roots.

The West Indian identity finds its most profound expression in music, dance and language, all of them coalescing in the calypso. Language in the Anglophone Caribbean context means some creolized form of English, with fragments from the Carib and Arawak substratum and from the adjacent Hispanic culture areas drifting into its orbit – as does the French patois of his native island, St Lucia, in the works of the greatest of Anglo-Caribbean poets, Derek Walcott.

Historically, local poets, particularly in Guyana, had experimented with dialect forms as far back as the late nineteenth century. But they used dialect in the main for comic sketches and scenes from low life, in the same way as the poet Paul Laurence Dunbar used Negro speech in the United States. Following in Claude McKay's footsteps, Victor Reid developed a modified form of Jamaican dialect in his novel of the Morant Bay rebellion, *New Day* (1949). In their search for a new identity, both V. S. Naipaul's protagonist in *The Mystic Masseur* (1957), who from Pundit Ganesh Ramsumair is gradually transmuted into G. Ramsay Muir, Esq., MBE, and Austin Clarke's Boysie, the Barbadian trying to become Canadian in *The Bigger Light* (1975), wrestle with 'something called language' like Jacob with the angel.

Derek Walcott slips easily from dialect:

O so you is Walcott?
You is Roddy brother?
Teacher Alix son?

into a sonorous, elevated form of English vibrating with hidden and apparent ironies. He sums up the problem of an imposed language and culture in the figure of Defoe's Robinson Crusoe, whose confusionist function is similar to that of John the Baptist in Okigbo's *Heavensgate*:

like Christofer he bears
in speech mnemonic as a missionary's
    the Word to savages,
its shape an earthen, water-bearing vessel's
    whose sprinkling alters us
into good Fridays who recite his praise,
    parroting our master's
style and voice, we make his language ours,
    converted cannibals
we learn with him to eat the flesh of Christ.

(Crusoe's Journal)

Mervyn Morris probes below the surface of the post-independence malaise caused by the glib use of fashionable labels such as 'black consciousness' and 'brotherhood' in the face of economic collapse both in the cane-growing rural areas ('raising cane') and in the city. In this context the dialect poem acquires a deadly precision:

Ol' plantation whither,
factory close down,
brothers of de country
raisin' Cain in town.

(Shadowboxing, 1979)

This critical appreciation would not be complete without an overview, however sketchy, of some of the most outstanding essays on individual authors in the volume. A choice is hard to make, and harder to justify, in view of the rather even quality of the various contributions.

Michael Gilles, in discussing the profile of Edgar Mittelholzer, etches out the psychic imbalance of his personality and his resultant angst of identity, which the author projected, among others, into several generations of the Groenwegel family in his *Kaywana* trilogy through a dual pattern of strength and weakness. Paradoxically, the white creole characters depicted in the novels of Jean Rhys, although 'untainted' in their genetic make-up, suffer from a similar crisis of identity exteriorized in sequestration, atrophy of the will, and death.

Samuel Selvon, who deals with the theme of initiation into manhood and the growth of a man's social awareness in his first novel, *A Brighter Sun* (1952) develops his character further in *Turn Again Tiger* (1958). In a similar process of maturation, albeit more ironically, his *Moses Ascending* (1975) enlarges upon the problem of West Indian emigration to Britain, which had been vividly portrayed in his earlier novel, *The Lonely Londoners* (1956), sharing the concerns of George Lamming in *The Emigrants* (1954). But Selvon distinguishes himself by his witty, anecdotal calypso style:

> Sam Selvon has moulded the folk tradition of the Caribbean into a recognised literary form, somewhat in the way Ralph Ellison used the blues in *Invisible Man*. (p. 124)

George Lamming, who masterfully unravels the interwoven pattern of individual and community life in Barbados in his early classic, *In the Castle of My Skin* (1953), shows an admonitory, prophetic vein in his later works, *Of Age and Innocence* (1958) and *Season of Adventure* (1960), where the archipelago and the adjoining headland coalesce into a mythic island, San Cristobal. He then leaves the present for the past in that *summa* of the West Indian quest for the self, *Natives of My Person* (1972), which covers the ground of his previous four novels all over again in a gigantic historical and allegorical sweep.

V. S. Naipaul is the antipode of the great myth-makers in West Indian poetry and fiction: a Brathwaite, a Lamming, a Wilson Harris. It is he who has most poignantly stated, often through caricature and satire, the dilemma of the Third World in general and the West Indies in particular. Bruce King in his essay on Naipaul takes a fresh and sympathetic look at the author and his works. He obviously rates his humaneness and his 'regenerative capacity' as a writer higher than does Wilson Harris, or the critic Kenneth Ramchand in his book, *The West Indian Novel and Its Background* (1970), although he deplores the absence of any 'fixed positions that are identifiably Naipaul's' (p. 178).

Whether dealing with the realism of Naipaul and Selvon, the highly symbolic merging of landscape and history in the novels of Wilson Harris, or the 'speculative vision of wholeness' in Edward Brathwaite's poetry, the approach adopted by Professor King's team of critics is always well balanced between sociological foundation, psychological penetration and aesthetic judgement. Limpidity of style without shallowness, as in Michel Fabre's essay on Samuel Selvon, is the hallmark of the volume, which forms an excellent introduction to the subject for the student of literature, and a near-comprehensive kind of stocktaking for the specialist. It is a far cry from the self-defeating, narcissistic type of criticism rampant these days which challenges the very primacy of literature.

This is not to say that a number of points made in the book are not arguable, or that certain minor stylistic or lexical blemishes have not infiltrated into the text, such as the unorthodox use of the word 'plebiscite' (p. 66) instead of 'plebeian masses', or 'plebs'. But on the whole, *West Indian Literature* is a model of cohesion, logical progression and careful editing. It is a worthy continuation, and in some respects an improvement upon, the editor's previous works: *Introduction to Nigerian Literature* (1972), *Literatures of the World in English* (1974), and his FESTAC anthology, *A Celebration of Black and African Writing* (1975), edited in collaboration with the late Kolawole Ogungbesan.

Together with the appearance in 1980 of the maiden issue of the *Journal of Caribbean Studies* (editor O. R. Dathorne) at the University of Miami, *West Indian Literature* represents an important landmark in our understanding of that tornado-torn corner of the globe which nearly two hundred years ago witnessed the first successful revolution in what we now call the Third World. If man's job is freedom, the thousand-fold thudding of bare feet in Toussaint L'Ouverture's Haiti marching down the corridors of history signified that the job was well under way. But freedom is an ongoing process, as the Guyanese poet Martin Carter makes us aware:

> I come from the nigger yard of yesterday
> leaping from the oppressor's hate
> and the scorn of myself;
> from the agony of the dark hut in the shadow
> and the hurt of things;
> from the long days of cruelty and the long nights of pain
> down to the wide streets of tomorrow, of the next day
> leaping I come, who cannot see will hear.
> (*Poems of Resistance*, 1954, p. 75)

Willfried Feuser

Index

Abeokuta Women's Union, 145
absurd theatre, 12–17
acculturation, 170–71
Achebe, Chinua, 166; *Arrow of God*, 167; *A Man of the People*, 63; *No Longer At Ease*, 146; *Things Fall Apart*, 155, 168
Adelugba, Dapo, 144
Ademoyega, A., *Why We Struck*, 157
aesthetic criticism (feminist), 37
Africa: ancestral, 122–5; Arab role, 111–17; colonization, *see* colonialism; commercial relations, 77, 88–9; Defoe on, 77, 78, 83, 88–9; Equiano on, 77–8, 80–81, 84–5, 88–9; European languages in, 164–9; European views, 3–4; French colonialism, 49, 51–2, 103–6; integrity of, 62, 63–4; leadership, 63, 66–7; literary history (female), 43–7; materialism, 106–7; rural, 20–22, 24, 26; urban, 23, 24, 27, 30, 35, 36–7, 45
Afro-West Indians, 118–21, 125
agriculture, 79, 83–4
Aidoo, Ama Ata, 44; *Anowa*, 171–2; *Our sister Killjoy*, 45
al-Qudus, Ihsan Abdul, *Thuqub fi al-thaub al-Aswad*, 116–17
al-Rashid, Dr Marwan Hamid, 111, 112
ALECSO, 112–16
alienation, 49, 52, 143
Allen, Walter, 41
Altizer, T. J. J., 5–6
America, 35–6, 43, 60–67, 93, 96, 117; racism in, 98, 99
androgyny concept, 39–41
Angelou, Maya, 105
Anglophone writers, 166, 173
Aniebo, Ifeanyi, *The Anonymity of Sacrifice*, 162
animals, symbolic, 69–71
Anowa (play), 170
antagonism, structural, 51, 56–7
anthropology, 8, 65
Antigone (Twi reworking), 64
Arab–African Connections, 112–16
Arabs (in Africa), 111–17, 123

archetypal criticism (feminist), 37–9, 47
Armah, Ayi Kwei, *The Beautyful Ones Are Not Yet Born*, 63; *Two Thousand Seasons*, 111, 112
assimilation (in Guinea), 19
Athenaeum, The, 129
Auden, W. H., 68
audience, 146–7; pre-awareness, 164–9
Austen, Jane, 35, 40, 42
autobiographical novels, 80, 93–109
autobiographies, 19–25, 39, 77–90; memory in, 95, 100, 144
Awe, Professor Olumuyiwa, 144
Awoonor, Kofi, 103, 105, 106

Bâ, Mariama, *So Long a Letter*, 45, 46
Ba Shiru, 35
Baker, Sir Samuel, 113–14
Bakunin, 53
Baldwin, James, *Go Tell it on the Mountain*, 94
Banham, M., reviews Etherton, 169–72
Bank of the Holy Spirit, 8–9
Baugh, Edward, 172
Beardslee, W. A., 5–6
Beckett, Samuel, 165; *Endgame*, 12–17; *Not I*, 12; Soyinka and, 12–17; *Waiting for Godot*, 12–17 *passim*
Behn, Aphra (*Oroonoko*), 85, 86
Beier, Ulli, 74
Bellow, Saul, *Henderson the Rain King*, 63, 64, 65
Benezet, Anthony, *Some Historical Account of Guinea*, 80–81, 83–4
Beti, M., *Sans haine et sans amour*, 173
Biafran War, 115, 157–62 *passim*; poetry, 68–72, 74–5
bin Sayed, Muhammed (Tippu Tip), 116
Black literary expression, 93–4, 107–9
blindness, use of, 12, 13–14
Boni, Nazi, 169
Bonneau, Richard, 4

Bosman, William, *Accurate Description of Guinea*, 83
Braddon, Mary, 41, 42
Brathwaite, Edward, 172, 176; *The Arrivants*, 173
Brecht, Berthold, 160
Britain, 4–5, 65; commercial relations with, 77, 88–9; reaction to Zulus, 127–39 passim; West Indian emigration to, 175; women novelists, 35, 37–9, 41–3
Brontë, Charlotte, 40, 41, 42, 43; *Jane Eyre*, 37, 38
Brontë, Emily, 40, 41, 42, 43
Brown, Lloyd, *Women Writers in Black Africa*, 34–5
butterfly, symbolic, 11

Caldecott, A. T., 127–8, 130
Caldecott, C. H., 128; *Descriptive History of the Zulu Kafirs*, 127, 132, 133–4, 135–6, 137
calypso, 119, 173, 175
Camus, Albert, 12; *L'Homme révolté*, 56; *Les Justes*, 49–51, 53, 54–8
cannibalism, 2–3, 65–6, 116
caricatures, 61–2, 63, 176
Carter, Martin, 177
Cartey, Wilfred, *Whispers from a Continent*, 93
Caseley-Hayford, A. and G., 44
Cecil, David, 41
ceremony of the Souls, 119–20
Césaire, Aimé, *La Tragédie du roi Christophe*, 49–55, 57–8
characterization: autobiographical novels, 94–6, 99–101; Beckett, 12, 13–14, 15–16; Camus/Césaire, 50–58; caricature, 61–2, 63, 176; Defoe/Equiano, 82–5, 87–8; female, 35–6; Soyinka, 12–13, 15–16, 148; Waugh, 65
Chevalier, Gabriel, *La Peur*, 162
childhood, 141–2, 143–4, 146; *see also* maternal loss
Chopin, Kate, 43
Christianity, 15, 71, 102, 122, 124, 146
Cinzano advertisement (symbol), 8, 10
civilization, 4, 7–9, 65–6, 102
Clark, J. P., *Aburi and After*, 74; *The Beast*, 71; *The Burden in Boxes*, 71; *Casualties*, 68–72, 74–5; *The Cockerel in the Tale*, 70; *Conversations at Accra*, 72; *Death of a Weaverbird*, 74; *Dirge*, 75; *Exodus*, 74; *Leader of the Hunt*, 71; *Night Song*, 75; *Ozidi*, 170; *The Reign of the Crocodiles*, 71; *Return Home*, 71; *Seasons of Omens*, 72; *Skulls and Cups*, 74; *Song*, 74; *Song of a Goat*, 71; *The Usurpation*, 74; *Vulture's Choice*, 70, 74; *What the Squirrel Said*, 70
Clarke, Austin, *The Bigger Light*, 174
Cobham, Rhonda, 172
Coleridge, 40
collective consciousness, 94, 97–100, 107
collectivism, 24, 28
colonialism, 5, 54, 88–9, 102, 155; African women and, 44, 45; Afro-Arab relations and, 111–15, 117; cultural development and, 170–71; French, 49, 51–2, 103–5, 106; independence and, 121–3
commerce, 3, 10, 77, 88–9
communalism, 45–6
Conde, Maryse, 45
Congo crisis, 115
Conrad, Joseph, 4, 165; *Heart of Darkness*, 60, 63
consciousness, 46, 118–19; collective, 94, 97–100, 107
Conteh-Morgan, John, reviews Egejuru, 164–9
contextual feminist criticism, 37
Cornevin, Robert, 3
creolization, 173
criticism, feminist, 34–47
cultural issues, 1, 10, 49, 138, 170–71; traditions, 3, 27–8, 34, 49

Dadié, Bernard, 2, 3–4, 5, 8–10, 11; *Climbié*, 94; *La Ville où nul ne meurt*, 1
Daily Worker, The, 142, 145
Dathorne, O. R., 176
Dash, C. M. L. (Rhys study), 172
Dash, J. M. (Brathwaite study), 172–3
Davis, Anne B., *The Dramatic Theory of Wole Soyinka*, 163
death (theme), 16, 49
decadence (images/symbols), 4, 7, 10
decolonization (African literature), 34
deculturation, 27–8
Defoe, Daniel; *The Adventures of Robinson Crusoe*, 77, 78–9, 82, 84–5, 174; *Colonel Jack*, 77, 82, 87–8; *The Life, Adventures and Pyracies of the Famous Captain Singleton*, 77, 79, 82–3, 84, 86, 89
Delany, Martin, 3
democracy, racism and, 98
destiny, 49–50, 52
dialect, West Indian, 174
diaries, simulated, 100–107, 108, 109
diaspora, literature of, 26, 33, 94

Dickens, Charles, 35, 36, 42; *Bleak House*, 130; *A Child's History of England*, 130; *Household Words*, 130; on Zulu life, 130–32, 133–8, 139
double articulation technique, 2
Douglass, Frederick, 105
Dove-Danquah, Mabel, 44
drama, 12–17, 169–72
Dunbar, Paul Laurence, 174

Easmon, R. Sarif, *The Black Madonna*, 152, 154bis; *Disenchantment*, 155–6; *The Feud*, 153–4; *First Night in Paris*, 152, 154–5; *For Love of Thérèse*, 152, 155; *Heart of a Judge*, 155; *Koya*, 154; *Last Night in Paris*, 152, 155; *The Mad Woman*, 155; *Michael Woode, District Commissioner*, 155; *No. 2 to Maia's Tailor*, 155; *Under the Flamboyante Tree*, 151, 155
Èdá (play), 170
Edwards, Paul, 80
Egejuru, P. A., *Black Writers; White Audience*, reviewed, 164–9
Ekwensi, Cyprian, *Divided We Stand*, 157; *Survive the Peace*, 157
Ekwuru, Andrew, *Going to Storm*, 157; *Songs of Steel* reviewed, 157–62
Eliade, Mircea, 5
Eliot, George, 37, 41, 42, 43
Eliot, T. S., 74
Ellmann, Mary, *Thinking About Women*, 37
Emecheta, Buchi, 35, 37, 38, 39, 44, 45, 46; *Destination Biafra*, 40–41
Emenyonu, E. N., 5
Emmanuel, J. A., 93
emotion, poetic, 70, 73, 74–5
Equiano, Olaudah, 148; *The Interesting Narrative*, 77–90
Etherton, Michael, *The Development of African Drama* reviewed, 169–72
ethics, politics and, 51, 54, 56, 58
ethnocentricity, European, 138–9
Europe, 3–4, 7–9, 28; colonialism, Afro-Arab relations and, 111–15, 117; ethnocentricity, 138–9; languages/literary tradition, 164–9; literary criticism, 34–5, 47; materialism, 106–7
evil, 5, 7–9, 17, 49–50, 54–7 passim
existentialism, 13, 15, 17, 25, 26, 28
experience, 32–3, 49–50, 82–3, 89; Black, 108–9; contextualized, 21–5; female, 37–9, 43

Fabre, Michel, 24–5; Selvon study, 172, 176

Fagunwa, D. O., 162
family relationships, 19–26, 28–32
feminism (in Africa), 45–7
    Women's Movement, 39–40, 142, 144–6
feminist criticism, 34; in African literature, 43–7; androgyny concept, 39–41; archetypal approach, 37–9, 47; discovery/recovery mode, 42–3, 47; female literary history and, 41–4; historical mode, 35–6, 38, 41–3; male writers and, 35–7; re-evaluative mode, 43–4, 47; sociological mode, 35–7, 38, 41–3
Feuser, Willfried, reviews Ekwuru, 157–62; reviews King, 172–7; 'A Tale of Tamed Tigers', 2
Fielding, Henry, 82
formalism (New Criticism), 37
Forsyth, Frederick, *The Dogs of War*, 157
France, 19, 49, 51–2, 103–5, 106
Francophone writers, 166–7, 169
freedom concept, 49, 51–2, 55
Freeman, E., 57
Fuller, Margaret, 43

Gaines, Ernest, *The Autobiography of Miss Jane Pittman*, 93–100, 108–9
Gardiner, Captain A. F., *Narrative of a Journey to the Zoolu Country*, 134
Garnett, Constance, 152–3
Gaskell, Mrs, 42
Gayle, Addison, 100
General and Impartial Review, The, 80
generic criticism (feminist), 37–8
genre, choice of (audience), 165, 168
Germany (colonization role), 113
Gibbs, James, *Critical Perspectives on Wole Soyinka* reviewed, 162–4
Gilbert, S. M., *The Madwoman in the Attic*, 38–9
Gilles, Michael (Mittelholzer study), 172, 175
Gilman, Charlotte, 43
Gods Are Not to Blame, The (play), 170
Godwyn, Morgan, 80
Gordimer, Nadine, 43
gothic novels, 38
greed (theme), 106–7
Greene, Graham, 2–3, 4, 6–8, 10; *Climbié*, 11; *Journey Without Maps*, 1; *The Lawless Road*, 5; 'The Lost Childhood', 5; *A Sort of Life*, 5
Gross, T. L., 93
Gubar, S., *The Madwoman in the Attic*, 38–9

Guinea, 19–20, 24, 30–32, 80–81, 83–4
Haiti, 51–2, 54, 118–19, 176
Haley, Alex, *Roots*, 65
Hamel, The Obeah Man (anon), 173
Harris, Wilson, 172, 176
Hawthorne, Nathaniel, 154, 155
Head, Bessie, 35, 38, 39, 44, 46
Heilbrun, C. G., *Toward a Recognition of Androgyny*, 39–40
Henn, T. R., 74
Heywood, Annemarie, 162
Heywood, Christopher, reviews Paton, 148–50
historical mode (feminist criticism), 35–6, 38, 41, 42, 43
history, 10, 71, 73, 144; female literary, 41–7; pseudo, 78, 89, 109
Hoffman, Léon-Francois, *Le Nègre romantique*, 2
hope/hopelessness, 15–16, 17, 108
Howarth, William, 95
humour, 5–6, 8, 9–10
Hutcheson, Francis, 80
Hutchinson, Joyce A., 25

identity problems, 27, 28, 173, 175; naming of slaves, 96, 101–2, 103
Igbo culture, 5, 158
Illustrated Weekly News, 129–30
images/imagery, 2–4, 13–15, 52, 74–5; mother, 20–25; patterns (women writers), 38–9; symbols and, 5–7, 69; woman, 35–6
imperialism, 111–12, 117
independence, 121–3; post, 44, 45–6
individualism, 22, 24, 27, 28; feminist, 45–7 passim
Invisible Man (novel), 93
Ipi Tombi (stage show), 139
Ireland, 69, 73–4
Irele, Abiola, 162, 167
Irving, Charles, 89–90
Isaacs, Nathaniel, *Travels and Adventures in Eastern Africa*, 132–4
Islam, 19, 45, 111, 112, 123–4, 158
Island, The (play), 170
Izevbaye, D. S., 162

Jackson, Blyden, 98
James, C. L. R., 173
Johnson, Samuel, 82
Jones, Professor Eldred, 34; *The Elizabethan Image of Africa*, 2
Journal of Caribbean Studies, 176
Journal of Sudanese Culture, 111
journeys, see travel books
Joyce, James, *A Portrait of the Artist as a Young Man*, 94
'Just Assassins', 53
juxtapositional technique, 71–2

Kane, Cheikh Hamidou, *Ambiguous Adventure*, 167
Kane, Mohamadou, 169
Kasoma, Kabwe, 170
Kettle, Arnold, 41
King, Bruce: *A Celebration of Black and African Writing*, 176; *Introduction to Nigerian Literature*, 176; *Literatures of the World in English*, 176; *West Indian Literature* reviewed, 172–7
King, Martin Luther, 108
King Kong (jazz opera), 139
Kinjeketile (play), 170
Kinkhead-Weekes, Mark, 163
Kosinski, Jerzy, *The Painted Bird*, 162
Kourouma, Ahmadou, 166, 169

L'Ouverture, Toussaint, 176
Lamming, George, 172; *In the Castle of My Skin*, 27–8, 32, 175; *Natives of My Person*, 175; *Of Age and Innocence*, 175; *Season of Adventure*, 118–21, 125, 173, 175
language, 5, 37, 61, 101, 105, 114, 147; Beckett, 13, 14–15, 17; Clark, 71, 72, 75; European (in African literature), 164–9; Soyinka, 12–15, 17, 75; West African, 152–4; West Indian, 173–4
Lawrence, Vincent, *An End to Flight*, 157
Laye, Camara, 24, 27; *L'Enfant noir*, 19–23, 25, 28–32; *Oedipus Tyrannus*, 20; *The Radiance of the King*, 63
Leech, John, 130
legislation, South African, 148–50
Lessing, Doris, 43
Lewes, George Henry, 43
Liberia, 2–3, 4–5, 6–8, 10–11
Lindfors, Bernth, *The Early Writings of Wole Soyinka*, 162
Little, Kenneth, 35; *The Sociology of Urban Women's Image in African Literature*, 36–7
London Zulu exhibition, 127–32, 136, 138
Lukács, Georg, 168

McCaffrey, Kathleen, 36, 45
MacDermot, Thomas Henry, 172
McKay, Claude, 174; *Banana Bottom*, 173
McLuhan, Marshall, 71–2
Madaule, Jacques, 7–8
Madiebo, Alexander A., *The Nigerian Revolution and the Biafran War*, 157

182 Index

Maes-Jelinek, Hena, 172
Magallat al-Thaqafat al-Sudaniyyah, 111
Mailer, Norman, 60; The Naked and the Dead, 162
Malraux, 49; La Condition humaine, 50
man: evil in, 7, 8–9, 17; existential, 13, 15, 17, 25, 26, 28; hope, 15–16, 17, 108; images, see images/imagery
Mandingo (Onstott), 65
Mandinka, 32
Marshall, Charles, 127, 128–9
materialism, 1, 8–9, 10, 106–7
maternal loss, 20–25, 27–32
Mau Mau revolt, 173
Mazrui, Ali, The Trial of Christopher Okigbo, 157
Mba, Nina, 145
memory, in autobiography, 95, 100, 144
men writers, feminist criticism, 35–7
Mercier, Roger, 169
metaphors, 38–9, 61, 69, 71
Middleton, Christopher, 160
Millett, Kate, Sexual Politics, 35–6
Milton, 39, 80
mimetic principle (art), 23, 68
Mitchell, Loften, Black Drama, 108
Mittelholzer, E., 172; Kaywana, 175
Modisane, Bloke, Blame Me On History, 26–7
Moer, Ellen, Literary Women, 38
Montesquieu, 80
Moore, Gerald, 164
Moore, Jack B., reviews Easmon, 151–6
moral issues, 36, 50, 69; practical politics and, 54–5, 56–8
Morris, Mervyn, 'Derek Walcott' study, 172; Shadowboxing, 172, 174–5
Mphahlele, Es'kia, Chirundu, 157
Mphahlele, Ezekiel, Down Second Avenue, 26
Munro, Ian (Lamming study), 172

Naipaul, V. S., 119, 172, 176; The Mystic Masseur, 174
naming (slaves), 95–7, 101–2, 103
narrative: double, 101, 102; slave, 95–100; techniques, 76, 78, 80, 82, 89, 94
Nechayev, 53
Négritude, 49
Ngugi, 36, 172; Trial of Dedan Kimathi, 170
Nigerian civil war, 115, 157–62 passim; poetry, 68–72, 74–5
nihilistic theories, 50, 53
Njau, Rebeka, 35, 36, 38, 39, 43, 46
novels, 168; feminist criticism, 34–47; pseudo-autobiographical, 80, 93–109
Nwapa, Flora, 35, 37, 38, 39, 45; Efuru, 44
Nwoga, D. I., 163

Obasanjo, Olusegun, My Command, 157
Ogot, Grace, 35, 44
Ogundipe-Leslie, Molara, reviews Soyinka, 141–8
Ogungbesan, Kolawole, 16
Okigbo, Christopher, 75; Heavensgate, 174; Path of Thunder, 71
Okpewho, Isidore, The Last Duty, 157
Oliphant, Margaret, 41, 42
Olsen, Tillie, Silences, 47
'organic form', Yeats', 73
Organization of African Unity, 115
Osofsky, Gilbert, 95
Ouologuem, Yambo, Bound to Violence, 44, 112
Ousmane, Sembène, 166
Ovonramwen Nogbaisi (play), 170
Owen, Wilfred, 69
Oyekunle, Segun, 170
Oyono, Ferdinand, Houseboy, 93–4, 100–107, 108, 109

pan-Africanism, 25, 27, 32, 123, 173
pan Arab-Islamism, 123–4
Pascal, Roy, 95
past (search for), 2–3, 118–25
paternalism (psychological attack), 105
Paton, Alan, Ah, But Your Land is Beautiful reviewed, 148–50; Cry, the Beloved Country, 150
Patterson, Orlando, Children of Sisyphus, 118, 173
personality, 72–3, 105–6
plays, 12–17, 169–72
Plievier, Theodor, Stalingrad, 162
poetry, war, 68–75
politics, 36, 49, 50, 64, 72, 163, 171–2; ethics and, 51, 54, 56, 58; moral idealism and practical, 54–8; South African, 148–50; women's involvement, 142, 145
Pope and papal wealth, 9, 10
Porter, Abioseh M., 36
Portugal (colonization role), 113, 115
Présence Africaine, 4, 169, 173
propaganda, 69
protagonist characters, 51, 53–4, 70
proverbs, African, 5, 10
pseudonyms, male, 39, 42
psychoanalysis, 1, 6–7
psychological: attack, 105–6; novels, 38, 42

race/racism, 65–6, 106; American, 98, 99, 109; collective consciousness, 94, 97–100, 107
Radiance of the King, 168
Ramchand, Kenneth, *The West Indian Novel and its Background*, 176
Ransome-Kuti, 142, 145
realism, 23, 32, 38, 109, 173
reality, 5, 49–50, 58
Redcam, Tom, *Becka's Buckra Baby*, 172
Reid, V. S., *The Leopard*, 173; *New Day*, 174
religion, 7, 15, 17, 96, 102; Roman Catholic, 3, 8–10; voodoo, 118–20; *see also* Christianity; Islam
Research in African Literatures, 35
revolution: moral idealism in, 54–5, 56–8; politics of, 50, 53, 54, 55–6
rhetoric, 14–15, 68–9, 70
Rhys, Jean, 172, 175
rhythm, 2, 73
Richardson, Dorothy, 41, 42, 43
Richardson, Samuel, 37
Rider Haggard, *King Solomon's Mines*, 117
Rigby, Lady Elizabeth, 37
Rome, 3, 5, 8–10
Rosenblatt, Roger, 93
Roumain, Jacques, *Gouverneurs de la rosée*, 173
Rousseau, 50
rural life, 20–24, 26, 27, 30, 45
Russia, 62, 66

Sainville, Léonard, 169
Sartre, Jean-Paul, 12, 49
Sassoon, Siegfried, 69
satire, 61–2, 176
schools, 4–5, 19–21
Schreiner, Olive, 43
Scott, Sarah, *The History of Sir George Ellison*, 88
self-awareness, 28, 45–6, 125
Selvon, Samuel, 172, 176; *A Brighter Sun*, 175; *The Lonely Londoners*, 175; *Moses Ascending*, 175; *Turn Again Tiger*, 175
Senghor, Léopold Sédar, 141, 165, 166; *Chaka*, 167
Sharjah Symposium (1976), 116
Sharpe, Granville, 80
Sharpeville, 149
Shelley, Mary, 43
short stories, 151–6
Showalter, Elaine, *A Literature of Their Own*, 41–3, 44
Sierra Leone, 3, 4, 6, 7
slavery, 52–5, 78, 85–8, 108, 123; Arab, 114–15; naming, 95–7, 101–2, 103; slave narratives, 93–100, 103, 108–9

Smedley, Agnes, 43
sociological criticism (feminist), 35–7, 38, 41, 42, 43
Sole Native Authority, 142, 144, 145
South Africa, 26–7, 148–50
Soyinka, Wole, 75, 166; 'Abiku', 148; *Aké* reviewed, 141–8; *A Dance of the Forests*, 142, 143, 148, 170, 171–2; *Death and the King's Horseman*, 148, 162, 164; *A First Death-Day*, 148; *Idanre and other Poems*, 143, 163; *The Interpreters*, 142, 148, 163; *Jero's Metamorphosis*, 12; *Madmen and Specialists*, 12–16 *passim*, 148, 170; *The Road*, 12, 13, 15, 16, 162; *Season of Anomy*, 157; *The Swamp Dwellers*, 12, 14, 16–17; *The Trials of Brother Jero*, 12
Spacks, Patricia Meyer, *The Female Imagination*, 37
Spectator, The, 129
steel drum music, 119, 120, 121
Stegeman, Beatrice, 'The New Woman in Contemporary African Novels', 45–6
Stephan, K., *Ein feiner Patriot*, 157
stereotyping, 35–7, 43, 62
suffering, 23, 49–50, 55, 57–8, 69
supernatural, 10–11, 30–31
superstition, 96
Swift, J., 61
symbols/symbolism, 5–11, 15–17, 69–71
Synge, 73

Taylor, Richard, reviews Gibbs, 162–4
Thackeray, W. M., 35, 42
theatre, 169–70, 171
themes, 12, 15, 17; choice of audience and, 165, 168–9
Third World countries, 112, 176
time notion, 13–14, 152
Times, The, 128–9
title pages (style), 78–9, 81
Todd, Olivier, *L'année du crabe*, 157
tonelle, religion of, 120, 121
traditionalism, African, 44–6 *passim*
tragedy, 49–51, 54, 56–8, 69–70, 75
travel books: Dadié, 1–5, 8–11; Equiano, 79, 82, 84; Greene, 1–8, 10–11; Laye, 19–23
Trollope, A., 35, 42
Tutuola, Amos, 147, 162
tyranny, Tsarist, 53, 55, 56

Umabatha (musical *Macbeth*), 139
Updike, John, *The Centaur*, 60; comparisons, 63–7; *The Coup*, 60–63; *Poorhouse Fair*, 60; *Rabbit, Run*, 60

urban life, 23, 24, 27, 30, 45; women (study), 35, 36–7
Vassa, Gustavus, see Equiano, O., Vaughan, J. Koyinde, 4
violence, 54, 55–7; in black autobiographies, 94, 97–9; in French colonialism, 103–5; psychological, 105–6
Voltaire, 61
voodoo, 118–20

Walcott, Derek, 172, 174; O Babylon!, 118
war, 115, 137, 157–62; poetry, 68–75
Watt, Ian, The Rise of the Novel, 38
Waugh, Evelyn, Black Mischief, 63, 65–6
wealth, criticism of, 8–11
West, Nathanael, Miss Lonelyhearts, 61–2
West Africa, 151, 152–3
West Indies, 27, 118–21, 172–7
Wharton, Edith, 40, 68
Wilberforce, 148
Williams, Denis, Other Leopards, 121–5
witchcraft, Zulu, 135–6
Wollstonecraft, Mary, 43

women: androgynous, 39–41; images of, 35–7; traditional African, 44–5; writers, 34–5, 37–47; see also feminism (in Africa); feminist criticism
Women's Movement, 39–40, 142, 144
Woolf, Virginia, 35, 38, 41, 42, 43; A Room of One's Own, 40
Wright, Richard, 27; Black Boy, 23–5, 28, 32, 105, 157
Wynter, Sylvia, 103; The Hills of Hebron, 118

Yeats, W. B., Easter 1916, 72–3; Meditations in Time of Civil War, 74; Nineteen Hundred and Nineteen, 73–4; The Second Coming, 74; September 1913, 73
Yoruba culture, 70, 142–3, 146; writers, 147, 162, 163
Young, J. H., 5–6
youth, rural African, 21, 24, 26, 32

Zimmerman, Everett, 85
Zulus, 167; Dickens on, 130–32, 133–8, 139; exhibition, 127–32, 136, 138

www.ingramcontent.com/pod-product-compliance
Lightning Source LLC
Chambersburg PA
CBHW070806230426
43665CB00017B/2511